AREA HANDBOOK
for the
HASHEMITE KINGDOM OF JORDAN

Coauthors

Richard F. Nyrop

Beryl Lieff Benderly
William W. Cover
Melissa J. Cutter
Newton B. Parker
Suzanne Teleki

Research completed September 1973

Second Edition

Published 1974

(This handbook supersedes DA Pam 550–34, November 1969)

DA Pam 550–34

Library of Congress Cataloging in Publication Data

Nyrop, Richard F.

   Area handbook for the Hashemite Kingdom of Jordan.

   Edition for 1969 by Systems Research Corporation.

   "DA pam 550–34."

   Bibliography: pp. 243–268

   Supt. of Docs. no.: D 101.22:550–34.2

   1. Jordan. I. Systems Research Corporation.

Area handbook for the Hashemite Kingdom of Jordan.

II. American University, Washington, D.C. Foreign Area Studies. III. Title.

        DS153.N93   **1974**   **915.695'03'4**   **74–11397**

For sale by the Superintendent of Documents, U.S. Government Printing Office
Washington, D.C. 20402—Price $6.30

FOREWORD

This volume is one of a series of handbooks prepared by Foreign Area Studies (FAS) of The American University, designed to be useful to military and other personnel who need a convenient compilation of basic facts about the social, economic, political, and military institutions and practices of various countries. The emphasis is on objective description of the nation's present society and the kinds of possible or probable changes that might be expected in the future. The handbook seeks to present as full and as balanced an integrated exposition as limitations on space and research time permit. It was compiled from information available in openly published material. An extensive bibliography is provided to permit recourse to other published sources for more detailed information. There has been no attempt to express any specific point of view or to make policy recommendations. The contents of the handbook represent the work of the authors and FAS and do not represent the official view of the United States government.

An effort has been made to make the handbook as comprehensive as possible. It can be expected, however, that the material, interpretations, and conclusions are subject to modification in the light of new information and developments. Such corrections, additions, and suggestions for factual, interpretive, or other change as readers may have will be welcomed for use in future revisions. Comments may be addressed to:

> The Director
> Foreign Area Studies
> The American University
> 5010 Wisconsin Avenue, N.W.
> Washington, D.C. 20016

PREFACE

The present *Area Handbook for Jordan* is the first revision of a study prepared for The American University in 1968 by the Systems Research Corporation and published in 1969. This revision retains some segments of the 1968 study but is basically a new work, particular attention having been devoted to the significant events of the 1969–73 period. Research on the study was concluded on September 28, 1973.

On October 6, 1973, the armed forces of Egypt and Syria attacked Israeli forces in the Sinai and the Golan Heights, areas that had been under Israeli occupation since the Arab-Israeli War of June 1967 (see ch. 2). Because the attacks were launched on Yom Kippur (the Day of Atonement—the most sacred of the holy days of Judaism), the Israeli government and many foreign observers called the ensuing battle the Yom Kippur war. Spokesmen for the government of Jordan, on the other hand, used the phrase Ramadan war because the fighting began during Ramadan, the Islamic month of fasting (see ch. 4).

From the outset there was uncertainty as to what Jordan would do, inasmuch as Jordan had lost its West Bank (see Glossary) to Israel in the 1967 war. A few hours after Israel was attacked, Israeli Minister of Defense Moshe Dayan warned that if Jordan entered the war it might experience a Black October to accompany the Black September of 1970 (see ch. 13). Dayan also admonished the residents of the Israeli-occupied Territory (the West Bank) to "continue their daily routines as on normal days." The West Bank Palestinians (see Glossary) generally followed Dayan's advice, and there were relatively few anti-Israel incidents, and those reportedly were minor.

The Palestine Liberation Organization (PLO) also sought to influence Jordan. PLO propaganda warned Jordan that its failure to join the battle posed a threat to the Arab cause. The PLO asserted that its guerrilla forces had a right to enter Jordan in order to attack Israeli forces in the West Bank, and the PLO complained bitterly when the Jordanian military blocked an attempted entry by PLO units. Although Dayan and other Israeli spokesmen asserted that a large Israeli military contingent had to be held out of the battle areas to patrol the border with Jordan, the PLO insisted that the absence of battle along the border was a betrayal of the Arab nation and reiterated its appeal to the citizens of Jordan to overthrow the monarchy.

King Hussein in the meantime maintained close contact with the presidents of Egypt and Syria. On October 10 the king's Supreme Defense Council called up some of the military reserves, established military volunteer centers, and announced the mobilization of all resources for "the military effort." These acts elicited a warning from Israeli Prime Minister Golda Meir, who observed that Hussein should recall the catastrophe of 1967 and "behave accordingly."

On October 13 a Jordanian official stated that units of the armed forces were moving into Syria to join the fighting. As of late December 1973 the official figures on Jordan's participation had not been publicly released, but foreign observers stated that between 2,000 and 3,000 men and about eighty tanks were sent to the battle zone in Syria. The Jordanians entered the fighting, but by October 22, when the combatant states agreed to a cease-fire, Jordanian casualties reportedly had been light, and none of the soldiers had been taken prisoner.

Jordan received immediate economic benefits from its modest military involvement. On October 17 the government of Kuwait announced that it would resume immediately the economic aid (the equivalent of US$46 million annually) that had been instituted after the 1967 war but terminated after the 1970 civil war (see ch. 10). In addition, Algeria and Tunisia resumed diplomatic relations, and the small shaykhdoms on the Persian Gulf announced that they would provide financial assistance to Jordan.

On October 22, 1973, the United Nations Security Council adopted Resolution 338, which called for a cease-fire and for implementation of Security Council Resolution 242 of November 22, 1967 (see ch. 2). Jordan at once accepted the terms of the resolution. During the next few weeks, Jordan and the other Arab states engaged in a series of diplomatic meetings in preparation for another Arab Summit Conference. On the eve of that conference, Hussein sought to clarify his position with respect to the Palestinians. In a speech on November 22, he declared, "We are the protectors of the Palestinian people's rights to determine their own fate.... After the retrieval of the [West Bank], we will give the Palestinians, wherever they may be, the opportunity to decide their course .... We will accept their decision." A few days later an official Jordanian spokesman stated that the Palestinians should make their decision in a "plebiscite under neutral, international supervision." The spokesman emphasized, however, that although the Jordanian government did not claim to be the representative of the Palestinians, it refused to "concede that claim to anyone." To give further emphasis to the point, Hussein's spokesman announced that Jordan favored the peace talks that were then scheduled to begin in Geneva on December 18, but that "Jordan will not participate ... if the Arab Summit Conference decides that the PLO is the sole legitimate representation of the Palestinian people."

Despite this warning by Hussein, the Arab Summit Conference, which met in Algeria November 26 through 28, did just that. It at first seemed probable that Jordan would not attend the Geneva peace talks, but after prolonged and intense consultations with other Arab governments—in particular Egypt and Saudi Arabia—and with the United States, Hussein changed his mind, and when the peace talks convened on December 21 under the joint auspices of the United States and the Soviet Union, a delegation from Jordan was present. Although the future of the peace talks was clearly impossible to predict, the initial meeting of December 1973 was the first time that the Arab states had engaged in face-to-face, public negotiations with Israel.

Up-to-date and accurate data and analytical information regarding Jordan were difficult to obtain. Although extensive use was made of consultants and of official reports by various governments and international organizations that were available to the public, much of the information was derived from secondary sources. The authors wish to express their gratitude to persons in various agencies of the United States government and to Jordanians residing in Washington, who were particularly helpful. The staff of the Joint Library of the International Monetary Fund and the International Bank for Reconstruction and Development was also very helpful.

The literature on Jordan is occasionally confusing because of the varying methods of transliteration used by scholars and other writers. The authors generally adhered to the system known as BGN/PCGN, the system agreed to by the United States Board on Geographic Names and the Permanent Committee on Geographical Names for British Official Use. A prominent exception to that system is the spelling used for the name of the reigning monarch. According to the BGN/PCGN system, the king's name would be spelled Husayn; the authors, however, followed the spelling used by the king, Hussein. The place names, again with minor exceptions, are those approved by the United States Board on Geographic Names in June 1971. All tons are metric unless otherwise specified.

COUNTRY SUMMARY

1. COUNTRY: Hashemite Kingdom of Jordan formed in 1950 after annexation of a portion of Palestine west of Jordan River. Kingdom is the successor to the Amirate of Transjordan formed by the United Kingdom in 1922 under its mandate from the League of Nations.

2. GOVERNMENT: Under provisions of the Jordanian constitution, King Hussein I rules as a constitutional, but almost absolute, monarch. Bicameral National Assembly composed of Senate, whose members appointed by the king, and House of Representatives, whose members in theory elected every four years by direct suffrage. As of late 1973 no election held since 1967.

3. SIZE AND TOPOGRAPHY: Of total territory of about 35,000 square miles, about 6 percent, known as West Bank (see Glossary), remained under Israeli occupation in late 1973. Jordan River, the Dead Sea, and series of wadis that extend south to the Gulf of Aqaba divide country into two regions known as the East Bank (see Glossary) and West Bank. Most of East Bank is sparsely inhabited desert.

4. CLIMATE: Generally hot and arid summers, cool variable winters. East Bank averages less than five inches rainfall annually, West Bank somewhat more.

5. POPULATION: In 1973 population of East Bank about 1.84 million, Palestinians (see Glossary) account for perhaps over 40 percent; about 60 percent of the Palestinians were refugees. Growth rate estimated at 3 to 3.7 percent annually.

6. LANGUAGE: Arabic official language. Only very small linguistic minorities.

7. RELIGION: Islam is official religion; Sunni Islam the most common branch. Religious minorities include Shiite Muslims; Christians, of whom Greek Orthodox are the most numerous; and very small numbers of other groups.

8. EDUCATION: Increasing literacy rate, estimated by government at 55 percent in 1970. Education free at all levels through university and compulsory for both sexes through ninth grade. In 1970 close to 90 percent of six- to eleven-year-olds, 65 percent of twelve- to fourteen-year-olds, 35 percent of fifteen- to eighteen-year-olds enrolled.

9. HEALTH: Water shortage and inadequate sanitation remain important causes of poor health conditions. One physician per 4,000 citizens, one dentist per 16,000 citizens, one nurse per 1,550 citizens. Common

diseases: tuberculosis, dysentery, typhoid, and trachoma.

10. JUSTICE: Three court systems: civil courts, consisting of magistrates courts, courts of first instance, courts of appeal, and the Court of Cassation (Appeals); Muslim and Christian religious courts, dealing with marriage, divorce, and inheritance; special tribal, military, industrial, juvenile courts and the High Court of Justice. No jury system; judges decide matters of law and fact.

11. ECONOMY: Known natural resources very meager. Only about 20 percent of land arable, rainfall highly erratic and frequently inadequate, yet agriculture major productive sector. From its inception country heavily dependent on large-scale loan and grant assistance from abroad.

12. FINANCE: Government's current and development budgets in large measure financed by foreign grants and loans; despite this aid, budgets in late 1960s and early 1970s had deficits, which were financed by banking system. During early 1970s there was a steady rise in prices.

13. TRANSPORTATION: Narrow-gauge, single-track Hejaz Railway runs from Syrian to Saudi Arabian border. About 1,750 miles of highways and secondary roads. Amman is the major international airport, and Al Aqaba is the sole seaport.

14. FOREIGN AID PROGRAMS: Mainly foreign grants to support the budget; development loans to support specified projects; United Nations Relief and Works Agency for Palestine Refugees in the Near East (UNRWA) to support refugees; and extensive military aid. Before 1957 most of aid not from UNRWA came from the United Kingdom; from 1957 to 1967, mostly from the United States; from 1967 to 1970, mostly from Kuwait, Libya, and Saudi Arabia; since 1970, mostly from the United States, Saudi Arabia, and various international lending agencies.

15. INTERNATIONAL MEMBERSHIPS: Since admission to United Nations in 1955 has participated in most specialized agencies. Member of the League of Arab States (Arab League) and attends most Arab summit meetings.

16. ARMED FORCES: Nearly 70,000 officers and men in military, almost 65,000 of them in the army. King is supreme commander. Defense expenditures in early 1970s averaged about 50 percent of total budgeted expenditures. Public Security Force (police) of about 7,500 under the Ministry of Interior.

JORDAN

TABLE OF CONTENTS

LIST OF ILLUSTRATIONS

LIST OF TABLES

SECTION I. SOCIAL

CHAPTER 1

GENERAL CHARACTER OF THE SOCIETY

In the fall of 1973 an important part of Jordan remained under the occupation of Israel, which had seized that area in the Arab-Israeli War of 1967 (see fig. 1). The rest of the country, popularly and officially known as the East Bank, existed in a condition similar to a state of siege under the firm rule of the constitutional but virtually absolute monarch, King Hussein I. Since his accession to the throne in 1953, Hussein has survived several coup and assassination attempts; in most instances his retention of power and life was a direct result of the loyalty to him of the armed forces. In late 1973 Hussein's ability to rule continued to depend upon the allegiance of the military, particularly the army and its officer corps, which were dominated by Transjordanians (see Glossary) and beduins (see ch. 5).

The political history of the country is brief. In 1922 the United Kingdom, operating under the sanction of a mandate from the League of Nations, created the Amirate of Transjordan; the boundaries of this new political entity were with minor exceptions those of contemporary East Bank Jordan. The British retained control over defense and external affairs, but they delegated extensive power to the man they chose as monarch: Amir Abdullah Ibn al Hussein.

In 1946 the British mandate over Transjordan was terminated, and the independent Hashemite Kingdom of Transjordan was established with Abdullah as king. During the Arab-Israeli War of 1948 the Transjordanian army, then known as the Arab Legion, seized and held a portion of the city of Jerusalem and part of what had been Palestine. In 1950 this area, which became known as the West Bank, was annexed by Abdullah, who then renamed the country the Hashemite Kingdom of Jordan.

The addition of the West Bank more than doubled the country's population and greatly enhanced the kingdom's economic potential. Although the West Bank included only 6 percent of the territory, it regularly provided well over one-third of the country's agricultural output (see ch. 12). Many of the holy places of Christianity, Islam, and Judaism are located in the West Bank, and the tourists to those sites were until 1967 the second largest source of foreign exchange earnings (see ch. 11). The West Bank residents, or Palestinians (see Glossary), were as a

1

group better educated and politically and socially more sophisticated than the largely rural and rustic Transjordanians, and the Palestinians added greatly to the nation's technical, administrative, and managerial skills. Because of the Palestinians' political sophistication, however, the annexation of the West Bank introduced political strife and internal divisiveness (see ch. 5; ch. 9).

Over 90 percent of the people of the East and West banks are Arab Muslims who share and, in varying degrees, act upon social and political attitudes that have characterized Arab civilization since well before the advent of Islam. Within this framework, however, the different experiences and values of the tribal Transjordanians and the sedentary, town-oriented Palestinians have made national unity and cohesion difficult.

Many of the commonly shared principles were explicitly adopted by the Prophet Muhammad in his role as the messenger of Islam; other principles and practices received implicit religious sanction as a result of observance and practice by Muhammad's immediate successors (see ch. 4). The Hashemite dynasty, which has no long-standing historic ties to the region, continues to rely upon this traditional attitudinal system in asserting its monarchical claims. Among Jordanians, the traditional attitudes are most specifically and unreservedly endorsed by the beduins. In addition to a commitment to such concepts as group independence, bravery, protection of the weak, and vengefulness, the beduins continue to reflect the ancient Arab concern with shame and honor and, although shame and honor adhere most immediately to the family, the concepts are also applied to larger social groups: the tribe, the nation-state, the Arab nation (see ch. 5).

These traditional attitudes include a legitimation and justification for certain aspects of hereditary authority. The beduins and other traditionalist Transjordanians therefore accept the Hashemite family—in this instance Abdullah, the first king, and his grandson Hussein, the reigning king—as legitimate rulers by virtue of their direct descent from the Prophet Muhammad (see ch. 2). The concept of the state becomes that of an immense tribe that is subject to the leadership and authority of the king as tribal brother, father, and first among peers. Within limits, therefore—that is, for as long as Hussein's public and private comportment conforms to this traditionalist concept and for as long as this concept holds its own against social change—Hussein may rely on the allegiance and support of most Transjordanians.

The Palestinians, on the other hand, generally view the Hashemite monarchical claims as anachronistic—suitable perhaps for a backward tribal community but not for a democratic, progressive, modernizing society. The nontribal Palestinian society lacks both the mode of life and the mind-set suited to Hashemite claims of leadership. The Jordanian constitution, which was promulgated in 1952, reserves sweeping, virtually unlimited power to the king, and many Palestinians

complain that they enjoyed more personal freedom and political participation during the British mandate period than they have under the
monarchy.

The inability of Hussein to end Israel's occupation of the West Bank
further erodes his already fragile claim to the loyalty and allegiance of
the Palestinians. Also, the defeat that Hussein's armed forces administered to the guerrilla forces in 1970 and 1971 undoubtedly enhanced his
prestige among most Transjordanians, especially among the beduins.
The Palestinians, however, whether living under Israeli rule, existing
in squalid refugee camps, or working as civil servants or commercial
entrepreneurs in Amman, generally viewed Hussein in 1973 as something less than a symbol of national unity.

Since the Arab-Israeli War of 1948 the refugees have posed a continuing and seemingly insoluble problem to the Near East in general and
to Jordan in particular. Although data relating to the refugees are subject to wide margins of error, in 1966 approximately 700,000 refugees
were registered with the United Nations Relief and Works Agency for
Palestine Refugees in the Near East (UNRWA) in all of Jordan. Immediately after the 1967 war an estimated 224,000 Palestinians (some
sources use figures as high as 375,000) fled from the West Bank to the
East Bank; some of these fled from camps in the West Bank, others
were refugees for the first time. Whatever the number, in 1973 Palestinians constituted about 40 percent of the East Bank population of
about 1.84 million, and over 60 percent of these East Bank Palestinians
were registered refugees.

The conquest of the West Bank by Israel had a shattering impact on
the Jordanian economy. In addition to the loss of the income derived
from tourists to Jerusalem, Jericho, Bethlehem, and the several other
holy sites, the national economy lost a large part of the remittances
from Jordanians working in foreign lands. A large percentage of those
Jordanians were from the West Bank and, although after 1967 this was
Israeli-occupied Territory, the workers continued to remit money to
their families resident there. In 1966 remittances totaled about JD10.6
million (for value of the Jordanian dinar—see Glossary) and were the
largest single source of foreign exchange earnings. In 1968 remittances
fell to about JD4.1 million but by 1972 had risen to an estimated JD7.4
million, a distant second in foreign exchange earnings (see ch. 11).
Overall, the West Bank in 1966 had contributed an estimated 40 percent of the nation's gross domestic product (GDP), and the abrupt termination of that contribution was keenly felt.

Although the economy was basically an agricultural one, in 1973 it
remained dependent on imported foodstuffs for many critical items
(see ch. 12). Of the approximately 29,400 square miles of the East Bank,
less than 20 percent was cultivable. Almost all of this land was in use,
but only about 10 percent was under irrigation. The low rainfall is unpredictable and, unless or until irrigation is extended to much more

3

land, there can be only marginal increase in the generally low crop yields.

About one-third of a working force of about 386,000 (approximately 21 percent of the East Bank population) was engaged in agriculture, mostly as subsistence farmers. In the early 1970s only about 5 percent of the people were nomadic or seminomadic (see ch. 3). During the early 1970s agriculture contributed somewhat less than 20 percent of the GDP, whereas industry (including mining, manufacturing, power and water, and construction) contributed between 16 and 18 percent. Industry accounted for about 50 percent of the country's exports, considerably more than agriculture.

Beyond its role as the major source of support to the monarchy, the military constituted an important factor in the economy. The military was the largest single employer; in fact, there were more men in uniform (nearly 70,000) than were employed in the industrial sector (between 35,000 and 40,000). During the late 1960s and early 1970s military expenditures, which were preponderantly for salaries and related expenses, regularly accounted for approximately 50 percent of the government's annual budgeted expenditures. The large number of men in the armed forces did not pose a drain on the available manpower, however. Unemployment remained high—ranging from 8 to 15 percent in the early 1970s—and the percentage of underemployed was probably higher. Many analysts suggested, therefore, that the armed forces served as a form of unemployment relief (see ch. 13). Perhaps more specifically, the military provided employment for the beduin and beduin-oriented segment of the citizenry, on whom the king depends and for whose welfare he manifests continuing concern (see ch. 5).

A serious problem for the government has been the physical one of coping with the rapid growth of cities, a growth that has exceeded not only all expectations and informed predictions but also the government's ability to provide social and welfare services. At the time of independence in 1946 the population of Amman was slightly in excess of 65,000; by late 1971 the population was just over 521,000, a more than sevenfold increase in twenty-five years. The neighboring cities of Az Zarqa and Irbid experienced sixfold increases during the same period.

The rapid growth has totally overburdened the already inadequate sewage treatment facilities, water supplies, public transportation, and many other social services (see ch. 6). The government has made great efforts in these fields, however, and in some areas has made significant progress. The educational system, especially for the first nine grades, has expanded at a rapid pace, and by the early 1970s elementary education was available to most of the population. In 1970 the government claimed that 55 percent of the adult population was literate, although some foreign observers suggested that this figure was inflated.

4

Underlying all Jordan's economic problems is the meagerness of its natural resources. Unlike most of its neighbors, Jordan has no known oil deposits. In fact, in 1973 the only known mineral deposit of commercial proportions was phosphate; the proven reserves were estimated at about 300 million tons, although the actual figure may be much larger (see ch. 12). Although the government in most spheres has not engaged in industrial or commercial ventures, it owned 64 percent of the Jordan Phosphate Mine Company, which mines, processes, and markets the phosphate ore. The company employed about 1,200 workers and was the largest industrial employer.

Until the 1967 war most phosphate exports (and many other non-agricultural exports) were shipped from Al Aqaba through the Suez Canal to markets in Lebanon, Turkey, and other Mediterranean markets. After the closure of the canal new markets were sought in South, Southeast, and East Asia, and a reduced volume was shipped overland through Syria to Lebanon. In 1971, however, Syria closed its border with Jordan, and hence Jordan lost access to its customers in the Mediterranean. By 1973 the border had been reopened, but Jordan had not yet recovered its earlier position in the Mediterranean markets.

In late 1973 the kingdom was in a period of relative calm, stability, and prosperity. Activities by political parties remained outlawed, and the government-owned radio and television and the government-controlled press engaged in no direct criticism of the regime (see ch. 7). The thirty members of the Senate were appointees of the king and were considered to be unreservedly loyal to him. The sixty-member House of Representatives in theory provided equal representation to the East and West banks, but no direct elections had been held since 1967 despite a provision for elections every four years (see ch. 8). The prime minister and his cabinet, all of whom are appointees of the king, are by law subject to control by the National Assembly, but during the late 1960s and early 1970s the legislators had made no serious attempt to challenge the king's near monopoly of political power.

From the 1950s to mid-1973 Jordan's relations with most Arab countries ranged from fair to very poor; the neighboring monarchy in Saudi Arabia and the distant monarchy in Morocco have been the only Arab governments that have regularly supported Hussein. Hussein has adhered to a pro-Western stance in international relations, reflecting, at least in part, his very heavy dependence on foreign, especially United States, economic and military aid; in 1972, for example, over 50 percent of the government's budgeted receipts were from foreign loans or grants (see ch. 11). Most Arab governments view the United States as Israel's primary benefactor and protector, and Jordan's reliance upon and close relationship with the United States is therefore strongly resented and loudly criticized. Some of the more radical Arab spokesmen, such as Libya's Colonel Muammar Qadhafi, openly advocate Hussein's overthrow, and in mid-1973 the politically moderate president of Tunisia suggested that Hussein could best serve the Arab cause by resigning so that a democratic government could be formed (see ch. 10).

Jordan's relations with Egypt and Syria have frequently been marred by acrimony and open hostility, but in September 1973 the three governments seemed to have resolved several points of disagreement and, by resuming formal diplomatic relations, to have laid the groundwork for future discussions. Much to the chagrin and dismay of perhaps a majority of the Palestinian refugees in Jordan and elsewhere, the Egyptian-Jordanian-Syrian agreements seemed to include a common desire to neutralize the Palestinian guerrilla groups, including those that attempted to overthrow Hussein in the 1970–71 civil war (see ch. 2; ch. 13). Shortly after the tripartite conference Hussein granted amnesty to several guerrilla leaders who had confessed that they had entered Jordan either to kill or to overthrow him, but Hussein's act was paralleled by one by the Syrian president, who placed new rigid controls on the guerrillas, including the closing of a guerrilla-operated radio station.

It should not be concluded, however, that Jordan's relations with Egypt, Syria, and other nonmonarchical Arab states will in the future be close, cordial, and cooperative. Hussein has in the past entered into numerous agreements with Egypt, Iraq, and (or) Syria, and in every instance the agreements were broken or repudiated by one or the other party. Jordan's political isolation within the Middle East has been lessened, however, as a result of the agreements.

CHAPTER 2

HISTORICAL SETTING

Jordan's central location as a trade crossroads and buffer between the settled region of the Mediterranean littoral west of the Jordan River and the desert to the east contributed significantly to the country's experience in ancient and more recent times. Until 1921, however, Jordan's history was that of a vaguely defined territory without a separate existence. Its earlier history, closely associated with the religions of Judaism, Christianity, and Islam, is therefore included in that of the surrounding states and contending empires of which it often formed a part.

By the time of the Ottoman Turkish conquest of 1517, three general geographic regions had developed distinct emphases and loyalties that continued to be identifiable in modern times: the villagers and town dwellers of Palestine, west of the Jordan River; the scattered villagers and tribesmen of northern Jordan, who tended to associate themselves with Syria; and the tribesmen of southern Jordan, who identified themselves with the deserts of the Arabian Peninsula to the south. Although most of them were Muslim Arabs, the integration of these somewhat differing backgrounds and regional orientations presented problems for the later Jordanian government in establishing the cohesion and identity of the state, a task that had not yet been accomplished in 1973.

Late in the nineteenth century, two political nationalist movements developed that were to affect the history of Jordan profoundly: Arab nationalism, articulated first in Lebanon and Syria; and Zionism, of European Jewish origin. Arising separately, these movements at length converged in Palestine and proved to be irreconcilable.

The state of Jordan first emerged immediately after World War I when Great Britain divided into two parts the mandate for Palestine that it had received from the League of Nations. The Arab Amirate of Transjordan was then established in the portion east of the Jordan River, within boundaries much the same as those of the East Bank (see Glossary) of Jordan in 1973. Great Britain supported as ruler the Hashemite prince (later King), Abdullah Ibn al Hussein, one of the principal figures of the British-aided Arab Revolt against the Turks in World War I. West of the Jordan River, direct British administration was set up in Palestine, and within this administration the Jewish national home promised by Great Britain to the Zionist organization in 1917 was implemented.

After a United Nations (UN) resolution of 1947 had endorsed the formation of separate Arab and Jewish states in Palestine, Great Britain gave up the League of Nations mandate on May 14, 1948, and at the same time the establishment of the state of Israel was proclaimed. Transjordan's Arab Legion then joined with forces of several other Arab states in the unsuccessful 1948–49 war against Israel. The end of these hostilities left Transjordan in control of the old portion of the city of Jerusalem and part of Palestine and with a trebled population, one-third of whom were refugees. The country's name was changed to the Hashemite Kingdom of Jordan, and in 1950 the holdings on the West Bank (see Glossary) were annexed. The West Bank was lost to Israeli control in the Arab-Israeli War of 1967.

Since 1950 perhaps the chief characteristic of the kingdom has been political and economic survivability under severe stress. Political survivability is illustrated not only in the continuing confrontation with Israel but in the series of crises erupting out of the inter-Arab tensions of the new nationalism after World War II; economic survival and development took place in a land devoid of major natural resources. Among the major factors responsible for Jordan's survival were the legacy of the period of British aid and guidance from 1921 to 1958, the United States programs of extensive economic and military aid after 1957, and the personality and leadership first of King Abdullah and then of his grandson, King Hussein I (Hussein Ibn Talal) (see ch. 8; ch. 9; ch. 13).

EARLY HISTORY

The Jordan Area and Ancient Israel

The region east of the Jordan River constituting the present-day state of Jordan was an important transit or connecting area in the great land bridge between Africa and Southwest Asia—composed of the northern reaches of the Arabian Peninsula, Palestine, Syria, and Mesopotamia—that is often referred to as the Fertile Crescent. At various times, in whole or in part, the area of Jordan was held by contending, successive empires to the east and west, by small local kingdoms, and by ancient Israel at its height. The principal centers of history affecting the country were located in the more populous coastal lands west of the Jordan River, the Egyptian empires on the Nile, the rival eastern empires of Mesopotamia and Persia, and the Arabian Peninsula on the south.

About 2000 B.C. large numbers of Semitic peoples known as Amorites, apparently from northern Syria, moved southeast into Mesopotamia and also southwest into the land of the Jordan River, called Canaan. By about 1500 B.C. the dominant population element on both sides of the Jordan River was Semitic.

8

About 1500 B.C. both Hittite marauders from Anatolia (Turkey) and Semitic people, called Habiru by the Egyptians, from northern Syria began to intrude upon Canaan. The Habiru have been identified also as early Hebrews. On the larger stage, the Egyptian and Hittite empires in 1280 B.C. entered into a treaty by which northern Syria was allocated to the Hittites, but southern Syria and the whole area of Canaan ostensibly remained under Egypt.

During the struggle between Egypt and the Hittites, Hebrew infiltration continued. The exodus of the Israelites from Egypt under Moses occurred about 1300 B.C., and the main phase of the Israelite conquest of Canaan under Joshua began apparently during the years 1250 to 1225 B.C. Only a few decades later another invasion of Canaan began, this by iron-using, Mediterranean sea people possibly from Crete, called Philistines. From them the area designation Palestine is derived; the modern Arabic word *Falastin* preserves the name intact.

The ancient kingdom of Israel was established about 1020 B.C. with the war leader Saul as first king. In the time of David, Saul's successor, the Israelite people were firmly united, the native Canaanites were subdued, and the Philistines were finally driven back into coastal enclaves between present-day Gaza and Tel Aviv. David expanded the realm well beyond the old tribal allocations made to the twelve tribes of Israel (three of which lay east of the Jordan River), and scholars have estimated that the population of the expanded realm contained more non-Israelites than Israelites. At its maximum extent, David's kingdom has been estimated to have stretched from the upper Euphrates River south to the Gulf of Aqaba. Amman was held briefly under David but broke away again after his death.

Under David's son and successor, Solomon, ancient Israel reached its peak of cultural splendor and influence, but after Solomon's death the realm split into two kingdoms: Israel, north of Jerusalem, and Judah, encompassing much of the former southern and western holdings, including Edom, that lay south of the Dead Sea. The balance of the territory that became Jordan in modern times included the desert areas where beduin tribal life prevailed, the Semitic kingdom of Ammon, and some of the land claimed by the Aramaic kingdom of Damascus.

Egypt, Assyria, Babylonia, and Persia

As the Egyptian power declined, the Assyrian empire rose among the Semitic peoples of the upper Tigris River region. In the early eighth century B.C. the capital of the northern Hebrew kingdom of Israel fell to the Assyrian king. The southern kingdom of Judah, although tributary to Assyria, preserved a shaky political independence for another 150 years. The rest of the area, including Jordan, was divided into provinces and ruled under Assyrian governors.

Assyria declined when confronted with the insurgent neo-Babylonian power of southern Mesopotamia. Nineveh, the Assyrian capital, fell in 612 B.C., and Babylon became supreme in the area, also defeating Egypt to the west. The kingdom of Judah was ended when Emperor Nebuchadrezzar II (605–562 B.C.) seized and destroyed Jerusalem in 586 B.C. Babylon, in its turn, was overthrown by the new imperial surge of the Persians under Cyrus II in 539 B.C.

Greece, Rome, and Byzantium

Alexander the Great of Macedon and his highly trained Greek army crossed the Dardanelles into Asia in 334 B.C. and, administering a crushing defeat to Persian forces, by 332 established Greek dominance in Syria, Jordan, Palestine, and Egypt. After his death in 323 the empire became divided among his governors general who, in Egypt, became the Ptolemaic line of pharaohs and, in greater Syria, the line of Seleucid kings. The city of Amman, in modern Jordan, was renamed Philadelphia during the Greek era.

The lands east and west of the Jordan River were thus caught again between rival realms. Both the Jews in Palestine and the Nabataeans east of the Dead Sea took advantage of the contention between the Ptolemaic and Seleucid empires. The Seleucid empire, having successfully displaced Ptolemaic efforts to absorb Palestine by 198 B.C., launched repressive measures against Jewish customs and religion. In 168 the Jewish revolt of the Maccabees erupted. The victories of Judas Maccabeus over the Seleucid Syrians were continued by his brothers, and in 143 a Jewish independent kingdom was reestablished under the line known as the Hasmoneans. This kingdom quickly expanded east of the Jordan but did not last long.

Rival claimants to the Hasmonean throne appealed for support in 64 B.C. to Pompey, the Roman commander who was then implanting Roman rule in Asia Minor, and in the following year the Roman legions seized Jerusalem. Petra, the Nabataean Arab kingdom that rose in southern Jordan after 800 B.C., was also taken. The period of Roman dominion began, followed soon by the start of the Christian era in Jerusalem, and was maintained despite revolts from A.D. 66 to 70 and from A.D. 132 to 135. After the 132–35 revolt, the Roman emperor Hadrian renamed the area Syria Palestina, renamed Jerusalem Aelia Capitolina, and dispersed the Jews. The Jews in the Palestine area, after these major repressions and dispersions, dwindled rapidly and, although a few remained, were not again to be a majority in the area for seventeen centuries.

By the Edict of Milan in A.D. 313 the Roman emperor Constantine permitted Christianity to develop as a recognized and tolerated religion. Constantine shifted his capital to Byzantium on the Bosporus Straits in 330, renaming the site Constantinople (present-day Istanbul). The holiest Christian place, however, was Jerusalem (see ch. 4). In the de facto partition of the Roman Empire in 395, the Jordanian area, along with most of the rest of the Middle East and North Africa remained under the eastern portion—the empire of Byzantium, which was ruled from Constantinople. The ruling families of Syria during this period were the Ghassanids, Christian Arabs loyal to Byzantium. They only intermittently controlled areas of Jordan south of Amman and were often in confrontation with the Arabs to the south, thus illustrating the rough differentiation between Syrian, or northern, Arabs and those having closest roots with the Arabian Peninsula to the south. This differentiation even then was not new in history and has continued to manifest itself in modern times.

By the seventh century A.D. Petra had gone deeply into decline. Byzantium and Persia fought a series of wars in the sixth and seventh centuries that devastated much of the central Middle East, and Persian forces were briefly in control of parts of Palestine and Jordan. The Persians were finally driven back in 927. The Christianized society in greater Syria and elsewhere in the empire, however, had become divided by war and by the doctrinal disputes of the early Christian church. It was at this time that a weakened Byzantium was hit by the new thrust of Islam surging out of the south, where religious ideology now formed a focus for the economic and population pressures in the Arabian Peninsula.

ISLAMIC CONQUEST AND ARAB RULE

By the time of his death in A.D. 632 the Prophet Muhammad had brought most of the tribes of the Arabian Peninsula under the banner of the new monotheistic religion of Islam (submission), uniting the individual, state, and society under the universalism of the all-powerful will of God. Adherents of Islam, called Muslims, collectively formed the Dar al Islam (House of Islam) (see ch. 4). By the middle of the seventh century Muhammad's successors carried the conquests of Islam north and east from the Arabian Peninsula and also westward into North Africa. Although most of the population west and east of the Jordan became Islamized, the small Jewish remnant in Palestine and the larger Christian groups on both banks preserved their identity.

After Muhammad's death at Medina, he was succeeded as spiritual and temporal head of all Muslims by his father-in-law, Abu Bakr, who ruled from A.D. 632 to 634. The occupant of this highest Islamic office became known as caliph, from the Arabic word for successor or deputy. Later the designation Commander of the Faithful was also used. Under Umar, who ruled from 634 to 644, external conquests were undertaken, and the government of conquered areas was organized. In 636 an Arab general crushed the Byzantine army at the Battle of Yarmuk River. Syria, Jordan, and Palestine were thus brought securely under Arab Muslim rule. Jerusalem itself was occupied by Umar in 638.

The scripture of Islam, or Quran, was compiled during the rule of the third caliph, Uthman. Uthman was assassinated and was succeeded by the Prophet Muhammad's cousin and son-in-law, Ali— the last of the four so-called orthodox caliphs. After a civil war among

Muslim factions, Ali moved his capital to Mesopotamia, where he was assassinated in A.D. 661. Thus began the great schism in Islam between the Shia, or supporters of Ali and his descendants as the true successors to the caliphate, and the Sunni, or those regarding themselves as orthodox followers of the Quran, who supported consensual succession. The Arab Muslims of Palestine and Jordan became and remained predominantly Sunni.

After Ali's murder his chief rival, Muawiyah, the Arab governor of Syria, proclaimed himself caliph and established his capital in Damascus. As Philip K. Hitti has written, Muawiyah initiated "a brand new style of the caliphate—monarchical, worldly, and anchored in Syria."

The Umayyad caliphs administered their territories much as the Byzantines and earlier empires had done—by the traditional mode of pyramidal, military-executive government with absolute and final authority held by the caliph, assisted by a few ministers, but with extensive power delegated to provincial governors general. The conqueror's law—in this case, the sharia (see Glossary), or Muslim law—applied only to those of the same faith as the conquerors. Civil law of personal status for non-Muslims was the law of their particular *millet*, or separate religious community. This system was to prevail throughout the world of Islam and survives in modified form in the legal system of present-day Jordan.

The Umayyad dynasty was overthrown in A.D. 750 by a rival Sunni faction, the Abbasids, who moved the capital to Baghdad. The Jordan area was remote from the center of power; it declined economically, retaining its beduin tribal way of life. The Jordanian area continued under Baghdad until the accession of the Shia Fatimid dynasty in Egypt in 969. After 1071 the Fatimids were displaced briefly by the Seljuk Turks.

Muslim expansionism and Muslim rule of the holy places in Jerusalem and Palestine at last aroused Western Europe and, late in the eleventh century, waves of Crusaders poured into the Middle East. The devastation of this invasion, mounted in the name of God as were the earlier Islamic and the ancient Israelite conquests, reached a climax in 1099 when the Crusaders took Jerusalem. Subsequently, the Latin Kingdom of Jerusalem was established and expanded east of the Jordan River, where the province of Outre Jourdain (Beyond Jordan) was formed. This may have been the first use of a form of the later term Transjordan, meaning the desert region east of the river and away from the more developed and populated coastal zone of Palestine.

In the mid-twelfth century the grand vizier of the Fatimid dynasty in Cairo was a Sunni scholar and soldier of Kurdish extraction named Salah al Din Yusuf Ibn Ayyub, better known to Western history as Saladin. Saladin became independent ruler of Egypt in 1174 and soon directed his forces against the Crusaders in Palestine and Syria. At the decisive battle of Hattin on the west shore of Lake Tiberias (Sea of Galilee), Saladin destroyed the Crusaders' army on July 4, 1187, and retook Jerusalem soon afterwards. Further campaigns reduced the Crusader domain to a small entity in what is now northern Lebanon, where the tiny state endured tenuously until 1291.

Saladin died at Damascus in 1193. His Ayyubid successors as sultans of Egypt and the revived empire quarreled among themselves, however, and the Syrian region broke up into small conflicting princedoms. The Ayyubid line was succeeded in 1260 by the Mamluk warlord sultans of Egypt. The Mamluks, after finally repelling successive Mongol invasions from the north and east, by the late fourteenth century held sway from the Nile to the Euphrates. Their power, weakened by internal factionalism, then declined, and Mamluk rule was confronted by the new power in the Middle East—the Ottoman Turks.

OTTOMAN TURKISH CONQUEST AND RULE

By the end of 1517 Syria, Jordan, Palestine, and Egypt had fallen to the Ottoman Turkish dominion. The stagnation into which Jordan and other Arab lands fell during the four centuries of Ottoman control left them out of phase with Europe and significantly affected their later history when independence was attained and nationalist self-development was attempted.

Led by an early succession of able sultans, the Ottoman Turkish dynasty had effectively defeated Byzantium and in 1453 ended that ancient regime by seizing Constantinople, which they renamed Istanbul and made their capital. Subsequent conquests spread the Ottoman domain rapidly over Anatolia and the Arab lands to the east, south, and west as far as Morocco and northwest into Europe as far as the walls of Vienna. The apogee of Ottoman power is usually considered to have been the reign of Sultan Suleyman I (reigned 1520-66), known to the West as Suleyman the Magnificent. Thereafter the empire began its decline.

The Ottomans ruled their domains through the traditional military-imperial system of viceroyalties, or governorates, each called a *vilayet* and headed by a pasha, or governor general, who ruled with complete authority in the name and at the pleasure of the sultan at Istanbul. Palestine, west of the Jordan River, became part of the *vilayet* of Beirut; and Jordan, east of the river, was part of the *vilayet* of Syria, of which Damascus was the capital.

In Jordan Egyptian influence briefly displaced Turkish influence from about 1831 to 1839 during the insurgence of the pasha of Egypt, Muhammad Ali, against the sultan. Egypt withdrew, however, under pressure of Great Britain and Russia, and Turkish governors returned. In 1900 the Turks, with German assistance, began construction of the Hejaz Railway, which by 1908 linked Damascus in Syria with the holy city of Medina in the Arabian Peninsula (see ch. 3). The original purpose was two-fold: to transport Muslim pilgrims to the Medina-Mecca pilgrimage sites and to enable better strategic control of the distant Arabian Peninsula. To protect the railway, as they had earlier endeavored to protect the caravan route, the Turks subsidized rival Arab tribal shaykhs along the way.

The Ottoman regime and its governors followed traditional patterns in employing the *millet* system of ruling minority religious communities. The Turkish codification of the Islamic sharia was utilized in towns and cities; in the desert, the less formal tribal customary law was followed. Generally, the governors and the governed remained strangers. As long as order was preserved, military levies were provided when called for, and taxes were paid, the Turkish administration was satisfied. Maintaining order, however, was not necessarily easy. Although the Turks were Muslims and the sultan in Istanbul was the caliph, the Turks were non-Arab, foreign oppressors in Jordan. The individualistic, fiercely independent beduins revolted against them when good opportunities arose. Serious uprisings occurred in the nineteenth century, in 1905, and again in 1910 and were put down by Turkish garrisons with some difficulty.

WORLD WAR I: ARABISM, ZIONISM, REVOLT, AND THE MANDATE

In the last two decades of the nineteenth century two separate movements developed that were to have continuing effects of the first magnitude not only for Jordan and Palestine but for all of the Middle East and North Africa. One was the Arab revival—first clearly identifiable in Syria and Lebanon. The other was Zionism—the Jewish revival rising in Europe, led by east European Jews, and articulating a quest for Jewish communal survival and identity in political terms.

Commencing about the same time, the two movements developed separately. Both were and became increasingly ultranationalistic and had other general resemblances—chiefly, the aim in each case of uniting in independence dispersed oppressed peoples considered to have elements of commonalty in culture, religion, language, and history. Both movements, however, were highly individual; their bases of objectives, attitudes, and action were different. They were to converge and confront each other finally in the geographical region of Palestine where, it was initially thought by some, they could develop in mutual accommodation. As history up to mid-1973 has shown, they were, in fact, to prove incompatible.

In Beirut, by 1875, a small number of Lebanese and Syrian intellectuals, both Christian and Muslim in composition and acclimated to Western thought by European-style education, were urging the study of Arab history, literature, and language to revive the Arab identity. By means of pamphlets and posters secretly printed and disseminated, they attempted to expose the oppressions of Ottoman rule and to arouse

Arab consciousness in the interest of autonomy or even independence. The idea of independence was expressed in context of a unity of "the Arab nation" as a whole. Because of tight Turkish security, this group atrophied after 1880.

During this time, but quite separately, a new spirit of Jewish identity was seeking expression in Europe. By 1890 the Odessa-based Society of Lovers of Zion was encouraging the movement of small bands of immigrants to Palestine. This effort met with constant difficulty from the Turkish governors and was not particularly successful. The missing dynamism for European Jewish nationalism was supplied by Theodor Herzl, an Austrian Jew and a well-known journalist in Vienna, who was dispatched by his newspaper to Paris in 1894 to cover the treason trial of a French army officer of Jewish faith, Captain Alfred Dreyfus. Appalled at the surge of anti-Semitism aroused in France by the Dreyfus case, Herzl shortly afterward conceived his plan for a Jewish homeland. Seized by a sense of mission, he then wrote his classic pamphlet *Der Judenstaat* (The Jewish State), published in 1897.

Herzl saw the problem primarily as a political-national question of international scope. Encouraged by the backing of Eastern European Jewish intellectuals, Herzl convened the First Zionist Congress at Basel, Switzerland, in August 1897. This body then founded the World Zionist Organization (WZO), with the stated aim "to create for the Jewish people a home in Palestine secured by public law."

In 1907 WZO set up an office in Palestine at Jaffa (Yafo), near which the Jewish city of Tel Aviv was founded in 1909. The small Jewish settlements, which became known as kibbutzim, evolved a distinctive system of communal living, and Jewish schools, press, and labor movements came into existence. Under stimulus of the second wave of immigration, the Jewish population in Palestine rose dramatically to some 85,000 by the start of World War I, or fully 12 percent of the total population. It declined, however, to about 8 percent by the end of the war.

Meanwhile, in Istanbul the Young Turk nationalist revolution initiated by the army-based Committee of Union and Progress had forced Sultan Abdul Hamid II, on July 24, 1908, to restore the Constitution of 1876 and later, in April 1909, had deposed him in favor of his aged brother, Mehmed V. These developments generated an initial wave of good feeling in the empire and aroused the hopes and expectations of its various nationalities.

After 1909, however, it soon became clear to Arabs and Zionists alike that the new Turkish nationalism was bent on increasingly centralized and intensified turkification of the Ottoman domains rather than the granting of local autonomies, to say nothing of independence. Arab opposition to the new Turkish despotism arose in two separate arenas. One developed among Arab intellectuals of Beirut and Damascus who enunciated the ideas of a new Arab nationalism but who at first sought autonomy within rather than secession from the Ottoman Empire. The second, more traditional in form, emerged among the remote desert tribes of Jordan and Arabia, who were politically inarticulate but resentful of outside control of any kind.

The Arab committees and clubs of Lebanon and Syria that had emerged in the first flush of optimism in 1908 were forced into clandestine political conspiracy in the form of secret societies, especially the Young Arab Society (Jamiyat al Arabiya al Fatat). The objectives became independence for all Arab societies, not only from Turkey but from foreign control of any kind.

The link between the urban Arab societies and the tribesmen in the desert was Hussein Ibn Ali al Hashimi, the grand sharif and amir of Mecca, the custodian of the Muslim holy places of Mecca and Medina and the Hejaz region of western Arabia. Hussein, head of the Hashemite branch of the Quraysh, the tribe of the Prophet Muhammad, was himself a descendent of the Prophet (hence, by Muslim usage, a sharif, or noble). He had four sons, the middle two of whom, Abdullah and Faisal, were to become major figures in Middle Eastern events during and after World War I.

Hussein and his sons had received Turkish as well as Arabic (but not Western) education and from time to time had spent enforced years of elite restraint in Istanbul. Sharif Hussein had been appointed prince of Mecca in 1908 because the Turks thought he would be a quieting influence, but once in office he did not prove to be as tractable as the Istanbul government had expected.

Both Abdullah, later king of Jordan and grandfather of the present King Hussein I of Jordan, and Faisal, later king of Syria (1919-20) and of Iraq (1921-33), were by 1915 associated secretly with the Arab nationalist societies of Syria and Lebanon, and it was partly through the sons' efforts that Sharif Hussein accepted from the northern societies what was called the Damascus Protocol as a basis for his later negotiations with the British. In return the northern societies accepted the Hashemites as leaders and spokesmen.

The first of the major events leading to the Arab uprising occurred with the visit of Abdullah in February 1914 to Lord Horatio Kitchener, the British agent and consul general at Cairo. Abdullah inquired about the possibility of British support if his father should raise a revolt against the Turks. Kitchener's reply was noncommittal, as Turkey was not then allied with Germany and World War I had not begun. The war broke out in August, however, and by early November Turkey was aligned with Germany and Austria-Hungary and at war with Great Britain, France, and Russia. Great Britain declared Egypt a protectorate and assigned Sir Henry McMahon as first British high commissioner; Kitchener was made British secretary of state for war and, in the changed circumstances, sought Arab support against Turkey. In Cairo McMahon conducted an extensive correspondence with Hussein between July 1915 and January 1916.

In a letter to McMahon in July 1915 Hussein specified an area for Arab independence under the "Sharifian Arab Government" consisting of the Arabian Peninsula (except Aden) and the Fertile Crescent of Palestine, Lebanon, Syria, and Iraq. In his reply of October 24, 1915, McMahon, on behalf of the British government, declared British support for postwar Arab independence, subject to certain reservations and exclusions of territory. As with the later Balfour Declaration, the exact meaning was not clear, although Arab spokesmen since then have usually maintained that Palestine was within the pledged area of independence. In any case, on June 5, 1916, Hussein launched the Arab Revolt against Turkey and in October proclaimed himself king of the Arabs. Supplies and money were provided by Great Britain for the tribal forces led by Abdullah and Faisal and various prominent shaykhs. British army technicians and advisers were also detailed from Cairo to assist the Arab irregular forces. Of these advisers, T.E. Lawrence (Lawrence of Arabia) was to become the best known.

Meanwhile, on May 16, 1916, the British and French governments concluded the secret Sykes-Picot Agreement. This undertaking, although allowing for a postwar Arab state on the Arabian Peninsula and an ill-defined plan for an international arrangement over Jerusalem and part of Palestine, divided the rest of the Ottoman domains in the Fertile Crescent between the two powers.

The outbreak of war had effectively prevented any further development of the Zionist settlements in Palestine, and the main efforts of this cause shifted to England, where discussion with Zionists was seen as having potential value to the pursuit of British war aims. The protracted negotiations with the British foreign office were climaxed on November 2, 1917, by the letter from Foreign Secretary Arthur James Balfour that became known as the Balfour Declaration. This document declared the British government's "sympathy with Jewish Zionist aspirations," viewed with favor "the establishment in Palestine of a national home for the Jewish People," and announced an intent

> to facilitate the achievement of this object, it being clearly understood that nothing shall be done which may prejudice the civil and religious rights of existing non-Jewish communities in Palestine.

Although painstakingly devised, the wording of this declaration was seen differently by different people and interests. Ultimately, it was found to contain undertakings that proved to be incompatible. The apprehensions of Hussein, Abdullah, and Faisal (not themselves Palestinians) were allayed by the British assurance that no one people in Palestine should be subject to another. Initially, there was substantial belief that Arabs and Jews could live there together under some sort of arrangement not yet set forth.

Also in November 1917, the contents of the Sykes-Picot Agreement were revealed by the Bolshevik government. Arab consternation at the contents was palliated by British and French reassurances, however, and by the fact that Allied military operations were progressing favorably. Al Aqaba was taken by Faisal's Arabs in July 1917, and Jerusalem fell to Field Marshal Edmund Allenby on December 9, 1917. Turkish forces remaining in Syria were subsequently defeated by the British and Arabs after hard fighting, and Faisal entered Damascus in triumph on October 1, 1918. The armistice with Turkey was concluded on October 31, 1918.

Faisal, as chief Arab delegate to the Paris Peace Conference convened in 1919, was a dramatic and eloquent advocate but could not prevail against the European power interests. He met with Chaim Weizmann, representing WZO, on January 3, 1919, and signed an agreement pledging the two parties to mutual cooperation under the Balfour Declaration concept. Faisal, however, wrote on the document that his signature was dependent upon fulfillment of Allied wartime pledges regarding Arab independence. Because these pledges were never fulfilled to Arab satisfaction, Arab leaders and spokesmen have consistently held the Faisal-Weizmann agreement to be invalid.

An American group known as the King-Crane Commission was appointed in 1919 by President Woodrow Wilson to investigate and report on the problem of disposition of Ottoman territories and the assigning of mandates. The commission, after extensive travel and surveys in Palestine, Jordan, and Syria, reported intense opposition to the Balfour Declaration, especially among the 90 percent Arab majority in Palestine, and warned against unlimited Jewish immigration or the imposition of a separate Jewish state. The commission's report of August 28, 1919, however, was not officially considered by the conference and was not made public until 1922.

From the Paris Peace Conference and the subconference of San Remo emerged the League of Nations Covenant and the mandate allocations making Great Britain the mandatory power for Palestine and Iraq and granting France the mandate for Syria and Lebanon. The mandate's terms reaffirmed the Balfour Declaration, called upon the mandatory power to "secure establishment of the Jewish national home," and recognized "an appropriate Jewish agency" for advice and cooperation to that end. The WZO was specifically recognized as that agency. Hussein, Abdullah, Faisal, and other Arab spokesmen opposed the mandate's terms because the League of Nations Covenant had endorsed the Wilsonian principle of self-determination of peoples and thereby, they maintained, logically and necessarily supported the cause of the majority—namely, the Arabs—in Palestine.

To British authority, pressed with heavy responsibilities and commitments after World War I, the objective of mandate administration was a peaceful accommodation in and development of Palestine by Arabs and Jews under British control. To Hussein cooperation with the Zionists had meant no more than providing within his intended

Arab kingdom a refuge for Jews. To the leaders of WZO, which by 1921 had a worldwide membership of about 770,000, the recognition in the mandate was simply a welcome first step on the way to attainment of a separate Jewish national state.

Arab-Jewish conflict in Palestine developed early and continued at an erratically rising tempo throughout the mandate period. Meanwhile, in Damascus Faisal had convened the General Syrian Congress in July 1919 and proclaimed Syria sovereign and independent. In March 1920 this congress reaffirmed the independence of both Syria and Iraq, and it declared Faisal king of Syria and Abdullah king of Iraq. In April, however, the San Remo conference carved out the mandates, and soon French troops began moving from Beirut into Syria. The French took Damascus on July 25, 1920. Faisal, thus deposed, fled to Europe and remained there until installed by the British as king of Iraq in 1921.

At the time of Faisal's ouster, his brother Abdullah was in what is now Jordan endeavoring to organize a countereffort against the French. It then became clear to Abdullah and the British that Abdullah was acceptable as ruler to the beduin tribes east of the Jordan, including the locally powerful Bani Sakhr. Palestine had not been specifically defined. After the British and French had agreed, under the Sykes-Picot guidelines, as to what constituted Lebanon, Syria, and Iraq, what was left over, by elimination, was the mandate of Palestine. This included, in effect, the territory of pre-June 1967 Jordan and Israel.

In March 1921 Winston Churchill, then colonial secretary, convened a high-level British policy council in Cairo. As a result of its deliberations, Great Britain divided the Palestine mandate along the Jordan River-Al Aqaba line. The eastern portion, or Transjordan, was to have an Arab administration, under British guidance, with Abdullah as amir. He was recognized as de facto ruler in April 1921. Revisions in the final draft of the mandate were made to give Great Britain much latitude in this area and were approved by the League of Nations Council in July 1922. A British memorandum in September 1922 excluded Transjordan from the zone of the Jewish national home. This division was aimed, as was British support of Faisal in Iraq, at satisfying wartime pledges to the Arabs. It was in this manner that what in 1973 was known as the East Bank of Jordan first came into being.

TRANSJORDAN AND MANDATED PALESTINE: 1921-39

The new entity of Transjordan at its inception in 1921 contained not more than 400,000 inhabitants. Of these, about 20 percent lived in four towns of 10,000 to 30,000 population. The balance were nomadic or seminomadic tribesmen or village farmers. British financial aid, later established on an annual subsidy basis, put minimum funds in the treasury, but Abdullah was initially faced with a severe lack of competent officials and civil servants.

With British assistance the problem of civil officials was gradually overcome. Government initially was simple, and Abdullah ruled directly with a small executive council, much in the traditional manner. British colonial administration concerned itself mainly with defense, financial, and foreign policy and left internal political affairs to Abdullah. Defense was initially assigned to the British Royal Air Force, which had a squadron stationed in Transjordan. A further problem of major proportions in the early years, however, was that of establishing public safety. Brigandage and tribal raiding were common, and the roads were not safe. In 1921 a reserve force to supplement the rudimentary police was organized by Captain (later Lieutenant Colonel) F.G. Peake, commonly known as Peake Pasha. In 1923 the police and the reserve force were combined into the Arab Legion. After a visit to London by Abdullah, Great Britain on May 15, 1923, recognized Transjordan as a national entity en route to independence with Great Britain in a special advisory and tutelary role.

From 1925 to 1939 Transjordan as a desert realm under the British aegis progressed slowly toward independence and modernization. Roads, communications, education, and other public services had slow but steady development, although not in as great degree as occurred in the more wealthy, populated, and accessible area of Palestine, where British administration was direct. Tribal troubles still broke out in Transjordan, as in the unrest of 1926 in the Wadi Musa-Petra area. In the same year senior British judicial and financial advisers were attached to Abdullah's government, and the Transjordan Frontier Force was formed. This body was a locally raised British army unit assigned to border guard duties and distinct from the Transjordan Arab Legion.

A further step in the direction of full self-government was taken in February 1928 when Great Britain and Transjordan executed a new treaty that relaxed British controls while still providing for a British resident to oversee financial and foreign policy matters. A constitution was promulgated in April 1928, and in April 1929 the Legislative Council, replacing the old Executive Council, was installed. In 1930 a campaign was launched to impose law and order and stamp out tribal raiding among the beduin. Major John Bagot Glubb (later, Lieutenant General Sir John Bagot Glubb), better known as Glubb Pasha, was transferred from Iraq as second in command of the Arab Legion under Peake. Glubb organized a highly effective beduin desert patrol consisting of mobile detachments based at strategic desert forts and equipped with good communications. Peake departed from Transjordan in 1939, and in April Glubb succeeded to full command of the Arab Legion. In January 1934 a new agreement with Great Britain allowed Abdullah to set up consular representation in Arab countries, and in May 1939 the Legislative Council was converted to a regular cabinet, or council of ministers.

In contrast with the comparative tranquillity and localism of Transjordan, the years after World War I were full of disturbance west of the Jordan River in British mandated Palestine. The Jewish Agency was established in August 1929 as the operational office for WZO in Palestine, and Jewish communal and quasi-governmental bodies developed steadily. In Zionist opinion Churchill's memoranda of 1922, subsequent commission reports, government White Papers, and regulation of immigration were evidence of British withdrawal from commitment and responsibilities. Royal commissions of 1929 and 1930, dispatched after outbreaks of violence in Palestine, recognized, as did later bodies, that the basic problem lay in the opposed positions of Zionism and Arab nationalism.

The rapid growth of anti-Semitism in Nazi Germany after 1933 augmented Jewish movement, legal or underground, to Palestine. Gravely disturbed at the increase in Jewish immigration and land acquisition, in April 1936 Palestinian Arabs formed the Supreme Arab Committee, later known as the Arab Higher Committee, under Haj Amin al Husseini and declared a general strike that assumed the proportions of a rebellion. The Arab Higher Committee was outlawed, and Great Britain dispatched the Peel Commission to Palestine. Its report, issued in July 1937, officially described the Arab and Zionist positions and the British obligations to each as irreconcilable and the existing mandate as unworkable. It recommended partition of Palestine into Jewish and Arab states with a retained British mandate over Nazareth, Bethlehem, and Jerusalem and a corridor from Jerusalem to the coast. The Twentieth Zionist Congress in 1937 rejected the proposed boundaries but agreed in principle to partition. Palestinian Arab nationalists firmly rejected all considerations of partition, although some favorable earlier sentiment apparently existed in Jordan.

The British government approved the Peel report and sent a technical team to make a detailed plan. This group, the Woodhead Commission, reversed the Peel Commission's findings and reported in November 1937 that partition was impracticable; this view was accepted. The British government then returned to the concept of peaceful accommodation between Jews and Arabs and called for a conference in March 1938 in London between the Jewish Agency and Arab representatives from Palestine and adjoining Arab states.

The conference failed to reach agreement, and the result was complicated by the fact that the Arab representatives refused, as they have since consistently done in comparable circumstances, to negotiate directly and openly with the Jewish Agency or, after 1948, with Israeli government representatives. On May 27, 1939, a new British White Paper was issued that extended British rule for ten years, limited Jewish immigration and land purchases in Palestine, and projected a Palestinian government at the end of the ten-year period subject to Jewish-Arab accommodation. This White Paper met a mixed Arab reception, being rejected by the Palestinian Arab Higher Committee. The Jewish Agency rejected it as a total repudiation of the Balfour Declaration and mandate obligations.

THE ESTABLISHMENT OF ISRAEL

During 1943 and 1944 Abdullah and his representatives had taken part in the inter-Arab preliminary discussions that resulted in the formation of the League of Arab States, or Arab League. Association with this cause identified Egypt with Arabism, an inclusion not previously clearly established. The Arab League was an outgrowth of older Arab nationalist visions of some kind of Fertile Crescent unity in the broad arc covering Palestine, Lebanon, Syria, Transjordan, and Iraq. Abdullah's concept of a Greater Syria under a Hashemite monarchy was familiar by this time and was opposed by new nationalists in Syria, by the Saudi Arabians, by the Zionists, and by France. In the end the Arab League became simply an association of sovereign states without real central unity or power. The league charter was signed at Cairo on March 22, 1945, by Syria, Egypt, Iraq, Lebanon, Saudi Arabia, and Transjordan, and the imam of Yemen signed on May 10.

On March 22, 1946, Transjordan and Great Britain entered into the Treaty of London, under which another major step was taken toward full sovereignty of the Arab state. Transjordan was proclaimed a kingdom on May 25 with Abdullah as king, and a new constitution replaced the obsolete document of 1928. Abdullah signed treaties of friendship and cooperation with Turkey and Iraq in 1947. His application for membership in the UN, however, was disapproved by a veto of the Soviet Union on grounds that the country was not fully independent. Also, Transjordan was not diplomatically recognized by the United States until January 31, 1949. A further treaty with Great Britain was executed in March 1948, under which all restrictions on sovereignty were removed except minimal considerations relating to defense and to British base and transit rights in Transjordan.

In Great Britain the Labour Party came to power in July 1945, and Ernest Bevin, as new secretary of state for foreign affairs and in implementation of the 1939 White Paper, limited Jewish immigration to Palestine. These actions in the postwar atmosphere inflamed Zionism and the Jewish Agency, and Palestine in effect became an armed camp. The Jewish Resistance Movement was formed in an attempt to unite or at least to coordinate the disparate Hagana, Irgun, and Stern paramilitary Jewish groups. Reprisals and counterreprisals between Jews and the authorities and between Arabs and the mandate authorities continued. The Palestinian Arab Higher Committee reappeared to oppose renewals of immigration.

The British in early 1947 decided to place the problem of Palestine before the UN, and on May 15, 1947, a special session of the UN General Assembly established the United Nations Special Committee on Palestine (UNSCOPS). On August 31 UNSCOPS issued a report supporting a geographically complex system of partition into separate Arab and Jewish states, a special international status for Jerusalem, and an economic union linking the three members. Supported by both the United States and the Soviet Union, this plan was adopted by the UN General Assembly on November 29, 1947.

On the next day the Arab Higher Committee totally rejected the plan and called for a general strike in Palestine; violence between Arabs and Jews mounted. The Zionist General Council stated willingness in principle to accept partition. The Arab League Council, meeting in December 1947, stated it would take whatever measures were required to prevent implementation of the UN resolution. Amid increasing conflict, representatives of the United Nations Implementation Commission were unable to function. In January 1948 Great Britain announced its intention to relinquish the mandate and to withdraw from Palestine on May 15, 1948, and it did so at that time.

Almost simultaneously forces of Egypt, Transjordan, Iraq, Syria, and Lebanon, with Saudi Arabian and Yemeni increments, advanced into Palestine. Arab units, except for the British-raised Arab Legion of Transjordan, were largely ill trained and had had little experience. Israeli forces, usually operating from interior lines of communication, included an estimated 20,000 to 25,000 European World War II veterans. The Arabs gained some initial success, but their advances were stemmed. By January 1949 the part of Palestine remaining in Arab hands was limited to that held by the Transjordan Arab Legion at the cessation of hostilities. Other Arab forces had been defeated or neutralized. This area was subsequently annexed by Jordan and commonly referred to as the West Bank. Abdullah had been particularly insistent that the Arab Legion must hold the part of the old city of Jerusalem containing the main Muslim holy places, and this had been accomplished (see ch. 4).

On May 29, 1948, the UN Security Council established the Truce Commission, headed by a Swedish diplomat, Folke Bernadotte, who was assassinated in Jerusalem by the Irgun on September 17, 1948. He was succeeded by an American, Ralph Bunche. This commission, which later evolved into the United Nations Truce Supervision Organization-Palestine (UNTSOP), attempted to devise new plans of settlement and arranged the truces of June 11 to July 8 and July 19 to October 14, 1948. Armistice talks were initiated with Egypt in January 1949, and an armistice agreement between Israel and Egypt was established on February 24; similar agreements were concluded with Lebanon on March 23, with Transjordan on April 3, and with Syria on July 20. Iraq did not enter into an armistice agreement but withdrew its forces.

THE HASHEMITE KINGDOM OF JORDAN, 1949–71

Stability and Isolation in King Abdullah's Last Years

Transjordan, one of the smallest of the Arab states and least blessed with natural resources of any kind, had done much of the fighting and had ended the war of 1948 in control of the only substantial part of Palestine remaining in Arab hands. This irregularly shaped area, which became commonly referred to as the West Bank, covered about 2,165 square miles (see fig. 1).

The population of Transjordan before the war had not exceeded 500,000. As a result of the war, some 900,000 to 1 million Palestinian Arabs became refugees. Of these, about 500,000 took refuge in Transjordan or in the West Bank. Most of these had to be accommodated in the refugee camps, in both banks. The camps were administered under the auspices of the United Nations Relief and Works Agency for Palestine Refugees in the Near East (UNRWA), set up in 1949. In addition, there were about 500,000 permanent residents, or natives, of the West Bank.

In December 1948 Abdullah declared himself king of Palestine, and in April 1949 he changed his country's name to Jordan. In April 1950 elections were held in both banks that were considered favorable by Abdullah, and on April 25, 1950, he formally annexed the West Bank to Jordan. This important step was immediately recognized and endorsed by Great Britain and was regarded by Abdullah as an act of responsibility on the part of Jordan. Within the Arab League, however, it was not generally approved, and monarchies and radical spokesmen alike condemned the move as a furtherance of Hashemite dynastic ambitions.

In 1951, faced with greater and more immediate problems and vulnerability than any other state in confronting Israel, Abdullah continued to search for a long-term, peaceful solution. Jordan alone of the Arab host countries extended full citizenship rights to the refugees. For security reasons, Abdullah did not favor the immediate internationalization of Jerusalem. In all these positions, he was opposed in the Arab League, finding support only from Hashemite kinsmen in Iraq. Radical socialist-nationalist propaganda, especially in Egypt and Syria, denounced him as a reactionary, medieval monarch and a tool of British colonial imperialism.

The Arab League debates after the Jordanian annexation of the West Bank were inconclusive, and Abdullah continued to set his own course. The East Bank during the period from early 1949 to early 1950 was relatively free from internal disturbance. The residual special relationship with Great Britain continued. Although not yet a member of the UN, Jordan supported the UN action in Korea and entered into an economic developmental aid agreement (under President Harry S. Truman's Point Four program) with the United States in March 1951.

The Assassination of Abdullah, Reign of Talal, and Accession of Hussein

On July 20, 1951, King Abdullah was assassinated as he entered the Al Aqsa Mosque in Jerusalem for Friday prayers. His grandson, the sixteen-year-old Prince Hussein, was at his side. Before he was killed by the king's guard, the assassin also fired at Hussein. The assassin was a Palestinian reportedly hired by relatives of Haj Amin al Husseini, a former mufti of Jerusalem, who was a bitter enemy of Abdullah.

Although many radical Palestinians blamed Abdullah for the reverses of 1948, there was no organized political follow-up after the murder of the king. Public disturbances were minor, order was quickly established by the Arab Legion, and a confused calm prevailed. The main political question was the succession to the throne.

Abdullah's son, Prince Naif, acted temporarily as regent, and some support existed for him to become king. The older son, Prince Talal, was in Switzerland receiving treatment for mental illness but reportedly had made much progress. It was widely believed that Abdullah would have favored Talal in order that the succession might then pass more easily to the young Hussein, Talal's son.

Accordingly, the government invited Talal to return and assume the throne, and he did so on September 6, 1951. During Talal's short reign he supported and promulgated a new constitution in January 1952, which still remained the basic instrument in mid-1973 (see ch. 8). Talal showed an inclination to improve relations with other Arab states, and Jordan in early 1952 joined the Arab League's Collective Security Pact, which Abdullah had rejected. Talal was popular among the people of the East Bank, who were not aware of his periodic seizures of mental illness. These increased in frequency and became clearly identified as schizophrenia.

On August 11, 1952, the prime minister presented to a secret session of the Jordanian legislature a report by three Jordanian Arab doctors and a recommendation that Talal be asked to abdicate in favor of Hussein. The legislature so decreed, and the abdication order was taken to Talal. He received it without surprise and acceded to it with dignity. He retired briefly to Cairo and then to a villa near Istanbul, where he lived quietly under medical attention until his death on July 8, 1972.

Hussein, who had been attending a private school in England, returned immediately to Jordan. Because he was under eighteen years of age, he could not, under the constitution, be crowned, and a regency council of three was therefore formed. Hussein decided to continue his education during the interim before he could come to the throne by attending the British Royal Military Academy at Sandhurst. After about six months, having attained eighteen years by the Muslim calendar, he returned to Jordan and, accompanied by much public ceremony, formally took the constitutional oath as king on May 2, 1953.

Early Reign and Survival of King Hussein I

When King Hussein I came to the throne, the chief influences that had thus far guided him were the example and teachings of his grandfather, the shocking experience of his grandfather's assassination, and his own education in conservative English schools. Hussein's own views, policies, and mode of operation were not yet firmly established. As king he had extensive legal powers. Although Jordan had become a constitutional monarchy, the constitution itself allowed the king to dismiss the National Assembly and to appoint the prime minister and other ministers at will. In addition, he enjoyed the traditional support of the East Bank Jordanian beduin tribes. The Arab Legion, paid for by a British subsidy, was composed mostly of intensely loyal beduin and British military officers.

Severe problems confronted the new king. Two-thirds of the citizens were Palestinians, whereas the government elite were mostly East Bank Jordanians, more conservative and traditional than the Palestinians whose spokesmen often reflected the new trend in radical Arab nationalism. In Cairo in July 1952 the successful coup d'etat of the Egyptian Free Officers movement headed by Gamal Abdul Nasser had overthrown the monarchy and established a republic. This example and the image of Nasser as the new champion of Arabism were, even by mid-1953, highly regarded by many Palestinians. Generally, and especially among the refugees, Great Britain, the United States, and the Hashemites were blamed by the Palestinians for their misfortunes.

Problems were magnified by the intensification during 1953 of border incidents with Israel that escalated in a succession of reprisals and counterreprisals between Palestinian infiltrators and Israeli forces. The Arab Legion endeavored to secure the armistice line and prevent infiltration, but its numbers were inadequate to provide complete and continuous coverage by day and night. Israeli forces during this time adopted the technique of massive retaliation that thereafter characterized their reaction pattern.

In 1953 and early 1954 an American plan for riparian distribution of the Jordan waters (the Eric Johnston plan) was tentatively accepted by Israel but, although recognized as technically sound from an engineering standpoint, was ultimately rejected by Jordan and the other Arab states concerned because it would involve coordination with and at least the implied recognition of Israel. In the stress of inter-Arab political relationships, it was impracticable for any Arab government to initiate settlement action with Israel, even if any had desired to do so.

In May 1953 Hussein designated as prime minister Fawzi al Mulqi, the former Jordanian ambassador to Great Britain and a liberal in comparison with Taufiq Abul Huda, whom he succeeded. By May 1954, however, internal tensions caused the Mulqi government to resign. Abul Huda returned to office, and his government was confirmed by the elections of October 16, 1954. A new financial aid agreement was made with Great Britain in December 1954, and Great Britain evinced an interest in coordinating its military and economic aid to Jordan with Jordanian participation in some kind of overall Middle Eastern defense system in the cold war between the West and the East. Jordan, however, preferred not to enter any great power pacts. Abul Huda's government was replaced in May 1955 by a new cabinet headed by Said al Mufti. Relations with Saudi Arabia were somewhat improved by an exchange of state visits by King Hussein and King Saud; also in 1955 Jordan was admitted to the UN.

The pattern of Western cold war alliances was extended on February 24, 1955, when Turkey and Iraq, later joined by Great Britain, Iran, and Pakistan, signed the United States-supported Baghdad Pact, which ultimately became the Central Treaty Organization (CENTO). Early in December 1955 the chief of the British general staff visited Amman to discuss conditions and terms under which Jordan might join the Baghdad Pact. The purpose of his visit was generally known, and radical Arab nationalist propaganda, especially from Palestinians and Radio Cairo, raised a storm of protest denouncing the pact and the monarchy as "tools of Western imperialism" and a "sellout to the Jews" and making other inflammatory charges.

The Mufti government resigned in disarray on December 13, and Hussein called upon a young former cabinet minister, Hazza al Majali, to form a new government. Majali was from a distinguished family of tribal shaykhs long predominant in the Karak region of south-central Jordan. He was known to be pro-Western, and after forming his cabinet, he stated without equivocation that he intended to take Jordan into the Baghdad Pact. Three days of mass demonstrations and rioting, raised by the political opposition, then followed in Amman.

The Arab Legion contained the mobs with minimal firing and casualties. Under this pressure, several of Majali's ministers resigned, and he then recommended a caretaker government. The mob dispersed, and Ibrahim Hashim became prime minister on December 20, 1955, followed by a regularized government under Samir Rifai on January 9, 1956. Order was restored. Jordan did not sign the Baghdad Pact but found itself again isolated in the Arab world.

On March 1, 1956, Hussein dismissed Glubb as commander of the Arab Legion, thus precipitating a diplomatic crisis that threatened to isolate Hussein from his principal ally, Great Britain. Some observers held that Hussein was advised to take this step as an act of defiance against Great Britain and of identification with the new Arab nationalism personified by Egypt's Nasser. Hussein stated that the decision was his alone, that he had found himself for some time in disagreement with Glubb over military organization and planning, and that the

British government ought not to identify this personal action as an official cause (see ch. 13). The British cabinet, however, took the opposite view and, although the British subsidy was not, in fact, then withdrawn, relations were strained for several years.

In May 1956 Hussein designated a young officer named Ali Abu Nuwar as major general and commander of the Arab Legion. The name of the force was officially changed to the Jordan Arab Army. Abu Nuwar was an advocate of Arab nationalism and elimination of foreign controls in the army and government. As chief of general staff, Abu Nuwar began his attempts to deanglicize the army and to break the tight pattern of its control by officers and men of Transjordanian beduin origin.

Border incidents with Israel were a continuing source of anxiety in 1956, and events reached a climax on October 10. At that time, in reprisal for a guerrilla attack on two farmers, an Israeli task group, supported by air and artillery, attacked the West Bank village of Qalqilyah, killing forty-eight. The Palestinians clamored for war, and in this atmosphere of crisis Jordanian politics took its brief venture into anti-Western radical nationalism.

In the parliamentary elections of October 21, 1956, the National Socialist Party received the most votes, and its leader, Suleiman Nabulsi, was designated by Hussein as prime minister (see ch. 9). Several National Front (communist) party members and members of the Baath Party (Arab Socialist Resurrection Party) also gained seats in the National Assembly, although independents and the older, conservative parties were represented about equally with the leftists. Nabulsi had become an ardent follower of Nasser and began to shape the policies of his government accordingly. Hussein entered a military pact with Egypt and Syria on October 24.

When Israel attacked Egypt in the Sinai Peninsula starting October 29, 1956, and the British and French invaded Port Said on November 5, Nabulsi suddenly became indecisive. Hussein, however, proposed that Jordan attack Israel at once but was urged personally by Nasser not to do so because Jordan's forces would be wasted in an action that by then was already lost. Jordan, as a result, did not become engaged in the brief Second Arab-Israeli War (1956). By early 1957, largely because of diplomatic pressures from both the United States and the Soviet Union, the Israeli, British, and French forces had been withdrawn from the Sinai. British participation in this attack made it politically imperative that Jordan end its special relationship under the 1948 treaty.

Hussein attended a conference with King Saud, President Nasser, and Syrian leaders at Cairo, January 18 and 19, 1957. Under the Arab Solidarity Agreement emanating from this conference, Saudi Arabia, Egypt, and Syria undertook, in the ratio of two-to-two-to-one, respectively, to pay Jordan a total annually of the equivalent of

US$35.8 million for ten years and thereby free Jordan from the British subsidy. An Anglo-Jordanian agreement of March 13, 1957, abrogated the basic Anglo-Jordanian treaty of 1948, terminated the British subsidy, and initiated the turnover of British installations and withdrawal of all British troops still in Jordan. As for the Arab Solidarity Agreement, Saudi Arabia made one quarterly payment; no one else paid anything.

The internal political scene in Jordan in early 1957 quickly shaped up as a power struggle between the monarchy and the Egypt-oriented government of Prime Minister Nabulsi. Hussein and the conservatives suspected that Nabulsi was maneuvering to disestablish the monarchy. Also, Nabulsi began negotiations aimed at opening diplomatic relations with the Soviet Union and securing Soviet arms aid. After the Egyptian-Soviet arms deal of 1955, the Soviet Union had increasingly supported the Arab cause against Israel and had begun by this means the establishment of a position of influence in the Middle East.

Hussein saw hopes of support in the Eisenhower Doctrine enunciated in January 1957 by the United States president as an offer of military and economic aid to those governments requesting help to save themselves from communism. Nabulsi rejected this doctrine. Political tension and Hussein's suspicions increased, and on April 10, 1957, exercising his constitutional prerogative, Hussein demanded the resignation of the Nabulsi government. On April 13 General Abu Nuwar made a statement to Said al Mufti, who was attempting to form a caretaker government, that was capable of being interpreted as an ultimatum that any new cabinet be approved by Abu Nuwar and the army officers of his staff aligned with him.

There followed a sequence of dramatic events that day and night that became known as the Zarqa affair. The public, sensing the explosive political atmosphere, had become restive in Amman. This was even more true of a large concentration of troops at the main army base at Az Zarqa, where rumors spread that the king was dead; taking Abu Nuwar with him, Hussein set off for Az Zarqa. En route he met several truckloads of troops who were overjoyed at seeing Hussein alive and who demanded the head of Abu Nuwar. At Abu Nuwar's request, the king sent him back to the safety of the royal palace and continued to Az Zarqa. There he spent several hours amid wildly enthusiastic demonstrations of loyalty to the throne and returned to Amman after reassuring and quieting the troops.

On the next day Hussein allowed Abu Nuwar to leave the country. He fled first to Syria, then to Egypt. Hussein appointed General Ali Hiyari, Abu Nuwar's cousin, as chief of general staff. On April 19 Hiyari followed his cousin in fleeing to Syria, and Hussein designated as his top commander a tough beduin officer, Habis al Majali, cousin of the forthright Hazza al Majali, whose brief term as prime minister had been disrupted by the Baghdad Pact riots. During the balance of

the month several cabinet crises occurred, as the remnants of the Nabulsi faction fought a rearguard action and external propaganda
against Hussein continued. Ibrahim Hashim, however, successfully
formed a government, and all political party activity was outlawed.

Hussein had won; what had counted was the loyalty of the combat
units of the army, and that loyalty clearly belonged to him. But Jordan
was beleaguered—Nasserism was arrayed against the king, the British subsidy was gone, the Arab Solidarity Agreement had evaporated,
the rift was wider than ever between the East Bank and the West
Bank, and Israel remained strong on the frontier. Hussein unequivo-
cally placed his country on the side of the West in the great power
global confrontation and sought a new principal source of aid—the
United States.

Crisis and Realignment with Western Aid

The United States replaced Great Britain as the major source of
foreign aid but under the Eisenhower Doctrine rather than by bilateral
treaty or alliance mechanisms. Existing economic aid programs were
expanded, and military aid was initiated. An airlift arriving at Amman
on September 9, 1957, brought a substantial amount of military equipment and was followed soon by shipments to Al Aqaba. Hussein, however, had to regard United States aid, no matter how welcome, as a
short- or intermediate-term solution because he did not control its
amount or origin and could not be certain how long it would last.

In seeking a viable, long-term arrangement for political stability in
face of the hostile Nasser-style revolutionary nationalism then prev-
alent in the Middle East, Jordan turned to neighboring Iraq. Iraq,
far larger than Jordan and more populous, was also far wealthier in oil
and other resources. It had usually supported Jordan in Arab councils,
although without deep involvement since the 1948 war. Its conservative government had taken Iraq into the Baghdad Pact in 1954 to
ensure continued Western support against the Soviet Union or, more
particularly, against radical Arab movements.

On February 1, 1958, the announcement by Egypt and Syria of the
integration of their two countries to form the United Arab Republic
(UAR) was greeted with high enthusiasm by the new nationalist
advocates of unity in the Arab world, but it made the situation of conservative or moderate regimes more perilous. The initial phase of
Jordanian-Iraqi negotiation was quickly concluded, and on February
14, 1958, a proclamation was issued in Amman by Hussein and King
Faisal II, Hussein's cousin, joining the Hashemite kingdoms of Iraq
and Jordan in a federation to be called the Arab Union. Faisal was to
be head-of-state; and Hussein, deputy head-of-state. Baghdad and
Amman were to alternate every six months as the capital. In May,
Samir Rifai became prime minister of Jordan; his predecessor,
Hashim, became prime minister in the new union.

Meanwhile, a severe political crisis had developed in Lebanon in connection with the presidential election. The incumbent government faction, conventional and Western oriented, was opposed by another faction of subversive and strongly pro-Nasser orientation supported from Syria. Civil disorders and violence mounted in May 1958. The Syrian Region of the UAR closed the Syria-Jordan border. In Lebanon full-scale civil war was averted, but the situation became so incendiary that the government requested United States assistance, and United States forces began landing at Beirut on July 15, 1958. An Iraqi motorized brigade, under the command of Brigadier Abdul Karim Qassim, seized control of Baghdad on July 14, 1958. King Faisal and the rest of the Iraqi royal family were seized and immediately shot to death. The Jordanian leaders Hashim and Suleiman Tuqan, who were in Baghdad at the time of the coup, were seized by the mob and killed.

Hussein, enraged with shock and grief, at first wished to throw the Jordan Arab Army into Iraq to revenge Faisal and restore the Arab Union but, advised by his chief civilian ministers, decided against this course. In Iraq the army and police supported the coup, and Qassim became president-dictator, taking Iraq out of the Arab Union and the Baghdad Pact.

Jordan was cut off as it had never been before: the Syrian and Iraqi borders were closed, and to the west lay Israel, whose intentions in this crisis were unknown but whose military capabilities were well known. Hussein appealed to both the United States and Great Britain. An emergency airlift of petroleum by the United States Air Force was instituted, and on July 17, 1958, British troops began to be airlanded at Amman. Ironically, these flights came in over Israel, since overflight clearances for alternate routes over Arab countries could not be secured in time.

The political atmosphere in Jordan after the coup in Iraq appeared for some weeks highly combustible, but the government, operating within a pattern of partial martial law, endured; the airlift continued, the British brigade was reinforced, the loyalty of the army remained unimpeached, and the Israeli frontier, after one incident in early June, continued to be quiet. During October a United States military survey mission was in Jordan, and a further phase of United States military aid was planned. By early November the British brigade was withdrawn; a British military advisory mission, however, remained with the Jordan army and air force.

On November 10, 1958, Hussein considered it safe to leave Jordan for Europe for a brief rest and took off in a small commercial aircraft marked with the Jordanian royal insignia. Over Syria he was first ordered by Damascus radio to land and then attacked by two Syrian MIG-17's that attempted, although without firing, to force him down. Taking evasive action at low altitudes, Hussein and the copilot returned the aircraft successfully to Jordanian airspace and to Amman. Wild enthusiasm and rejoicing, especially among the Jordanian military forces, immediately broke out because of the king's escape. On the following day morale was further boosted by the arrival of the first two of six transonic British fighter aircraft provided by United States offshore procurement for the Jordan air force. These two incidents, the king's escape and the delivery of the Hawker Hunters, taken against the background of United States and British aid, did much to relieve the high tension of the previous six months.

On May 6, 1959, Rifai turned over the prime ministership to Hazza al Majali, an act leaving no doubt as to where Jordan's orientation lay. United States aid of all kinds amounted to more than US$50 million annually. The rebuilt port of Al Aqaba, with twelve new oil storage tanks, new berthing facilities, and a new phosphate loading plant, was opened (see ch. 12). Diplomatic relations were resumed in August 1959 with the UAR, and border incidents with Israel were less frequent than the low-level subversive infiltration attempts intercepted from Syria. Hussein visited King Saud in February 1960, and relations with Saudi Arabia began to improve. At the same time, however, anti-Israel agitation began to mount again.

On May 28, 1960, Prime Minister Majali and the director of the United States aid program in Jordan signed the East Ghor Canal Agreement for an irrigation scheme of 17,500 acres in the Jordan valley (see ch. 3). A few days later Majali and the United States ambassador concluded an agreement for a project that would assist the desert areas. Advances in education, public services, and other fields were also made or planned. A new paved highway from Amman south across the desert to Maan was dedicated in November 1960, and a shortened highway from the Jericho vicinity up to Jerusalem was opened in January 1963.

The two-year period of relative tranquillity was broken on August 29, 1960, when Prime Minister Majali was assassinated by a heavy time bomb charge concealed in his desk. Twelve people were killed, and some fifty were injured by this bomb and another that exploded about twenty minutes later. Again, as at the time of Abdullah's assassination, no organized political follow-up appeared. Curfew was declared, and beduin troops moved into Amman. Some analysts speculated that the conspirators expected the assassination to generate a public uprising. Precisely the opposite occurred, however, as Hussein quickly formed a new government with his chief aide, Bahjat al Talhouni, as prime minister. The assassination plot was traced to Syria and further identified with Cairo, although in later years this identification was not pressed. Four suspects were caught, convicted, and hanged. The army was, for a time, concentrated near the Syrian border. The threat of Israel remained, however, and Syria was not invaded.

The Majali tragedy proved to be an external rather than an internal crisis. Domestic calm prevailed, extending to the general acceptance of Hussein's marriage to Antoinette Gardiner on May 25, 1961. (Hussein had been first married on April 19, 1955, to Sharifa Dina Abdul Hamid al Aun of Cairo. This marriage, after the birth in 1956 of a daughter, was dissolved in 1957.) Antoinette Gardiner, upon conversion to Islam and marriage to the king, became Princess Muna. Four children were born to this union: Prince Abdullah (1962); Prince Faisal (1963); and the twin princesses, Zein and Aisha (1968). Abdullah was technically crown prince until April 1965, when the king, by constitutional processes, shifted the designation to his own younger brother, Prince Hasan (see ch. 8). The king's marriage to Princess Muna was dissolved on December 21, 1972. On December 26, 1972, Hussein married Alia Tuqan, of a prominent Palestinian family, and she became queen.

In January 1962 Wasfi al Tal became prime minister, and in December 1962 the resumption of limited political party activity in Jordan was permitted. Samir Rifai, succeeding Tal in March 1963, was able to remain in office only about one month. A caretaker government under the king's great uncle, Sharif Hussein bin Nasir, was confirmed in office after new elections in July 1963, and the year closed in a conciliatory atmosphere at home and abroad. Diplomatic relations had been opened for the first time with the Soviet Union in August 1963, but Soviet offers of military equipment were not accepted.

Development and Disaster: 1964–67

By early 1964 Arab governments and Palestinian spokesmen had become seriously alarmed at the intention stated by Israel in 1963 to draw water from Lake Tiberias in order to irrigate the Negev Desert in southern Israel. President Nasser thereupon invited the Arab heads-of-state to attend a summit conference in Cairo in January 1964. From his new position of strength, both internally and externally in the Arab world, Hussein promptly accepted the invitation and took the occasion to resume diplomatic relations with the UAR. (Technically, despite the Syrian secession of September 28, 1961, Egypt retained the name United Arab Republic until September 2, 1971, when it again became the Arab Republic of Egypt.)

At the conference the principal issue was the Jordan waters question. Israel, with its pipeline nearing completion, had announced the intention to take from Lake Tiberias quantities of water approximating the allocations of the 1954–55 Johnston plan. The conference, despite Syria's militant rhetoric, excluded war with Israel, at least for the time being, because of the absence of unified Arab political and military systems.

Instead, three alternative courses of action were approved: the diversion of the tributary sources of the Jordan River north of Lake

Tiberias in Lebanon and Syria; the establishment of the United Arab Command under an Egyptian commander; and the formation of the new Palestine Liberation Organization (PLO), to be headed by a former Jerusalem lawyer, Ahmad Shukairy, as the recognized focus for Palestinian expression and resistance against Israel. The Cairo Conference of January 1964 ended in a euphoric atmosphere of goodwill and brotherhood.

Talhouni succeeded Nasir as Jordanian prime minister in July 1964, pledging his government to implement the spirit of the Cairo Conference "according to the king's instructions." The revived Jordan-UAR friendship was cultivated; Jordan entered the Arab Common Market in August 1964; and in September Hussein attended the second Arab summit at Alexandria. In May 1965 Jordan, along with nine other Arab states, broke off relations with the Federal Republic of Germany (West Germany) because of its recognition of Israel. Jordan and Saudi Arabia on August 9, 1965, signed an important agreement defining for the first time the boundary between the two countries. By this agreement Jordan gave up some territory in the southeast but was able to gain an extension of about twelve miles down the gulf from the crowded port of Al Aqaba.

Shukairy, famous for the often hysterical violence of his political rhetoric, was to play a role in Palestinian history somewhat analogous to that of the old mufti, Haj Amin al Husseini, one of the principal architects of the Arab disasters of 1948 and 1949. Shukairy organized the PLO at a conference in Jerusalem on May 28, 1964. The PLO objective, according to the Palestine National Charter produced at the conference, was the liberation of Palestine in cooperation with all Arab states but without interfering in their internal affairs or claiming sovereignty on the West Bank. Almost from the start, trouble developed with Hussein's government and was apparent in February 1965 when the king called on Tal to become prime minister again. The rift between the PLO and the government was far advanced by the time of the third Arab summit in September 1965.

Essentially, conflict arose because the PLO, despite its stated intentions to the contrary, attempted in practice to assume governmental functions, such as taxing Palestinians and distributing arms to the villagers, acts that infringed on Jordanian sovereignty. In December 1964, with Syrian assistance, the guerrilla organization called Al Fatah was formed in Damascus under leadership of a Palestinian refugee, Yasir Arafat. Al Fatah and PLO raids and sabotage were carried out against Israel without clearance from either the United Arab Command (which in practice did not become strongly organized) or the Jordanian military. Jordanian policy since 1949 had been and continued to be one of avoiding border incidents and terrorism that would generate reprisal and possibly an untimely war. State policy and the guerrilla policy were thus at odds as to the mode and timing of operations.

Al Fatah attacks, although planned in Syria, were most often launched into Israel by infiltration through Lebanon or Jordan. Israeli reprisals against selected Jordanian West Bank villages became increasingly severe and frequent from May 1965 onward. Syrian policy and propaganda became increasingly extremist, and in July 1966, when Hussein cut off Jordanian official endorsement and support for the PLO, both that organization and the Syrian government openly turned against him with all the devices of propaganda at their disposal. Jordan and Syria had broken ground for a dam on the Yarmuk River in May 1966, but the project was soon suspended because of the tension between the countries. The proposal to divert Jordan River tributaries had proved too dangerous because of Israeli harassment and had in effect been abandoned.

In reprisal for the terrorist attacks by the guerrillas Israel, on November 13, 1966, destroyed the Jordanian village of As Samu with an attack by a reinforced brigade. Although Israel was censured by the UN, the public clamor and rioting against the Jordan government that broke out among the Palestinians of the West Bank exceeded any previous experience. As in the past, Hussein restored public order by use of the army. Political pressure against Hussein mounted, however, along with clashes and incidents on the Syria-Jordan border; and after the uneasy winter of 1966 Hussein again designated Nasir as head of another interim government.

Tension mounted on the Israeli-Syrian border, where a serious land and air engagement took place on April 7, 1967, in which Syria was reported to have lost six aircraft. The UAR was severely criticized by Syria and also by Jordan for failing to send support. After general elections on April 23 the moderate Saad Juma became Jordanian prime minister. In mid-May the UAR commenced on extensive military buildup in the Sinai Peninsula in response to Syrian allegations that it was in imminent danger of invasion by strong Israeli forces grouped in attack posture. The UAR declared a state of emergency on May 16 and on May 18 demanded removal of the United Nations Emergency Force from the Sinai. This demand was acceded to by United Nations Secretary General U Thant and immediately carried out.

On May 22, 1967, President Nasser announced that the Strait of Tiran, at the entrance to the Gulf of Aqaba, would be closed to Israeli shipping, and Israel immediately declared this action to be a cause of war. Hussein quickly decided that it would not again be possible, as in 1956, for Jordan to stay out of the conflict. He got in touch with Nasser, proceeded to Cairo, and on May 30, 1967, unhesitatingly signed a military alliance with the UAR, not only in response to political pressures at home but also in fulfillment of basic pan-Arab commitments.

The tempo of scattered firing along the Arab-Israeli borders increased. On the morning of June 5, 1967, declaring itself surrounded and with danger of attack increasing daily, Israel launched a massive air assault that effectively eliminated UAR, Jordanian, Syrian, and Iraqi air forces on the ground. Israeli follow-up ground attacks successively engaged and routed the UAR army in the Sinai, defeated the Jordanians on the West Bank, and finally overpowered the southwestern Syrian defenses. By June 11 a cease-fire had been established, and Israel was in possession of, among other areas, Jordan's West Bank, including all of Jerusalem.

Of all the Arab states Jordan, which could least afford it, lost most in the war. Government figures list 6,094 killed or missing. The best one-third of its agricultural land and its main tourist centers were lost. Jerusalem was wholly in Israeli hands; the Israeli parliament legislated the annexation of the old city on June 27, 1967. (The United States did not recognize this annexation.) During the short war more than 200,000 refugees—many of whom had first been refugees from the 1948-49 war—fled from the West Bank to the East Bank. Hussein and his government survived, but the outlook for the country had never been darker than on June 11, 1967.

Postwar Survival and the Guerrilla Crisis

In the wake of the war Hussein and his government were confronted with the critical problems of a shattered economy, the welfare and management of the refugees, the need for external aid and readjustments in international relations, the requirement for a rapid rebuilding of the Jordanian army and replacement of its losses, and the loss of the West Bank to Israel. Internally, however, the major problem was the continuing confrontation with the Palestinian guerrilla organizations—also known as commandos, or fedayeen.

The West Bank, which became known as the Israeli-occupied Territory, was under the control of Israeli Defense Minister Moshe Dayan, who allowed a general continuation of local administration on the West Bank subject to the maintenance of order and overall Israeli security control. In time, Dayan's "open bridges" policy allowed a tightly controlled flow of personnel and produce back and forth across the Jordan, and some of the new refugees returned to the West Bank. The general refugee situation was alleviated in Jordan, although far from solved, by the humanitarian efforts of such agencies as the UN, the International Red Cross, and the American Near East Refugee Association. Agriculture's contribution to the Jordanian economy was seriously dislocated by the war, but the important East Bank phosphate industry was unhurt and was expanded after the war (see ch. 12).

The Arab League heads-of-state met at Khartoum at the end of August 1967. The conference, generally considered to represent the views of Arab moderates, reached four major decisions: oil production, suspended by the oil states during the war to be resumed; continued nonrecognition of and nonnegotiation with Israel, individually or collectively; continued closure of the Suez Canal and the elimination of all foreign military bases in Arab territory; and provision of financial subsidy aid to the UAR and Jordan by the oil-rich states of Saudi Arabia, Libya, and Kuwait. The total annual subsidy, promised for the indefinite future, amounted to the sterling equivalent of US$378 million, of which Jordan was to receive about US$112 million. Donor states at first regularly paid their shares in quarterly installments, but Libya and Kuwait withdrew their support to Jordan during the 1970-71 war between the Jordan government and the guerrillas.

In addition to the Khartoum subsidies, Jordan also received grants from the shaykhdoms of Abu Dhabi and Qatar and a special grant of US$42 million from Saudi Arabia for arms purchases. Great Britain provided an emergency loan to cushion the immediate effects of the June 1967 war and later extended further long-term credits. West Germany, with whom Jordan had resumed relations, also extended certain development loans. Although the direct United States subsidy had been terminated, substantial long-term loans were extended to Jordan for emergency relief, development, and military assistance, and in February 1968 United States arms shipments to Jordan were resumed. By such means and its own meager resources, Jordan averted financial disaster.

On November 22, 1967, after months of diplomatic wrangling, the UN Security Council adopted Resolution 242 as a guideline for the settlement of the 1967 war. The principal provisions of this resolution proclaimed the inadmissibility of territorial aquisition by war and called for withdrawal of Israeli forces from areas occupied in the 1967 war; termination of all states of belligerency; acknowledgment of the sovereignty of all states in the area within secure and recognized boundaries; freedom of navigation on all international waterways in the area; a just settlement of the refugee problem; and the designation of a special UN representative as a contact betwen the states concerned.

In time Jordan, the UAR, and Israel accepted this resolution in general but with distinctly varying policy interpretations. Hussein rested his case for a settlement of the 1967 war squarely on this resolution, such settlement not implying an overall solution to the general Arab-Israeli problem. In the six years after 1967 both Jordanian and Egyptian policy at length admitted to at least a de facto recognition of Israel, but the question of the Israeli attitude toward the occupied territories, the procedural complexities of negotiation, and the implacable opposition to negotiated settlement by the radical Palestinians and other Arab nationalists in Syria, Libya, and elsewhere prevented it.

Hostilities with Israel did not end with the cease-fire on June 11, 1967. On the Jordanian front the guerrilla organizations, especially

Al Fatah, became increasingly active after June 1967 and attempted to employ the methods of the so-called wars of national liberation in the style of the Provisional Revolutionary Government of South Vietnam (Viet Cong) and within a doctrinal framework of ill-digested Maoism.

The irregular forces of the PLO had played little part in the war. After the Arab failures in conventional warfare against Israel, however, the seemingly cheap and effective methodology of guerrilla war was seized upon by Palestinian nationalists as the new instrument through which Israel could be defeated. In December 1967 Shukairy was replaced as head of the PLO by Yahya Hammouda. Hammouda was succeeded in February 1969 by Arafat, who continued also as head of Al Fatah and its action arm, Al Asifah. By early 1970 at least seven fedayeen organizations became identified in Jordan. Other than Al Fatah, the most important was the Popular Front for the Liberation of Palestine (PFLP), led by George Habbash (see ch. 9). Although the PLO sought to integrate these various bands and announcements were made from time to time that this had occurred, they were never effectively united.

At first by genuine inclination and then by political necessity, Hussein sought accommodation with the guerrillas and provided training sites and assistance. In Jordan's internal politics, however, the main issue from mid-1967 to mid-1971 was the struggle for political control between the government and the guerrilla organizations. The guerrillas, based in the refugee camps, gradually became virtually a state within a state; money and arms, from both the Arab states and private individuals, were easily secured.

As the guerrilla effort mounted, Israel retaliated quickly and with increasing effectiveness. In March 1968 an Israeli brigade attacked the Jordanian village of Karameh, said to be the guerrilla capital. Damage was inflicted, but the Israeli force was driven back with substantial loss by the fedayeen and the Jordan army. This action was cited as a great fedayeen victory.

Israel launched further heavy attacks at Irbid in June 1968 and at As Salt in August. The constricted area and generally open terrain of the West Bank did not provide the kind of concealment and refuge featured in classic guerrilla operations, and the Palestinian population failed to provide the universal "friendly sea" of Mao Tse-tung's doctrine in which the guerrilla could "swim like a fish." The guerrillas' main activities in Jordan increasingly appeared to turn away from fighting Israel and to be directed instead to the overthrow of Hussein.

A major guerrilla-government confrontation occurred in November 1968 when the government sought to disarm the refugee camps, but civil war was averted by a compromise that favored the Palestinians. In June 1969, in another major reprisal aimed at forcing

Jordan to curb the guerrillas, Israeli forces blew up key sections of the East Ghor irrigation canal, previously damaged in the 1967 war. Severe confrontations between the Jordan army and the guerrillas occurred again in February and June 1970, including several more assassination attempts against Hussein, but were settled by further concessions to the guerrillas and the removal of antifedayeen officers from top army commands. The guerrillas were at the height of their political power in Jordan, but the army and the tribal shaykhs of south Jordan, held in check only by Hussein's word, were increasingly restive.

Fighting between army and guerrilla forces broke out late in August 1970. At the end of the first week in September, the PFLP hijacked three European airliners and forced them to land at a Jordanian desert field. The passengers were held hostage for the release of certain guerrillas, and the aircraft were blown up. All hostages were eventually released, most of them by mid-September.

Hussein's patience was exhausted. On September 16 he formed a military cabinet, recalled Field Marshall Habis al Majali as army commander, and gave the order to suppress the guerrillas. On September 17 Jordan armor and infantry units attacked the guerrilla strongholds in Amman. Within three days the guerrillas were defeated in Amman, although not totally driven out. Fighting in Amman was heavy, with much destruction and loss of life. The number of those killed on all sides has been responsibly estimated at up to 3,500, although guerrilla propaganda then and later cited much higher figures (see ch. 9).

Meanwhile, on September 19 a force of at least 200 Syrian tanks invaded northern Jordan to assist the guerrillas. The Syrian invasion force was fully withdrawn by September 25 after suffering at least 50-percent tank losses from Jordanian armor and air strikes and from logistical problems. Syria was at the same time influenced by the possibility of Israeli intervention, by diplomatic pressure and possible intervention by the United States, and by separate diplomatic pressures from the Soviet Union.

With the Syrian invasion thrown back and the guerrillas mostly driven from Amman, Hussein and his government once more had survived. Assassination attempts gainst Hussein again had failed. The crisis of 1970 was regarded, however, as having been the most serious of the many threats to the government during its history.

On September 26, 1970, Hussein restored a civilian cabinet with Ahmad Tuqan as prime minister, and on September 27 the king proceeded to Cairo to attend a summit conference hastily summoned by Nasser to reestablish inter-Arab peace. At the urging of Nasser and other Arab heads-of-state, Hussein and Arafat entered into a new agreement to keep the peace and maintain the identity of both the Jordan government and the guerrilla movements. The Tunisian premier, Bahi Ladgham, undertook to head a commission to oversee implementation of the agreement.

Hussein and Arafat signed a further agreement on October 13, 1970, in Amman that appeared highly favorable to the guerrillas. In practice, however, the Jordanian army and security forces quietly began the steady reassertion of Jordanian law and sovereignty. Guerrilla refusals to comply were cited as violations of the agreement, and arrests were made. At the end of October Hussein again called on Tal to become prime minister. By early 1971 the systematic, piecemeal mop-up of the guerrillas had proceeded so far as to cause Ladgham to suspend efforts to enforce the Cairo agreement. Syria, the UAR, Algeria, and Libya all denounced Jordan verbally. In Syria, however, a more pragmatic wing of the Baath Party had come to power in November 1970, and by early April 1971, as the last of the guerrillas were forced from Amman, the Syrian party press suddenly changed its line by calling upon the fedayeen to become realistic. On June 5, however, Al Fatah and six other remnant bands called for a new effort to overthrow Hussein.

On July 13, 1971, Jordanian army forces launched a coordinated attack on the last guerrilla redoubt in the area and seized it by July 18. All bases were destroyed, and all the bands in Jordan were broken up. About 2,500 prisoners were taken. The contest for political control in Jordan between the government and the guerrillas of 1967 to 1971 was finished. King Hussein and his government were again firmly in control of the country (see ch. 9; ch. 13).

CHAPTER 3

GEOGRAPHY AND POPULATION

The territory of Jordan totals almost 35,000 square miles, but in mid-1973 roughly 6 percent of the kingdom remained under Israeli occupation as a consequence of the Arab-Israeli War of 1967 (see ch. 2). The occupied territory, known as the West Bank (see Glossary), contains about 50 percent of the better agricultural land and many of the more important urban centers, such as Hebron, Jerusalem, and Nabulus (see fig. 1).

The country is landlocked except at its southern extremity, where about sixteen miles of shoreline along the Gulf of Aqaba provide access to the Red Sea. A great north-south geological rift, forming the depression of the Jordan River valley, Lake Tiberias (Sea of Galilee), and the Dead Sea, is the dominant topographical feature dividing the country into the two regions known as the East Bank (see Glossary) and the West Bank. The depression itself is one of the hottest and most forbidding areas in the entire Fertile Crescent. Throughout history it has been a barrier between the lands of the east and the territories bordering the Mediterranean Sea on the west.

More than anything else the distribution of rainfall continues to determine the pattern of permanent settlement. By far the great majority of the population lives in the northern part of the country on either side of the Jordan River where there is enough rainfall to support cultivation. Almost 82 percent of East Bank territory is sparsely inhabited desert; the population is concentrated in the northwestern corner, accessible to the Jordan River system and the site of major urban centers.

Arable land is the country's most valuable if limited resource. The East Ghor Canal, completed in 1963, brought much of the northern Jordan valley under irrigation, and in early 1973 plans were well under way to impound the waters from some of the side valleys to provide extra water supplies for the East Ghor Canal system. The Jordan valley itself was the site of major development efforts in 1973. Projects for land reclamation; the further exploitation of water resources; and the construction of roads, bridges, dams, and electrical plants were in early stages of implementation.

Because of alterations in the national territory as a result of warfare and occupation, there have been extreme fluctuations in the number of inhabitants as well as massive population shifts since 1946. The first, and as of 1973 the only, full official census was held in 1961 during a period of relative territorial stability but, because of the redistribution of much of the population after the Arab-Israeli War of 1967, the 1961 census data furnish only conditionally valid premises for projections for the early 1970s.

The population of Jordan including the Israeli-occupied West Bank totaled an estimated 2,583,000 in 1973; the East Bank population at the same time was about 1,837,000. Refugees from the West Bank and from other Israeli-occupied Arab lands accounted for approximately one-third or more of the East Bank population. According to some authorities, 40 percent or possibly one-half of the total population of Jordan were refugees and displaced persons from Israeli-occupied territories. Estimates regarding the absolute number of refugees are subject to wide margins of error because of duplications in refugee registration, underreporting of refugee deaths, and a high degree of mobility within this group.

Urbanization and official efforts at resettlement were the two major trends governing population redistribution during the early 1970s. In the East Bank difficult economic conditions in the countryside and a constant stream of refugees have stimulated migration to the major cities of the northwest, and nearly 30 percent of the East Bank population lives in Amman, the national capital. The government has been at least partially successful in settling the country's approximately 117,000 nomads in special areas bordering the eastern desert. Medium-sized agricultural communities are planned in the Jordan valley to settle refugees and rural migrants who would otherwise flock to the cities.

Only a little over 20 percent of the East Bank population is in the working force. Agriculture and services employ about one-third each of the working population; industry and trade engage about one-tenth each. Unemployment during the late 1960s was estimated to be in excess of 10 percent but according to some sources had declined somewhat by 1972. The problem of surplus unemployed unskilled workers persisted, however, in addition to which a substantial number of technically qualified persons emigrated to neighboring countries to seek employment (see ch. 11).

GEOGRAPHY

Boundaries

Except for small sections of the borders with Israel and Syria, Jordan's international boundaries do not follow well-defined or natural features of the terrain. The boundaries were established by various international agreements and, with the obvious exception of the border with Israel, none was in dispute in 1973.

The border with Israel is based on the Armistice Demarcation Line agreed upon in April 1949 by Israel and what was then Transjordan, after negotiations under the auspices of a United Nations (UN) mediator. In general the border represents the battle positions held by the Arab and Israeli forces when a cease-fire went into effect and has no relation to economic or administrative factors.

Until the Israeli occupation after the 1967 war, the demarcation line divided the city of Jerusalem between Jordan and Israel, Jordan holding the old city and most of the holy places and Israel, the newer city on the west. The western boundary of Jordanian territory, both south and north of Jerusalem, generally follows a line where the high ground of Judea and Samaria begins to fall off to the lower plains and valleys along the Mediterranean coastline. At Qalqilyah, west of Nabulus, the border is only about ten miles from the sea.

The June 1967 hostilities between Jordan and Israel, resulting in the occupation of all of the West Bank of Jordan by Israeli forces, were halted along a cease-fire line that, at least temporarily, became the border between the two countries. This line followed the course of the Jordan River south from the mouth of the Wadi al Yabis to the head of the Dead Sea; north from the Wadi al Yabis the cease-fire line coincided with the demarcation line of 1949.

The boundaries between Jordan and neighboring Syria, Iraq, and Saudi Arabia do not have the special significance of the border with Israel, and they have not materially hampered the nomadic people in their movements. By the time political boundaries were drawn across the deserts around Transjordan after World War I, practically all the nomadic tribes of the country had been established for some time in territories lying wholly within the confines of the new state. To take care of the few cases where it had been traditional for tribal peoples to move back and forth across the country's borders, agreements with neighboring countries recognized a principle of freedom of grazing and provided for a continuation of migratory practices, subject to certain regulations.

The border between Jordan and Saudi Arabia, only partially delimited by a series of agreements between Great Britian and the government of what eventually became Saudi Arabia, was first formally defined in the Hadda Agreement of 1925. This together with other agreements resulted in a border maintained amicably in a sort of status quo until 1965. In that year Jordan and Saudi Arabia concluded a bilateral agreement that realigned and completely delimited the boundary. The realignment resulted in some exchange of territory, and Jordan's coastline on the Gulf of Aqaba was lengthened by about twelve miles.

The boundary passes through arid, virtually rainless, and almost entirely unpopulated desert or semidesert country. Easier access to the Gulf of Aqaba and a few scattered wells are the only gains of strategic value to Jordan. The boundary agreement of 1965 also established a zone in which the two parties would share petroleum revenues equally if oil were discovered and promised to protect the pasturage and watering rights of nomadic tribes inside the newly exchanged territories.

Administrative Divisions

In mid-1973 the East Bank was divided into five major divisions known as governorates (*alwiya;* sing., *liwa*), which in turn were subdivided into a number of subordinate jurisdictions known as *aqdiya* (sing., *qada*). (The West Bank, when under Jordanian administration, had had three governorates.)

For many years all of the extensive desert region east of the Hejaz Railway, which lies east of and roughly parallel to the north-south rift, constituted a separate administrative division under the special Desert Administration. Early in 1967 an end was put to this arrangement, and responsibility for the desert region was divided among the adjacent governorates of Irbid, Al Asimah, Al Karak, and Maan by extending their boundaries due east from the line of the railway to the Saudi Arabian border. Each governorate is centered on one of the country's main towns, each of which for many years has been the political and economic hub of the surrounding area.

Ground Forms and Drainage

In relief the country consists mainly of a fairly high plateau divided into ridges by valleys or gorges and has a few mountainous areas. Fractures of the earth's surface are evident in the great geological rift that cuts like a trench across the whole length of the country near its western borders. This system has been the scene of repeated earthquakes whose destructive power is attested by the ruins of temples and other buildings of antiquity to be found throughout the country. No severe shocks, however, have been recorded for several hundred years. In the north, extending southeast from the border with Syria, there are extensive fields of broken lava and basaltic rock. In places the lava is classed as fairly recent, but there has been little volcanic activity in the historical past.

By far the greater part of the country east of the rift depression is desert, displaying the landforms and other features associated with great aridity. Most of the land is, in fact, a part of the great Syrian (or North Arabian) Desert. There are broad expanses of sand and dunes, particularly in the far south, together with salt flats. Occasional jumbles of sandstone hills or low mountains support only the most meager and stunted vegetation, which comes briefly to life after the scanty winter rains.

Because rainfall is so deficient, the drainage network is coarse and incised. In many areas the relief is such as to provide no eventual outlet to the sea, so that sedimentary deposits accumulate in basins where all moisture evaporates or is absorbed by the ground. Toward the depression in the western part of the East Bank, the desert rises and gradually becomes the Jordanian highlands—a steppe country of high, deeply cut limestone plateaus with an average elevation of about 3,000 feet and occasional summits reaching 4,000 feet in the north and over 5,000 feet in the south.

The western edge of this plateau country forms an escarpment along the eastern side of the Jordan River–Dead Sea depression and its continuation south of the Dead Sea. Most of the wadis that provide drainage from the plateau country into the depression carry water only during the short season of winter rains. But they are sharply incised, have deep, canyonlike walls, and—wet or dry—can be formidable obstacles to travel. On its western side the depression is hemmed in by another escarpment that descends quite abruptly from the crest line of the heights of Samaria and Judea. The wadis that form tributaries on this side are very short and contribute only a meager, intermittent flow of water. This area receives moderate amounts of rainfall, and rain-fed agriculture supplemented by irrigation from local wells is possible in some localities.

The lowland area south of the Yarmuk River to the northern end of the Dead Sea is intensely cultivated through irrigation from the East Ghor Canal, which runs parallel to the Jordan River. Cereals, maize (corn), tobacco, groundnuts (peanuts), and some fruits are the chief crops (see ch. 12). Demand from the neighboring oil-producing Arab countries and lessened competition from the agricultural producers of the West Bank have stimulated the spread of new kinds of cash crops, including tomatoes, melons, citrus fruits, artichokes, and potatoes. Agricultural production has been further stimulated by government programs to prevent soil erosion and flash flooding and by officially sponsored agricultural extension work. Nomad pastoralists from the steppe lands customarily brought their animals to this area for grazing during the summer months, but official grazing controls have been introduced since the mid-1960s to protect cultivated lands. Since that time the development of small dams at the outlets of tributary streams from the plateau has significantly increased the region's agricultural potential, but the development of that potential has been handicapped by unsettled frontier conditions since 1967.

The Jordan River flows through the northern reaches of the depression from sources on Mount Hermon on the border between Lebanon and Syria. It is a short river, but from its mountain headwaters, some 100 miles in an air line north of its mouth at the Dead Sea, its streambed drops from an elevation of about 9,000 feet above sea level to nearly 1,300 feet below sea level. Before reaching Jordanian territory the river forms Lake Tiberias, whose surface is about 700 feet below sea level. Flow farther to the south is regulated by a low dam at the southern end of the lake. The river's principal tributary is the Yarmuk River, which near its junction forms the boundary between Israel on the northwest, Syria on the northeast, and Jordan on the south. The Az Zarqa River, second main tributary of the Jordan, rises and empties entirely within the East Bank (see fig. 2). In early 1973 the river was being developed to provide irrigation of the lower eastern Jordan valley.

From its confluence with the Yarmuk River south to the Dead Sea, the Jordan River meanders through a valley between three and fifteen miles wide. The valley comprises an alluvial floodplain up to one mile wide and higher terraces below the highlands on either side. The course of the river is very sinuous and is constricted in some places by cascades or rapids. Except in such places, the river proper is from sixty to 250 feet wide and from three to six feet deep throughout the year.

The flow of water released into the Jordan at the outlet of Lake Tiberias has been reduced and the river's salinity during low water season increased to alarming levels because of Israel's diversion of the waters. Jordan valley irrigation schemes, of major importance in this water-deficient country, have relied increasingly on run-of-river diversion from the Yarmuk and Az Zarqa rivers. A major project to irrigate some 20,000 acres in the Jordan valley was announced in early 1973 by the Jordan Valley Organization; the area is to serve as a resettlement zone for some 130,000 people (see ch. 12).

The Dead Sea, which the Jordan River enters at a surface elevation of nearly 1,300 feet below sea level, occupies the deepest depression on the land surface of the earth. The depth of the depression proper is accentuated by the mountains and highlands paralleling it, which rise to elevations of 2,500 to 4,000 feet above sea level. The sea's greatest depth is about 1,300 feet. Its bottom thus reaches down to a point some 2,600 feet below sea level. Toward its southern end a barren peninsula juts from the east to divide the Dead Sea into a larger and much deeper northern basin and a very shallow southern basin only about ten feet deep. Covering an area of about 370 square miles, the entire body of water is some fifty miles long and has a maximum width from east to west of about ten miles.

An inland lake with no outlet, the sea's water level is maintained by the balance between inflowing water from the Jordan River and tributary wadis and evaporation from the sea's surface. Because of very high temperatures throughout most of the year, the evaporation loss has been estimated to exceed an average of 5 million tons of water per day. Rainfall over the Dead Sea itself is negligible, and a high rate of evaporation gives the water an average salinity of nearly 25 percent—seven times that of the ocean and too salty to support animal or plant life. Most of the salts in the water consist of magnesium and sodium chlorides, but in addition there is a rich variety of other soluble minerals, such as potash and bromines, which can be extracted by solar evaporation.

South of the Dead Sea a continuation of the depression, known popularly as the Wadi al Arabah, rises gradually through a region of barren desert until it reaches sea level about halfway to the Gulf of Aqaba. Thence the wadi's rise continues to an elevation of about 900 feet above

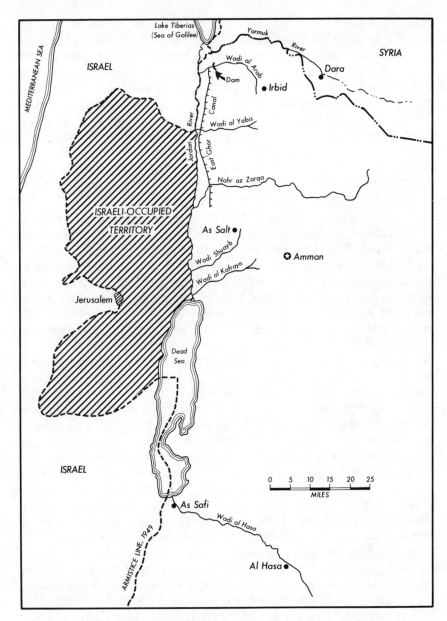

Figure 2. Man-made Features and Principal Rivers of Jordan

sea level only forty miles from the head of the gulf. Here there is a divide between drainage lines running north to the Dead Sea and south to the Gulf of Aqaba.

Climate

The major characteristic of the climate is the contrast between a rainy season from November to March and very dry weather for the

47

rest of the year. With hot, dry, uniform summers and cool, variable winters during which practically all of the precipitation occurs, the country has a Mediterranean climate. Although the relief of the ground may introduce local variations, in general, the farther inland from the Mediterranean Sea a given part of the country lies, the greater are the seasonal contrasts in temperature and the less the rainfall. Atmospheric pressures during the summer months are relatively uniform, whereas the winter months bring a succession of marked low-pressure areas with accompanying cold fronts. These cyclonic disturbances generally move eastward from over the Mediterranean Sea several times a month and may result in precipitation, provided there is sufficient inflow of moist air from the south.

By far the greater part of the East Bank receives less than five inches of rainfall per year and may be classified as a dry desert or steppe climatic region. Where the ground rises to form the highlands east of the Jordan River valley precipitation increases to around twelve inches in the south and twenty or more inches in the north. The Jordan River valley itself, lying in the lee of high ground on the West Bank, forms a narrow climatic zone that may receive up to twelve inches of rain annually in its northern reaches, dwindling to less than five inches at the head of the Dead Sea. Except for the desert area generally east of Jerusalem and Hebron overlooking the Dead Sea, the hills and plateaus of the West Bank are fairly well watered, receiving between fifteen and twenty-five inches of rainfall per year.

Rainfall throughout the country is exceedingly variable, not only in the total for any given year but in the amount falling during any particular period within the year. Rains of cloudburst proportions are not uncommon and may be preceded or followed by protracted dry weather.

On the average the country's long, hot summer reaches a peak during August. January is usually the coolest month. The fairly wide ranges of temperature during a twenty-four-hour period are greatest during the summer months and have a tendency to increase with higher elevation and distance from the Mediterranean seacoast. For example, the range at Amman during August averages about 25°F, whereas for January it is about 15°F. The corresponding figures for Jerusalem, which is nearer to the coast, are about 3°F lower. Daytime temperatures during the summer months often exceed 100°F. In contrast, the winter months bring moderately cool and sometimes cold weather, especially at the higher elevations. Except in the rift depression, frost is not uncommon during the winter. It snows from time to time in Jerusalem and more frequently in Amman.

For a month or so before and after the summer season hot, dry air from the desert, drawn by low pressure, may produce strong winds from the south or southeast, which sometimes reach gale force. Known in the Middle East by various names including the *khamsin*, this siroccolike wind is dry and is usually accompanied by great dust clouds. Its

48

onset is heralded by a hazy sky, a falling barometer, and a drop in relative humidity below 10 percent. Within a few hours there may be a rise in temperature of 40°F to 50°F. These windstorms ordinarily last only a day or so, but they cause much discomfort and can destroy crops by desiccating them.

The *shamal* is another wind of some significance, but one that comes from the north or northwest, generally at intervals between June and September. Remarkably steady during daytime hours but sinking to a breeze at night, this wind may blow for as long as nine out of ten days and then repeat the process. It originates as a dry continental mass of polar air and is warmed by its passage over the Eurasian landmass. The dryness of the *shamal* allows intense heating of the earth's surface by the sun, resulting in high daytime temperatures that become moderate, however, after sunset.

Minerals and Soils

Exploration up to 1973 indicates that the country is poorly endowed with mineral fuels and metallic ores. Oil, a major resource in many parts of the Middle East, has not been found in any commercially feasible quantity despite extensive geological investigation and deep test drilling. There are no known beds of coal. Manganese ore has been found in considerable quantity some twenty-five miles south of the Dead Sea but is of questionable value because of its high copper content (see fig. 3). Other metallic minerals, notably iron and barite ores, are present but only as minor occurrences. In early 1972 explorations near the port of Al Aqaba uncovered extensive copper deposits estimated to be capable of an annual yield of 25 million tons of ore with an average of 1 percent pure copper content, a level that makes extraction commercially feasible.

The most important mineral resource under exploitation in 1973 was phosphate rock; reserves were estimated at 307 million tons (see ch. 12). The largest deposits were located at Wadi al Hasa about ninety miles south of Amman; others were at Ar Rusayfah between Amman and Az Zarqa. Potash and various soluble salts from the Dead Sea have become economic assets. Limestone for building and making cement is plentiful, and the country has clay, feldspar, ocher, gypsum, and marble.

The local differences that mark the country's pattern of rainfall— a decisive factor in soil formation and modification—are reflected in the kinds of soil to be found. Desert soils prevail in the east and in all the East Bank territory except the uplands adjoining the Jordan valley where rainfall is abundant.

Desert soils in their extreme forms are but surface layers of various kinds of rock debris showing little sign of chemical alteration or structural breakdown. The desert soil in the east, consisting of pebbles, rock fragments, and sand of varying degrees of coarseness, is very alkaline and lacks organic matter. Farther west where the elevations rise toward the uplands and rainfall increases, the soil has a finer, more sandy texture and is gray or shading to brown in color. It has a small proportion of humus but is still highly alkaline and generally includes gypsum close to the surface.

The higher land stretching along both sides of the rift depression and reaching from the Dead Sea north to the Syrian border has a range of brown, loamy soils. Less alkaline than desert soils, they are intermixed with humus and mineral elements derived mainly from limestone or, in some places, from igneous material such as lava. These soils show little leaching of plant nutrients and are easily eroded. In the Jordan valley, where the terraces are formed by old sea deposits, the subsoil consists mostly of salty marl covered by a thin, superficial layer of nonsaline arable topsoil with minimal leaching potential.

The West Bank hills and valleys of Samaria on the north, Judea, west of Jerusalem, and Hebron, on the south have a special soil characteristic of many Mediterranean areas known as terra rossa. This soil, formed from limestone under a special climatic regime of ample winter rain and severe summer drought, is low in humus content but is enriched by iron oxides and silica. Somewhat alkaline, terra rossa has a high iron content, which gives it a red color that becomes yellowish in areas of higher rainfall. It is quite fertile and suitable for vines and olive trees but is easily eroded, as may be observed in many parts of the West Bank.

Man-made Features

The country's only rail line, the narrow-gauge, single-track Hejaz Railway, was built in the early 1900s to accommodate pilgrim traffic between Damascus (Syria) and Medina (Saudi Arabia). South of Maan the railway was largely destroyed during World War I but was partially restored during the 1960s. In 1972 Jordan operated some 277 miles of track from Dara in Syria via Amman and Maan to Ras an Naqb, about forty-three miles north of the port of Al Aqaba. In accordance with an agreement among Syria, Jordan, and Saudi Arabia, the Hejaz line was being reconstructed, the Maan-Al Mudawwarah section in Jordan having been completed in 1972. The new line was designed to carry some of the 500,000 pilgrims who travel to and from Mecca each year, although for many pilgrims road and air traffic have become the preferred forms of transportation.

Construction of an eighty-eight-mile railway branch from Hattiya, on the main line between Maan and the Saudi Arabian border, to Al Aqaba was begun in 1972. Although designed mainly to carry phosphate shipments from Al Hasa, the railway is part of a major development effort to link industrial and agricultural areas.

According to information available in early 1973, the country as a whole had about 1,750 miles of highways in 1969, Amman serving as a

road transportation center for the East Bank. The total mileage included some 1,070 miles of primary and 610 miles of secondary roads. More than 80 percent of the primary and 66 percent of the secondary roads were paved. Because of the country's configuration and the pattern of settlement, the main roads have a north-south orientation, and short connections run east and west to link a system that served all the main towns and cities but was not altogether adequate to handle domestic and foreign trade. Some of the feeder roads to the agricultural areas of the Jordan valley and to the northern highlands were poorly maintained. On the East Bank a main highway, following the general alignment of the Hejaz Railway as far south as Maan and then continuing in a southwesterly direction, connects Amman and the country's only seaport, Al Aqaba. The road from Maan to Al Mudawwarah was completed in 1970.

The main highway connecting East and West banks runs from Amman to Jerusalem, crossing the Jordan River at the Allenby Bridge (see ch. 2). There is another major connection that crosses the river farther north at the Damiyah Bridge and continues to Nabulus. In mid-1973 the border was closed (see ch. 10). The main transportation artery of the West Bank is a north-south highway from Hebron in the south that passes through Bethlehem, Jerusalem, Ram Allah, Nabulus, and Janin.

Highway development projects in the Seven Year Program for Economic Development (1964–70), generally known as the Seven Year Plan, allocated some 50 percent of highway funds to road maintenance. New construction projects were planned, but some of these had to be abandoned because of the war in 1967. The Al Aqaba-As Safi road, for example, which was designed to serve the Dead Sea potash development project near As Safi, was halted after it was one-quarter completed. During the early 1970s official road construction programs stressed expansion of the network in the Amman area and improvement of the highway links with Iraq, Syria, and Saudi Arabia. Construction of a new eleven-mile-long road between Amman and Az Zarqa was proposed in 1972 to serve as one of the key sections of the country's road network. The road would serve important phosphate deposits that are mined about midway between Amman and Az Zarqa as well as the country's only oil refinery (near Az Zarqa) and a cement plant near the capital.

When Israel came into being in 1948, Jordan found itself cut off from its natural access to the sea at Jaffa (Yafo) and Haifa. Beirut in Lebanon had excellent facilities, but to depend on this seaport meant to depend on a land route through Syria and Lebanon to reach it. In order to stay within Jordanian territory, the government decided to develop a port at Al Aqaba as its outlet to the sea. By the mid-1960s the construction and improvement of port facilities and land communications with the rest of the country had been completed, and Al Aqaba was serving overseas trade. Port facilities included two general berths 1,000 feet and 700 feet long and seven main transit sheds, providing a covered storage area of 40,000 square feet. In 1967 a berth to receive phosphate ships up to 100,000 tons capacity and two large phosphate storage areas were built. Oil-handling facilities were added at a later date. In early 1973 the port had a capacity of 800,000 tons of general cargo a year but was used mainly for shipping phosphate.

The country's major international airport is near Amman; by 1973 the annual volume of passenger traffic at that airport had reached 125,900 people. Official plans in late 1972 called for the construction of a new airport at Zeeyza, about nineteen miles south of Amman. A new airport had been built at Al Aqaba and began to handle traffic in mid-1972. Smaller airfields are located near Al Mafraq and Az Zarqa. The government-owned Royal Jordanian Airline operates both domestic and international flights.

The Trans-Arabian Pipeline (Tapline) crosses Jordan from Saudi Arabia to Sidon, Lebanon. The thirty-inch principal pipeline, which has a capacity of 475,000 barrels per day, supplies the eight-inch branch pipeline leading to the Az Zarqa oil refinery.

Since the mid-1950s there have been a number of plans among Arab countries for developing and making use of the water resources of the Jordan River basin. Sharp political differences and lack of financial means have frustrated attempts to draw up a plan agreeable to all the countries concerned. Jordan, however, undertook a development project of its own and in 1958 began the construction of the East Ghor Canal. The forty-four-mile canal was completed in 1963 to irrigate 30,000 acres of land on the eastern slope of the Jordan valley known as the East Ghor (see ch. 12).

The Khalid ibn al Walid Dam on the Yarmuk River was built to divert part of the river's flow into the East Ghor Canal. In 1972 official efforts focused on the development of dam and irrigation works on the Az Zarqa River. In early 1973 the river was diverted from its usual course through a special tunnel, making possible the construction of the King Talal Dam. Located nineteen miles west of Jarash, the dam and its ancillary plant and canals will irrigate some 12,000 acres in the Jordan valley. Upon completion of the main dam in 1974 four storage dams of varying sizes will operate on the Az Zarqa's major side wadis.

Settlement Patterns

The 1961 census indicated that a little over half the population of the country lived in villages, about 44 percent lived in the fully urban areas, and a diminishing number of nomadic or seminomadic tent dwellers accounted for not quite 6 percent of the population. Since 1961 the urban population has been growing at the rate of almost 4.5 percent annually, exceeding the overall population growth rate and almost doubling the rate of growth of the rural population. It was estimated that nearly half the country's total population would be urban by 1975.

The majority of the settled rural people live in villages near the fields they cultivate. Many of these villages were originated by groups from nomadic tribes, but some villages were formed by countryfolk who moved there by choice from other farming areas generally lying farther west. Others were established by people who were required to move by their rulers. Still others were developed when farm families found it possible to establish new homes closer to the fields they worked.

Typically, the villages are small, averaging only about 400 inhabitants in East Bank territory and about twice that on the West Bank. The actual size varies considerably from region to region and is related to the productive capacity of the surrounding farmlands. The larger villages are usually found in the more fertile areas, where families are able to reach their fields without having to travel too far. Most of the inhabitants are farmers, but there are generally a few tradesmen and shopkeepers to provide specialized services.

Although the majority of urban settlements are small rural towns with populations under 10,000, the overwhelming proportion of the urban population lives in the five relatively large cities. These include Az Zarqa and Irbid, both the sites of budding industries with populations between 30,000 and 100,000, and As Salt and Ar Ramtha, which have between 10,000 and 30,000 inhabitants. Amman, the capital, was the largest and fastest growing city with about 500,000 inhabitants in early 1973, representing nearly 30 percent of the East Bank's total population. The city has been a main receiving area for rural migrants and refugees, its population growing at an annual rate of 6.9 percent between 1952 and 1961 and of 6 percent since the late 1960s. Amman's boundaries have been repeatedly expanded and by the late 1960s encompassed an area of about twenty square miles beyond the original municipal boundaries. All the urban centers are situated on main lines of travel and are the sources of modernizing influences for the neighboring areas.

Camps of nomadic beduins are found mainly in an area about 248 miles long and some 155 miles wide east of the railway line. Settlements of seminomads are found near the Qaal Jafr and Azraq ash Shishan oases. The former is the site of a government-sponsored agricultural project to settle the beduin population; a similar settlement has been established near Al Hasa, center of the phosphate industry.

A new kind of settlement, the refugee camp, emerged in the wake of the Arab-Israeli War of 1948. The original refugee settlements were tent camps, but these have yielded in most places to rows of galvanized steel, aluminum, and asbestos shelters (huts). According to information available in mid-1973, there were ten refugee and six so-called emergency camps (the latter for refugees displaced after 1967) with a total of about 281,000 inhabitants. Most of the camps are located near the major cities in the northwest. In each of the three most populous refugee camps the number of inhabitants exceeded 30,000.

Resettlement projects calling for the establishment of medium-sized rural settlements on newly irrigated lands have figured prominently in government development plans. According to official announcements in early 1973, some 137,000 people are to be resettled in the Jordan valley, pending the completion of an irrigation project that will expand the valley's irrigated area by some 20,000 acres. The plan calls for construction of thirty-eight villages, including 50,000 housing units.

POPULATION

Size and Growth

The 1961 official census placed the national population at 1,706,200. Since 1967 the constant ebb and flow of refugees from the occupied territory has made it difficult to estimate the number of persons living in the East Bank. According to the United Nations Relief and Works Agency for Palestine Refugees in the Near East (UNRWA), about 224,000 people who fled from the West Bank immediately after the hostilities were admitted to UNRWA refugee camps in the East Bank; other sources, however, placed their total number at approximately 320,000. Another census was planned for 1970 but was postponed because of the civil strife during that year (see ch. 2). Official Jordanian population estimates available in early 1973 were compiled in 1971 on the basis of projections from the 1961 census and revised crude birthrates. According to these estimates, the national population in 1971 totaled 2,423,000, of which 1,723,000 lived in the East Bank. UNRWA estimated that the population on both banks of the Jordan during the same year included some 830,000 refugees; of the total, more than 550,000 lived on the East Bank.

Emigration, immigration, and visits contributed to the fluctuation of the number of inhabitants in the country at any given time. In 1972 various observers estimated that some 100,000 Jordanians were residing abroad compared with 60,000 at the time of the 1961 census. In 1971 about 598,000 people—mostly Jordanians and other Arab nationals— entered the East Bank as visitors or tourists, and some 600,000 departed. An increase in the volume of visitors from the Israeli-occupied Territory was reported in early 1973, more than 200,000 people from Arab countries crossing the Jordan River during the previous year.

The population has been increasing at an estimated annual rate well in excess of 3 percent. For the early through the mid 1960s UN sources established an estimated growth rate of 3.1 to 3.2 percent, and a growth rate of between 3.4 and 3.5 percent was projected by the same sources for the early 1970s. According to some Jordanian official sources, however, these percentages were based on unrealistically low death rates, and the country's true population growth rate was more likely to have averaged about 2.9 percent annually between 1962 and 1972. UN and other international sources, however, in early 1973 used an annual growth rate of between 3.2 and 3.3 percent for 1971 and 1972. In 1972 the Population Reference Bureau, calculating with a growth rate of 3.3, predicted a doubling of the population in twenty-one years.

No official policy has been adopted on birth control although King Hussein is one of the signatories of the World Leaders' Declaration on Population. The government has supported family planning programs offered under private auspices, however. Abortion is illegal but in practice may be performed on medical grounds, and the use of contraceptives is not prohibited by law.

Family planning information and services are available from the clinics of the Jordan Family Planning and Protection Association founded in 1963. The association operated nineteen clinics, which provided contraceptive services to more than 3,200 new and about 38,600 previous patients in 1970. Birth control supplies and educational services are offered by the Women's Federation of Jordan and the Near East Council of Churches. Moreover, the Women's Federation of Jordan has launched a countrywide birth control information campaign, opened planned parenthood clinics in the major cities, and established prenatal and child welfare centers.

Age, Sex, and Vital Statistics

According to official projections of the Jordanian Department of Statistics available in early 1973, almost 46 percent of an estimated total population of 2.4 million in 1971 was under fifteen years of age, reflecting an estimated annual increase of 4 percent in this age-group since the 1961 census. About one-third of the people under twenty-four years old in 1971 were below the age of five. Almost half of the total population was between fifteen and sixty-four years of age, and only a little over 3 percent was sixty-five years or older. Because of the youthfulness of the population there was a high ratio between the dependent and the working population. For every 100 individuals of working age (fifteen to sixty-four years old) in 1970 there were some eighty-nine children under fourteen years of age.

According to the official projections the sex ratio in 1971 remained approximately the same as in 1961—about 103 males for every 100 females. There were more males than females under twenty-five years old, but women were slightly more numerous than men in the twenty-five to fifty-five age-group; above that age the numbers of men and of women were approximately the same. Other official population estimates on the number of inhabitants by sex on the East and West banks reflect a massive exodus of males from the West Bank since 1967. In that year there were 122 males for every 100 females on the West Bank, whereas the corresponding ratio on the East Bank was 109 to 100. In 1971 there were only ninety-three men for every 100 women in the West Bank, and the sex ratio in the East Bank remained about the same—108 men for every 100 women. All of the foregoing data should be viewed with great caution, however, chiefly but not exclusively because of the resistance by a large percentage of the population to questions relating to women in the family, particularly to young women.

Because of incomplete registration and underreporting, vital statistics represent estimates. UN and other expert sources in early 1973 reported a birthrate of between forty-six and forty-seven per 1,000 population and a death rate of between thirteen and sixteen per 1,000. The latter represents an adjustment by demographic experts of the official rate of about five per 1,000, considered to be unrealistically low. The rates were computed during the mid-1960s and applied to both the East and West banks. No rates were available for the early 1970s. According to UN sources, 77,758 live births and 7,233 deaths were reported in the East Bank in 1971.

Density and Distribution

In 1971 the overall population density for all of Jordan was estimated to be sixty-five per square mile; the East Bank had an estimated population density of forty-nine per square mile. There were wide regional variations, however, ranging from 273 per square mile in the settled areas to about three per square mile in the vast expanses of desert.

In 1971 the five governorates of the East Bank showed population totals ranging from 972,000 in the governorate of Al Asimah (which includes the capital city of Amman) to about 60,000 in the governorate of Maan (see table 1). More than 90 percent of the population lived in the western portions of the three northern governorates of Al Asimah, Al Balqa, and Irbid, although these portions constitute only about 8 percent of East Bank territory. The populations of Al Asimah and Irbid, which since 1961 have received most of the refugees and rural migrants, increased by 124 percent and 79 percent, respectively.

Refugees accounted for much of the population concentration in the northern-northwestern regions of the East Bank. After the Arab-Israeli War of 1967 approximately 300,000 refugees fled from the West Bank and from other Israeli-occupied areas to the major cities and refugee camps located in the northwest of the East Bank, augmenting an already large refugee population. At the same time, the artillery shelling and guerrilla activites in the Jordan valley area immediately after the June war caused many East Bank villagers in that area to seek shelter farther east, mostly in the capital and in other major cities. Further dislocations and shifts occurred after the civil war in the fall of 1970, increasing the population of emergency refugee camps by more than 9,000.

Table 1. Population of East Bank Governorates of Jordan, 1961 and 1971

Governorates	1961[1]	1971[2]
Al Asimah	433,619	972,000
Al Balqa	79,057	110,000
Irbid..	273,976	491,000
Al Karak	67,211	90,000
Maan	46,914	60,000
TOTAL	900,777	1,723,000

[1] 1961 figures derived from census.
[2] 1971 figures are official estimates.

Source: Adapted from *Statistical Yearbook, 1971*, XXII, Amman, 1972, p. 2.

Working Force

In 1973 data on the size, age and sex characteristics, and employment rates of the working force were fragmentary and were based on sample surveys. According to this tentative data, the East Bank working force in 1970 totaled about 350,000, approximately 21 percent of the population. The various surveys suggest a very low participation of women in the working force. According to a 1971 manpower survey, for example, an estimated 63 percent of the males between twelve and sixty-five years of age were in the working force, whereas only 6.5 percent of the women of that age group were listed in the working force.

In 1970 an estimated 14 percent of the working force was unemployed. By mid-1972 the unemployment rate had reportedly declined to 8 percent, apparently reflecting the economic upswing that began in 1971 (see ch. 11). Observers were agreed, however, that the unemployment rate would be much higher were it not for the low rate of participation by women.

Most new entrants into the urban labor market during the late 1960s and early 1970s found employment in the various government services. Industry absorbed only a small proportion of jobseekers because government subsidies were extended mostly to enterprises utilizing sophisticated technical machinery but a relatively small number of workers. Development plans during the early 1970s called for the creation of some 70,000 jobs, mostly in agriculture and in industries devoted to the development of natural resources, but information on the implementation of the plan was not available in mid-1973.

According to a 1970 survey, the majority of the working population in that year was employed in agriculture and in services (see table 2). Comparison of the survey with data derived from the 1961 census indicates that there had been little change in the proportion of agricultural workers over the decade, although some experts have suggested that employment in this sector (growing at a rate of 3.5 percent annually) has increased since 1967, probably because of the expansion of irrigated land area. Smallholders and family workers accounted for more than half of the agricultural labor force during the late 1960s, a proportion that probably remained the same in 1973.

Table 2. Employment of the Working Force of Jordan by Economic Sector, 1961 and 1970
(in percent)

Sector	1961	1970
Agriculture	33.4	32.9
Mining and quarrying	2.3	0.9
Manufacturing	7.7	6.0
Electricity	0.5	0.3
Construction	10.1	2.0
Wholesale and retail trade, restaurants, and hotels	7.7	6.6
Transport, storage, and communications	3.6	3.1
Financing, insurance and real estate, and business services	n.a.	1.1
Community, social, and personal services	13.3	9.7
Government services (including armed forces)	14.1	23.4
Total Employed	92.7	86.0
Seeking work	7.3	14.0

n.a.—not available.

Most of the approximately 21,000 industrial workers were employed in small, craft shop enterprises employing five or fewer workers. Enterprises with over 100 workers—nearly all located in the Amman-Az Zarqa area—employed less than 20 percent of the industrial labor force. Flour milling; oil pressing; and shoe, textile, futniture, and cement making were the largest employers in the manufacturing industry. Production was disrupted and employment declined in the larger enterprises after the 1967 war and again after the civil strife of 1970 (see ch. 2). Many of the artisan enterprises, however, took on additional workers from the ranks of refugees.

Employment in other Arab countries, especially in Kuwait and Saudi Arabia, is an important outlet for Jordanians seeking work. Many people leaving for these countries to find work are university trained and possess valuable skills. Their emigration constitutes a brain drain but helps to alleviate domestic unemployment.

A significant portion of the working force is literate, but there is a shortage of technical skills (see ch. 6). Vocational courses enrolled only about 9 percent of the secondary school students in the early 1970s. The shortages were less noticeable during the sluggish economic activities of the middle and late 1960s, but after the economic upswing of 1971 there was much official and private concern over the severe shortage of technical and middle level managerial manpower. On-the-job training on a limited scope is offered by some of the larger enterprises, but average employers find the cost of such training exorbitant.

CHAPTER 4

RELIGIOUS LIFE

Over 93 percent of the people of Jordan adhere to Sunni Islam (see Glossary), and the religion is one of the primary cultural influences in the country, particularly on rural people. Although observance is not always orthodox, devotion to and identification with the faith is high. To a considerable extent Islam bolsters and legitimates the throne (see ch. 9). Sunni Islam, in addition, is the established religion, and as such its institutions receive government support.

Religious minorities include Christians of various denominations, a small number of Shiite Muslims, and adherents to other faiths. As a significant sector of the biblical Holy Land, Jordanian territory, especially the West Bank (see Glossary), contains a large number of shrines and holy places sacred to various combinations of Muslims, Christians, and Jews. Problems of access to and administration of these sites have for some time exacerbated problems on the international level.

ISLAM

Tenets

In A.D. 610 Muhammad, a merchant belonging to the Hashemite branch of the ruling Quraysh tribe in the Arabian town of Mecca and later known as the Prophet, began to preach the first of a series of revelations granted him by God through the Angel Gabriel. Muhammad denounced the polytheistic paganism of his fellow Meccans. Because the town's economy was based in part on a thriving pilgrimage business to the Kaaba and numerous pagan shrines located there, Muhammad's vigorous and continuing censure eventually earned him the bitter enmity of the town's leaders. In A.D. 622 he and a group of his followers were accepted into the town of Yathrib, which came to be known as Medina (the city) because it was the center of his activities. The move, or *hijrah*, known in the West as the Hegira, marks the beginning of the Islamic era and of Islam as a force on the stage of history; the Muslim calendar, based on the lunar year, begins in A.D. 622. In Medina Muhammad continued to preach, eventually defeated his detractors in battle, and consolidated both the temporal and spiritual leadership of all Arabia in his person before his death in A.D. 632.

After Muhammad's death his followers compiled those of his words regarded as coming directly from God as the Quran, the holy scriptures of Islam; some of his other sayings and teachings as well as the precedents of his personal behavior, recalled by those who had known him during life, became the *hadith*. Together they form the Sunna, a comprehensive guide to the spiritual, ethical, and social life of the Muslim.

The *shahadah* (literally, testimony) succinctly states the central belief of Islam: "There is no god but God (Allah), and Muhammad is his Prophet." This simple profession of faith is repeated on many ritual occasions, and recital in full and unquestioning sincerity designates one a Muslim. The God preached by Muhammad was not one previously unknown to his countrymen, for Allah is Arabic for God rather than a particular name. Rather than introducing a new deity Muhammad denied the existence of the many minor gods and spirits worshiped before his ministry and declared the omnipotence of the unique creator, God. Islam means submission to God, and he who submits is a Muslim. Muhammad is the "seal of the Prophets"; his revelation is said to complete for all time the series of biblical revelations received by the Jews and the Christians. God himself is believed to have remained one and the same throughout time, but men had strayed from his true teachings until set aright by Muhammad. Prophets and sages of the biblical tradition, such as Abraham, Moses, and Jesus (Isa), are recognized as inspired vehicles of God's will. Islam, however, reveres as sacred only the message, rejecting Christianity's deification of the messenger. It accepts the concepts of guardian angels, a Day of Judgment, general resurrection, heaven and hell, and eternal life of the soul.

The duties of the Muslim form the five pillars of the faith. These are *shahadah* (recitation of the creed); *salat* (daily prayer); *zakat* (almsgiving); *sawm* (fasting); and *hajj* (pilgrimage). The believer is to pray in a prescribed manner after purification through ritual ablutions at dawn, midday, midafternoon, sunset, and nightfall. Prescribed genuflections and prostrations are to accompany the prayers, which the worshiper recites facing toward Mecca. Whenever possible, men pray in congregation at the mosque with a prayer leader, and on Fridays they are obliged to do so. Women may also attend public worship at the mosque, where they are segregated from the men, although most frequently those who pray do so at home. A special functionary, the *muaddhin*, intones a call to prayer to the entire community at the appropriate hours; those out of earshot determine the proper time from the sun.

In the early days of Islam the authorities imposed a tax on personal property proportionate to one's wealth; this was distributed to the mosques and to the needy. In addition, freewill gifts were made. Almsgiving, although still a duty of the believer, has become a more private matter. Properties contributed by pious individuals to support religious activities were usually administered as religious foundations, or *awqaf* (sing., *waqf*).

The ninth month of the Muslim calendar is Ramadan, a period of obligatory fasting in commemoration of Muhammad's receipt of God's revelation, the Quran. During this month, all but the sick, the weak, pregnant women, soldiers on duty, travelers on necessary journeys, and young children are enjoined from eating, drinking, smoking, or sexual intercourse during the daylight hours. The pious well-to-do usually do little or no work during this period, and some businesses close for all or part of the day. Since the months of the lunar calendar revolve through the solar year, Ramadan falls at various seasons in different years. A fast in summertime imposes considerable hardship on those who must do physical work. The fast is widely observed, especially in rural areas. Each day's fast ends with a signal that light is insufficient to distinguish a black thread from a white one. Id al Fitr, a three-day feast and holiday, ends the month of Ramadan.

Finally, all Muslims at least once in their lifetime should, if possible, make the hajj to the holy city of Mecca to participate in special rites held at several spots there during the twelfth month of the lunar calendar. The Prophet instituted this requirement, modifying pre-Islamic custom to emphasize sites associated with God and Abraham, father of the Arabs through his son Ishmael (Ismail). The pilgrim, dressed in a white seamless garment (*ihram*), abstains from sexual relations, shaving, haircutting, and nail paring. Highlights of the pilgrimage include kissing the sacred black stone; circumambulation of the Kaaba, the sacred structure, reputedly built by Abraham, that houses the black stone; running seven times between the mountains Safa and Marwa in imitation of Hagar, Ishmael's mother, during her travail in the desert; and standing in prayer on Mount Arafat. The returning pilgrim is referred to as a hajj and is entitled to the honorific "al Haj" before his name. Id al Adha marks the end of the hajj month.

The permanent struggle for the triumph of the word of God on earth, the jihad, represents an additional general duty of all Muslims. Although this has in the past been used to justify holy wars, modern Muslims see it in a broader context of civic and personal action. In addition to specific duties, Islam imposes a code of ethical conduct encouraging generosity, fairness, honesty, and respect and forbidding adultery, gambling, usury, and the consumption of carrion, blood, pork, and alcohol.

A Muslim stands in a personal relationship to God; there is neither intermediary nor clergy in orthodox Islam. Those who lead prayers, preach sermons, and interpret the law do so by virtue of their superior knowledge and scholarship rather than because of any special powers or prerogatives conferred by ordination.

Early Development

During his lifetime Muhammad was both spiritual and temporal leader of the Muslim community; he established the concept of Islam as a total and all-encompassing way of life for man and society. Muslims believe that God revealed to Muhammad the rules governing decent and proper behavior, and it is therefore incumbent upon the individual to live in the manner prescribed by revealed law and upon the community to perfect human society on earth according to the holy injunctions. Islam traditionally recognizes no distinction between religion and state. Religious and secular life merge, as do religious and secular law. In keeping with this conception of society, all Muslims have been traditionally subject to the sharia, the body of religious law (see Glossary). A comprehensive system of law, the sharia developed gradually during the first four centuries of Islam, primarily through the accretion of precedent and interpretation by various judges and scholars. During the tenth century, however, legal opinion began to harden into authoritative doctrine and the figurative gate of interpretation (bab al ijtihad) gradually closed. Thenceforth, rather than encouraging flexibility, Islamic law emphasized maintenance of the status quo.

In A.D. 632, after Muhammad's death, the leaders of the Muslim community consensually chose Abu Bakr, the Prophet's father-in-law and one of his earliest followers, to succeed him. At that time some persons favored Ali, the Prophet's cousin and husband of his favorite daughter Fatima, but Ali and his supporters (the so-called Shiat Ali, or party of Ali) eventually recognized the community's choice. The next two caliphs, Umar, who succeeded in 634, and Uthman, who took power in 646, enjoyed recognition of the entire community. When Ali finally succeeded to the caliphate in 656, Muawiyah, governor of Syria, rebelled in the name of his murdered kinsman Uthman. After the ensuing civil war, Ali moved his capital to Mesopotamia where in a short time he too was murdered.

Ali's death ended the last of the so-called four orthodox caliphates and the period in which the entire community of Islam recognized a single caliphate. Muawiyah then proclaimed himself caliph from Damascus. The Shiat Ali, however, refused to recognize Muawiyah or his line, the Umayyad caliphs; the Shiat Ali withdrew in the first great schism and established a dissident sect known as the Shia, or Shiites, in support of the claims of Ali's line to a presumptive right to the caliphate based on descent from the Prophet. The larger fraction of Islam, the so-called Sunni, claims to follow the orthodox teaching and example of the Prophet as embodied in the Sunna.

Originally political in nature, the differences between the Sunni and Shiite interpretations rapidly took on theological and metaphysical overtones. Ali's two sons, Hasan and Husayn, killed in the wars following the schism, became martyred heroes to the Shiites and repositories of the claims of Ali's line to mystical preeminence among Muslims. The Sunnis retained the doctrine of leadership by consensus, although

Arabs and members of the Quraysh, Muhammad's tribe, predominated in the early years. Reputed descent from the Prophet still carries great social and religious prestige throughout the Muslim world. Meanwhile, the Shiite doctrine of rule by divine right became more and more firmly established, and disagreements over which of several pretenders had the truer claim to the mystical power of Ali precipitated further schisms. Some Shiite groups developed doctrines of divine leadership far removed from the strict monotheism of early Islam, including beliefs in hidden but divinely chosen leaders and spiritual powers that equaled or surpassed those of the Prophet himself.

The early political rivalry remained active as well. Shiism gained political dominance of Iraq, Persia, and Yemen. In the early 1970s Shiites were numerous in Syria and were found in all Muslim countries. Except for the approximately 1,000 Shishan, who adhered to Shia, Jordan's Muslims were Sunni (see ch. 5).

The early Islamic polity was intensely expansionist, fueled both by fervor for the new religion and by economic and social factors. Conquering armies and migrating tribes swept out of Arabia, spreading Islam with the sword as much as with suasion, and by the end of Islam's first century, Islamic armies had reached far into North Africa and eastward and northward into Asia. The territory of modern Jordan was among the first to come under the sway of Islam; by A.D. 638 Muslim armies had penetrated into it (see ch. 2).

Although Muhammad had enjoined the Muslim community to convert the infidel, he had also recognized the special status of the "people of the book," Jews and Christians, whose own revealed scriptures he considered perversions of God's true word but nevertheless in some sense contributory to Islam. These peoples, approaching but not yet having achieved the perfection of Islam, were spared the choice offered the pagan—conversion or death. Jews and Christians in Muslim territories could enjoy the freedom to live according to their own religious law and in their own communities if they accepted the position of dhimmis, or tolerated subject peoples. This status entailed recognition of Muslim authority, additional taxes, prohibition of proselytism among Muslims, and certain restrictions on political rights.

The Ottoman Empire, of which Jordan was a part for 400 years, was accordingly organized around a system of *millets,* or religious communities (see ch. 2). Each organized religious minority lived according to its own particular canon law under the leadership of recognized religious authorities who both represented it to the outside world and supervised its internal communal life. This form of organization preserved and nourished the cultural differences that, quite apart from theological considerations, distinguished these peoples. The *millet* system prevented the full integration of non-Muslims into the general life of the Muslim people. Applied throughout the Ottoman Empire and frequently combined with residential segregation by religion, it has had enduring influence on the social structure of all the countries of the Middle East and is in large part responsible for the general association of religion and nationality. Within the Jordanian judicial system religious law remains in effect in matters concerning personal status (see Religion and Politics, this ch.) (see ch. 5; ch. 8).

Popular Religion

Despite their strong identification with and loyalty to Islam, many persons, especially the uneducated and those in rural areas, have incorporated into their religious life a number of beliefs and practices different from and even antithetical to the teachings of orthodox Islam. Authorities attribute at least some of these accretions to pre-Islamic beliefs and customs common to the area.

Religious devotion and piety carry tremendous prestige, especially in the villages, and villagers tend strongly to associate traditional practices with the rules of religion. Although often in fact unassociated with the teachings of Islam, these customs, as well as the general veneration for the past and for elders, frequently take on the force of religion. Beduin rituals in particular are said to emphasize reverence for ancestors. In many places it is customary to react to events not with original expressions but with one of a number of accepted and traditional maxims or sayings. Deviation from customary behavior in this and other respects is often viewed as irreligious and disrespectful.

In his daily life the villager and poor urbanite depend heavily on the will of God, which is held responsible for all occurrences. The expression *inshallah* (God willing) accompanies any statement of intention, and the expression *bismallah* (in the name of God) accompanies the performance of most actions. Such matters as the climate, the distribution of wealth, and the birth of children are popularly believed to be beyond any human agency. It is believed, for example, that each child brings with him his own means of earning a livelihood and therefore a future guaranteed by God. Nevertheless, villagers believe that, in matters that they may control, God expects them to work diligently.

Divine retribution for bad deeds is a constant fear. Many adverse conditions, such as storms, disease, crop failures, natural disasters, or general misfortune, appear to villagers as punishments for specific misdeeds. In addition, the Last Day (Day of Judgment) looms before every villager as a time he will be called to account for all the actions of his lifetime. The Quranic notion of the guardian angel is very influential. On the shoulders of each person, villagers believe, ride two angels. The one on the right records those actions worthy of commendation while the one on the left keeps track of those worthy of punishment. The total weight of this testimony will determine the individual's fate on the Last Day.

Numerous other spiritual creatures inhabit the world of the villager. Evil spirits known as jinns (*jan*), fiery intelligent beings that are capable of appearing in human and other forms, cause all sorts of malicious mischief. Some persons, such as epileptics, are believed to harbor them. For protection villagers carry in their clothing bits of paper inscribed with Quranic verses, and they frequently pronounce the name of God. A copy of the Quran keeps a house safe from the jinns. The evil eye, which can be foiled by the same means, can also cause hardship. In addition, angels, who are made of light, can come to earth on special missions; for example, one guards the spot at which a person died.

Despite Islam's unequivocal teaching that God is one and that no being approaches him in sanctity, many people accept the notion that certain persons (saints) have a special quality of personal holiness and affinity to God that is known as *baraka*. The intercession of these beings is believed to help in all manner of trouble, and most localities have at least one shrine (*maqam*) of such a person. Devotees often visit the shrine of their patron, especially seeking relief from illness or barrenness. Observers have noted that many of the less orthodox beliefs are somewhat more common among women than among men because the social segregation of the sexes prevents women from taking part in much of the formal religious life of the community.

Despite the extreme reverence in which Islam is held, strict adherence to the five pillars is not common. For example, Jordanian observers have noted that many villagers do not fast for the entire month of Ramadan. They do, however, avoid breaking the fast in public. Most people do not tithe to support religious institutions, nor are pilgrimages to Mecca or public prayer common among villagers. Nevertheless, most people try to give the impression that they fulfill their religious duties. Obvious or conspicuous disbelief among villagers earns the nonconformist the opprobrious title *kafir* (unbeliever) as well as social ostracism.

RELIGION AND POLITICS

Islam and the State

Islam is an important organizing principle in the Jordanian political system. King Hussein, as scion of a royal family long associated with Mecca rather than the territory of his kingdom, derives the loyalty of his most devoted subjects, the beduin, primarily from his status as a member of the Prophet's subtribe and as one of his direct descendants (see ch. 8). The inclusion of the proper name Hashemite in the country's name indicates the symbolic power of this claim.

Indeed, Yosef Akheimer quotes a beduin tribesman as follows: "We believe with all our hearts that the king is a direct descendant of Muhammad. We will brook no argument on this point. . . . We protect the king not because he is our ruler but because he is the symbol of our state. . . . The king is the symbol of purity and the worship of God. And so the preservation of the Hashemite line is the guarding of our religion, our heritage, and our continued existence."

Despite the overwhelmingly Islamic nature of the country, however, the constitution guarantees freedom of worship to non-Muslims. In addition, nine of the sixty seats in the House of Representatives, or 15 percent of the seats, are reserved for the Christian community, which constitutes about 6.5 percent of the population.

The Ministry of Awqaf, Islamic Affairs, and Holy Places acts for the government in religious matters. The government pays the salaries of Islamic religious teachers and maintains mosques, religious schools, and other Islamic structures. Its financial control allows the government to limit to some extent the independence of religious leaders. In 1955, furthermore, a law imposed governmental censorship on the sermons and speeches presented in mosques. The government sometimes attempts to use the authority of the ulama (sing., *alim*), the body of recognized Islamic scholars, to strengthen support for government policies.

Religious courts are an integral part of the Jordanian judicial system. Government-appointed judges (*qudah*; sing., *qadi*) hear cases involving divorce, inheritance, marriage, guardianship, and religious endowments that they judge according to the sharia. Appellate jurisdiction in these matters belongs to the Court of Cassation (Appeals) in Amman. In 1971 sharia courts of primary jurisdiction and appeals handled 3,275 cases. The Greek Catholic, Greek Orthodox, and Roman Catholic communities each have their own religious courts as well, which in 1971 handled 122, fifty-two, and forty-seven cases, respectively.

The Problem of the Holy Places

The West Bank, occupied by Israeli forces since the Arab-Israeli War of 1967, contains numerous sites sacred to three major world religions, jurisdiction over and administration of which have created sensitive and difficult problems, particularly in the international arena. Although numerous sites associated with biblical figures sacred to Jews or Muslims or both, as well as numerous places associated with incidents in the life of Jesus, are scattered throughout the Israeli-occupied Territory, a truly astonishing concentration of holy places lies within or near the walled city of Jerusalem (see fig. 4).

As the locale of the last days of Jesus, the ancient capital of the Jewish kingdom, and the scene of the Prophet's nocturnal ascent to heaven, the city is without peer in Christianity and Judaism and is the third holiest city in Islam. Possession of Jerusalem has therefore been a major source of contention. Proclaimed an international city under the 1947 armistice, it came under Jordanian domination in 1948. During the twenty years until it fell to the Israelis in 1967, several ancient synagogues were destroyed, and Jewish religious pilgrimage was not allowed. During Israeli tenure Muslim religious observances have been permitted, but a number of Muslim mosques have reportedly been de-

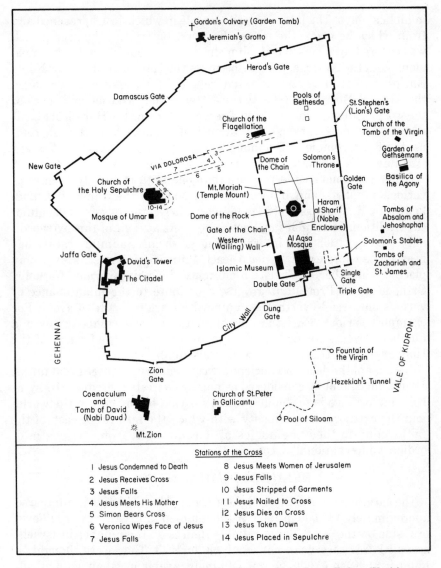

Source: Adapted from National Geographic Society, *Holy Land Today*, Washington, 1964; and Bertha Spafford Vester, "Jerusalem, My Home," *National Geographic*, CXXVI, No. 6, December 1964, p. 831.

Figure 4. Principal Holy Places in the Vicinity of the Walled City of Jerusalem

stroyed, and the number of Muslim pilgrims has understandably diminished drastically (see ch. 10).

The sensibilities of the three faiths particularly converge on Mount Moriah, or Temple Mount. Here, on a flat rock face, is the legendary spot where Abraham offered to sacrifice his son, Ishmael according to Islam, or Isaac according to Judaism. On this site later stood the Temple of Solomon and then the Temple of Herod, the ritual center of Judaism in biblical days. The latter was the temple in which Jesus preached and from which he drove the moneychangers. Later still, the sacred rock was covered by a massive Muslim shrine, the Dome of the Rock which, along with the Al Aqsa Mosque, occupies the Haram al Sharif, or Noble Enclosure. Arson by an Australian religious fanatic severely damaged the Al Aqsa Mosque in 1969, to the extreme consternation and shock of the world's Muslim community. The wall enclosing the Haram al Sharif rests in part on several courses of ancient stone that are the sole remnants of the Temple of Solomon. Thus, a portion of it is the Western (Wailing) Wall, the most sacred place of Judaism.

Other locations sacred to more than one faith include the tombs of various prophets and biblical figures, such as the Tomb of David, known to Muslims as Nabi Daud, which lies close to the Coenaculum, the traditional site of Jesus' Last Supper. As a result of this extraordinary juxtaposition and intermingling of shrines, administration has been quite complex. In general, each faith administers its own holy places. A number of Christian churches, including various Catholic, Orthodox, and Protestant groups, contribute to the maintenance of various shrines. Nevertheless, animosities are difficult to avoid. For example, various Christian denominations have competed over a number of years for prerogatives in such places as the Church of the Holy Sepulchre, traditional site of Jesus' tomb.

Because of the deep and ancient attachment to it by three great faiths, Jerusalem cannot be considered as merely contested territory. Its symbolic importance is probably as great as that of any city in the world, and the extraordinary tenacity with which the faithful of each of the faiths cling to their memories of it removes it from the realm of ordinary international discourse.

RELIGIOUS MINORITIES

The largest non-Muslim religious group, the Christians, numbered approximately 180,000 in 1965. Although many Christians were known to reside on the West Bank, reliable figures on the number in Israeli-occupied Territory were not available in 1973. They were thought to number at least 70,000. Overwhelmingly Arabic in language and culture, Jordan's Christians are disproportionately represented among the more economically prosperous. Some observers have suggested that Christians began to emigrate from the country during the 1960s, fearing governmental instability. In 1973, however, figures supporting this supposition were not available. Despite their Arabic culture, many Christians belong to churches whose liturgical languages are other than Arabic.

The Greek Orthodox Church, claiming more than 90,000 adherents in 1968 in Jordan, is the largest Christian group in the country. With an elaborately organized clerical hierarchy headed by a patriarch, the Greek Orthodox Church administers most of the Christian shrines in

Jerusalem and other West Bank towns. The Greek Orthodox patriarch of Jerusalem is the supreme religious leader of the Greek Orthodox community in Jordan and Israel. The liturgical language of the church includes both Greek and Arabic. The higher clergy, however, are predominantly of Greek descent. Also present are small numbers of Syrian and Armenian Orthodox.

The Greek Catholic (Melkite) Church in Jordan is headed by the patriarch of Antiochia, Jerusalem, and Alexandria, who in turn is subject to the authority of the pope in Rome. The higher and lower clergy generally are Arabs, and Arabic is used throughout most of the liturgy. The greater part of the more than 60,000 Greek Catholics in 1968 lived on the West Bank.

The Roman Catholic (Latin) Church, with about 16,000 adherents in 1968, has its own patriarch, who is also subject to papal authority. Several other Catholic groups, each headed by a patriarch who is in turn subordinate to Rome, are represented. These include several hundred Syrian Catholics and Armenian Catholics. Some European Catholics are members of religious orders, such as the Dominicans, Carmelites, and Franciscans.

The approximately 11,000 members of the different Protestant denominations by 1968 had been converted primarily from the Orthodox and Catholic churches. Muslims seldom convert to any other faith. Protestant communities, resulting generally from American and European missionary activities, are also represented by the personnel of various international organizations. Some Protestant groups have established schools and hospitals throughout the country, principally on the West Bank, and have also constructed a few unpretentious churches.

The Christian churches generally receive financial contributions from affiliated churches around the world, especially for the maintenance of Christian shrines, convents, and monasteries. Rivalries concerning dogma as well as control over certain religious sites exist among various Christian groups, particularly between the Catholic and Orthodox denominations of the same language background. Violent religious conflicts, however, seldom occur, either among the Christians or between the Christians and Muslims. The Christian churches also have their own ecclesiastical courts that decide matters of alimony, divorce, succession, or annulment.

In 1968 non-Christian religious minorities included a few, less than 300, Samaritans and different branches and sects of the Muslim faith. The Samaritans, members of an ancient Jewish sect whose members claim descent from the house of Joseph, accept only the Pentateuch, the first five books of the Bible. They worship on Mount Gerizim, where in ancient times they had a temple. The small community of Druzes, who live in the area near the Syrian border, are members of a sect that originally derived from the Ismaili branch of Shiite Islam. The Druzes, primarily located in the mountains of Lebanon and in southern Syria, have many secret beliefs and maintain that Hakim, the sixth Fatimid caliph, was divine in nature and is still alive and in hiding. A small settlement of Bahais, another sect that split off from Shia, inhabit the village of Adasiya in the north Jordan valley.

CHAPTER 5

SOCIAL SYSTEM

The geographic and demographic entity that functions as the Hashemite Kingdom of Jordan is the result of a series of historical accidents largely unrelated to the social structure of the country. Vast international forces rather than indigenous necessities have consistently molded the form and development of the country. The Amirate of Transjordan, dominated by beduin or tribal groups, was created out of the land remaining after the British and French had carved up their respective mandates; the territory that came to be known as the West Bank (see Glossary), composed mainly of Palestinian (see Glossary) villages and towns, was the land seized by the Jordanians during the Arab-Israeli War of 1948 (see ch. 2). Neither territory had previously functioned as a discrete unit, and the nation they became when they combined was further burdened with a bitter and unassimilated refugee population. This uneasy alliance of two quite disparate social systems ended in the abrupt and even more uneasy amalgamation of their peoples in a single territory after the Arab-Israeli War of 1967.

As in many unions of unwilling partners, the Palestinian and Transjordanian (see Glossary) peoples have found living together in harmony difficult and coalescence into a single, self-sonsciously united people impossible. Not only a sense of mutual historical animosity and grievance separates them. Much deeper and older differences of culture, values, social organization, and way of life have prevented the consolidation of the various elements into a unitary and self-consistent social organization. Naseer Aruri probably understates the case when he writes, "Gaps in the social structure have militated against the development of a consensus. Such gaps separated Palestinians and [Trans] jordanians, beduins and townsmen. . . . Their struggle has not centered on specific interests but on 'total ways of life'."

The main proponent of national unity, the monarchy, early built its precarious political foundation on the quasi-tribal loyalties of the East Bank (see Glossary) beduin who represent a traditional tribal organization of pastoral warriors. The dominant cultural form in the pre-1948 East Bank, tribalism also exerted a powerful influence over the villages of the area. Palestine, on the other hand, was a sedentary society of villagers and city dwellers, many of whom were literate, well educated, and westernized (see ch. 6). Sophisticated and highly politicized, the Palestinians only grudgingly accepted the paternalistic rule of a dynasty and nation to which they had no historic tie. The clash of these two cultural traditions has been a leitmotiv of Jordanian society and politics since amalgamation of the banks.

The upheaval precipitated by recurrent wars, the pull of government employment, and other factors have brought so many Palestinians to the East Bank that by 1973 they constituted about 40 percent of the population there. In addition, their cultural influence surpasses their numbers. Palestinians constituted over two-thirds of pre-1967 Jordanian society, and their cultural influence has challenged or overwhelmed that of the East Bank for a number of years. In 1971 Eliezer Ben-Moshe wrote that "the Palestinians dominate Jordan today because of numerical superiority and also because they constitute the social, cultural, and economic elite of Jordanian society. In essence, every year 'Palestinianization' of the whole of Jordan is increasing despite the Hashemite ruler's efforts to block it."

Jordanian society, then, is an uneasy combination of two quite different traditions. Before the intrusion of the Palestinian element, traditional Transjordanian society functioned fairly smoothly, if in a manner far removed from modern life. This relatively coherent system has been swamped, however, by masses of Palestinians who, arriving as fleeing individuals rather than as social units, have subjected it to nearly intolerable strain. The seemingly inert camp-bound refugee population has, in addition, acted as a true catalyst, convulsing the country in turmoil while remaining impervious to assimilation.

CLEAVAGE AND COHESION

Rather than forming an integrated system, the ethnic, cultural, ecological, and social groups of Jordan exist to a large extent as isolated elements. Although many Middle Eastern societies have been described as mosaics of distinct and often conflicting groups, the Jordanian situation is probably more fragmented than most because of the forcible uprooting that many citizens have endured. No consistent system of stratification or values binds all or even most of the people into one unit. In fact, different stratification criteria, based on often contradictory values, operate among the various groups.

Nor do the value systems of the various cultural traditions encourage the adoption of new loyalties. In traditional society, whether tribal, rural, or urban, loyalty did not generally extend beyond the limits of real or presumed kinship. Furthermore, the Palestinian sense of grievance and outrage, nourished for a quarter century in refugee camps and city neighborhoods and exacerbated by the civil strife of 1970, has precluded loyalty to the monarch. The quasi-tribal nature of the king's ties to the beduin and the extreme importance of the beduin-based army in maintaining social order have, on the other hand, precluded the adoption of institutions and procedures more congenial to the Palestinians.

Probably the most important force favoring cohesion of the society as a whole is the Arab-Islamic cultural tradition common to the overwhelming majority of Jordanians. Except for a small percentage of Christians, most of whom are Arabs, and other extremely small groups of adherents to other religions, Jordanians are Arab Muslims, the vast majority being members of the Sunni branch of Islam (see ch. 4).

Apart from a small number of Christian nomadic tribesmen, unique in the Middle East, and other relatively small groups such as the village-dwelling adherents of the Samaritan religion, members of minority groups generally live in cities and towns, where they occupy a disproportionate share of posts in government, business, finance, and the professions. To a large extent Christians control banking, although some observers suggest that the Christian population may be diminishing through emigration.

The Circassians, a Sunni Muslim community of approximately 12,000 descendants of families brought from the Caucasus in Ottoman times in order to provide in the territory an element loyal to the sultan, are concentrated in Amman. They have long been important in government, business, and similar pursuits. Despite their small numbers, for example, in 1938 they constituted 7.3 percent of the non-British government officials in Transjordan. Twenty-six of the thirty-three cabinets between 1947 and 1965 included one or more Circassians. A 1928 law guaranteed them one member of the lower house of parliament for each 5,000 people, as opposed to one member for 27,000 people among Arab Muslims. Circassian families are prominent in landowning, commerce, and industry.

The only significant non-Sunni element is the small group of Chechens, another Caucasian people. Most non-Arab Christians are Armenian. Observers note, however, that the distinctive community life that formerly characterized the minorities has been decreasing as more and more individuals, especially the young, pass into the general population through assimilation, intermarriage, and adoption of the prevailing speech.

The Arabic language is a potent force for unity throughout the Middle East. Rich in synonyms, rhythmic, highly expressive and poetic, it can have a strongly emotional, almost hypnotic, effect on its speakers and listeners. As the medium of the Quran, believed to be the literal word of God, it has been the vehicle of the historic glories of Islamic civilization. The emotional attachment of Arabic speakers to the beauties of their language is far greater than that of most peoples to their native tongues, and poetic eloquence has long been the most admired cultural attainment and sign of cultivation in the Arab world. In villages and nomadic tribes as well as among literate city dwellers, Arabic speakers have long striven to display in their speech an extensive command of traditional or classic phrases and locutions. The speaker and writer traditionally strove for an elaboration and circumlocution in both spoken and written forms that often strikes Westerners as flowery or verbose. Beauty of expression has long been valued above factual accuracy; only among the technically educated has this preference begun to shift.

One of the more widely spoken languages in the world, Arabic is the mother tongue of 50 million people from Morocco to the Arabian Sea. It is related to other Semitic languages, such as Aramaic, Phoenician, Syriac, Hebrew, various Ethiopic languages, and the Akkadian of ancient Babylonia and Assyria.

Throughout the Arab world the language exists in three forms: the classical Arabic of the Quran; the literary language developed from the classical and known as modern standard Arabic, which has virtually the same structure wherever used; and the local form of the spoken language. All educated Arabs tend to be functionally bilingual—in modern standard Arabic and their own dialect of spoken Arabic. Even uneducated Arabic speakers—in Jordan about half the population— can usually comprehend the general meaning of something said in modern standard Arabic although they cannot speak it themselves and often have difficulty understanding it. Classical Arabic is known chiefly to scholarly specialists; many men have memorized Quranic phrases by rote but cannot be said to speak the classic form.

Dialects of spoken Arabic vary greatly throughout the Arab world. Jordanians speak one common to Syria, Lebanon, Jordan, and parts of Iraq and, like people speaking other dialects, they proudly regard theirs as the best. Nevertheless, few people believe that their dialect is actually good Arabic in the sense of conforming to the ideal. Although they converse in colloquial Arabic, they generally agree that modern standard Arabic, the written language, is superior to the spoken form because it is closer to the perfection of Quranic language. Arabs generally believe that the speech of the beduin resembles the purer classical form most closely and that the local dialects used by the settled villagers and townsmen are unfortunate corruptions.

Within the same region a city dweller speaks slightly differently from a villager, and a tribesman significantly differently from either. Even within villages, quarters often display some differences. Each variety of the language has some different sounds and different ways of expressing ideas, and the vocabulary includes words fitted to the specific way of life of its speakers. Grammatical structure differs as well.

Because of the different forms of the language, therefore, the unifying influence of Arabic operates mainly among the literate; and in an important sense the loyalty of many literate people to the Arab Nation militates against a specifically Jordanian solidarity. In any case, countervailing traditional centrifugal forces, based mainly on the deeply felt loyalty to those of similar ancestry and family, are very strong. For example, both tribesmen and villagers in modern Jordan distinguish the peoples of Qays, or northern, from those of Yamani, or southern, descent. Running back to a pre-Islamic distinction among tribes in Arabia, this criterion differentiates the descendants of biblical ancestors, Ismail and Qahtar, respectively. Over many generations groups and communities have identified with one or the other faction, and the distinction retained political importance into modern times.

THE COMPONENTS OF SOCIETY

Traditional Transjordanian Society

Before the convulsive events of the post-World War II period thrust it onto the center stage of international affairs, the territory that is now the East Bank of Jordan was a provincial backwater of the Ottoman Empire and then later a small and weak desert amirate (see ch. 2). Straddling the transitional area between the "desert and the sown," it was marginal to the movements of social and intellectual change that began sweeping the Arab world in the nineteenth century. The area exhibited the symbiosis between the nomad of the desert and the sedentary agriculturalists that was traditional throughout most of the Middle East. Although ringed by the hinterlands of Jerusalem, Baghdad, and Damascus, it lacked a significant urban center of its own until the late 1940s; consequently, it did not display the artistically, intellectually, commercially, and governmentally sophisticated form of Arabic high culture characteristic of urban life. The basic form of organization in Transjordan was (and for much of the non-Palestinian population remains) tribal, and the basic dynamic, the stylized raiding and trading relationships among the various tribes and between the tribes and villagers.

The Tribes

Jordan is unique among primarily sedentary Middle Eastern countries in that the central government depends for its most significant political support on the beduin tribes. Constituting perhaps 5 percent of the population, the beduins come under the purview of the Office of Tribal Affairs, which was established in 1969 under the supervision of the intelligence agency. This office serves as a link between the central government and the tribes, supplying the tribes with weapons and financial subsidies and attempting to strengthen their loyalty to the king in his struggle with antiroyalist Palestinian elements. King Hussein I, mindful of the intensely personal nature of his ties with the nomads, visits them often, socializing in their tents and playing the role of a paramount supertribal shaykh.

People of tribal origin constitute, in addition, a disproportionate share of the Jordan army, particularly at senior command levels (see ch. 13). The opportunity for a lucrative, secure career that also carries high prestige and conforms to traditional martial tribal attitudes has for half a century drawn recruits from the desert into the desert-based Arab Legion under the British and its successor force, the Jordan Arab

Army. Army service has been one of the most important influences for social change among nomadic tribes because it fosters a desire for education and for a new style of life. In the words of Joseph Chelhod, "An educated beduin means an abandoned tent."

Because of its dependence on the tribes, the central government has not been able, unlike most other Arab governments with significant nomadic populations, to put pressure on the tribes to become sedentary. Nevertheless, many have voluntarily become sedentary, encouraged by the loss of traditional economic bases of raiding and protection of caravans. According to government figures nearly 50 percent of the nomadic population had become sedentary in the twenty years preceding the early 1960s. In the 1950s the nomadic population was estimated at between 150,000 and 220,000 nomads and seminomads; 1971 government figures placed the nomads at 53,000 and seminomads at 42,500. Important tribes, such as the Bani Sakhr and Huwaytat, were at least partially sedentary. Nevertheless, external conditions can cause the nomadic population to fluctuate.

At the founding of Israel, for example, a number of tribes of the Negev Desert, such as the Tarabin, Azazimat, and Jarabat, crossed into Jordan, taking over the former pasturelands of settled tribes and nearly doubling the nomadic population. As a result of these often contradictory trends, tribal groups exist at all points between the extremes of total nomadism and total sedentariness.

The true beduin tribe is a fully nomadic group based on camel herding. The tribes and animals exist in symbiotic relationship; the camels supply most of the food and other needs of the beduins; and the tribesmen assure the animals' survival by locating and guiding them to adequate pasturage. This fine adaptation to an extremely demanding ecological niche requires a versatile, portable technology that is, of its type, extremely sophisticated. It also requires a high degree of very specialized knowledge and a flexible social structure that expands and contracts according to need.

Camel tribes have traditionally been larger and more powerful than those herding sheep and goats. Because of the greater speed and the less frequent need for water of their animals, the beduins range over larger territories and go deeper into the desert. The cycle of the pastoral year consists of progress between traditional summer camping areas, close to the border of the "sown" with its assured water supply, and traditional winter camping areas deep in the desert, which become usable as pasturage after the fall rains. The tribes tend to camp in relatively large groups in summer and to split into smaller, ranging groups to exploit the more scattered water supplies available in winter. Each tribe exploits a territory to which it has traditional use rights, although the paths of various tribes sometimes cross, leading to conflict. In general, the extremes of the annual migration may be as much as 100 to 120 miles apart or farther. Nomads traditionally have not respected international borders, and some tribes still cross one or more international boundaries on their yearly travels (see fig. 5).

The tribal social structure is based upon the ramification of patrilineal ties between men. A tribe is a group of related families claiming descent from a supposed founding ancestor. Within this overall loyalty, however, descent from intermediate ancestors defines several levels of smaller groups. In cases of conflict, groups of kinsmen mass at the appropriate level of opposition. For example, the grandsons of brothers form two groups in opposition to each other, but they form one unit in opposition to the descendants of the brother of their common great-grandfather.

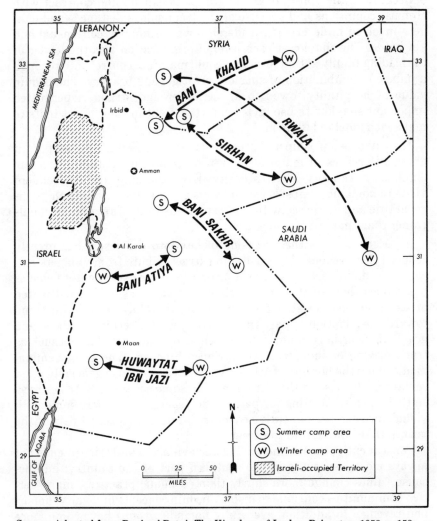

Source: Adapted from Raphael Patai, *The Kingdom of Jordan*, Princeton, 1958, p. 158.

Figure 5. Traditional Migration Patterns of Selected Nomadic Tribes in Jordan

Beduins have traditionally exhibited to the highest degree the attitudes surrounding the concept of honor. Any slight or injury to a member of a tribal group was an injury to all members of that group; likewise, all members were responsible for the actions of any fellow tribesman. Honor inhered in the family or tribe and in the individual as the family's or tribe's representative. Slights could only be erased by appropriate revenge. Consequently, bloody and escalating feuds between tribes or subtribes often resulted from murder or slights to women. Although in a case of intratribal conflict individuals with blood ties in both groups often attempted mediation, conflicts between tribes were not usually amenable to negotiation.

Because of the ability of tribal groups to expand and contract with climatic conditions and because of the tremendous distances and dangers involved in desert life, leadership was ordinarily consensual and kin based. The shaykh at each level of organization was the leader of the leading family at that level and could maintain control only through a judicious combination of suasion, prestige, and bravery. The beduin value of hospitality, owed to any traveler and stranger, permitted important shaykhs to use lavish entertainment in their guest tents to make men indebted to them.

The extreme hardship and precariousness of desert life do not permit great differences in material possessions, and the attitudinal system emphasizes equality and fraternity. Even the king, on his frequent visits to nomadic camps, is called by his given name rather than by his royal title and is treated with the respect due to the first among equals rather than that due to a monarch.

In recent decades the extension of law into the desert has greatly reduced the freedom of the tribes to extract tribute from villagers and caravans, an important source of income, and the use of motor vehicles has robbed them of their monopoly on mobility beyond the cultivated areas. There has existed for some time, therefore, a definite trend toward the adoption of part-time cultivation and herding of sheep and goats, alone or in combination, as well as of other occupations such as truck driving or industrial work. Sheep breeders tend to be seminomadic along the borders of "the sown." Cultivators also generally must remain fairly close to their croplands. In some cases entire tribes have settled down to farming for part of the year, and in others some individuals become permanently sedentary while others spend part of the year with the animals in the desert.

Consequently, the distinction between villagers and tribesmen is not always clear, especially in the southern part of the country; and because values change more slowly than economic practices, many settled communities continue to display beduin concepts of loyalty, honor, and revenge. In addition, even fully nomadic groups have come more and more fully into the national orbit with the advent of the transistor radio, which is found in tents in the farthest reaches of the desert. It is probable, furthermore, that gradual permanent settlement of nomadic tribes will continue, possibly at an increasing rate. Because permanent settlement of nomads is in effect the expansion of the "sown," availability of water is an important determinant of its speed and success. Government irrigation and water control projects presage an increasing productivity of agriculture and therefore an increasing probability of successful settlement (see ch. 3; ch. 12).

Despite his passing as the viable ruler of the desert, the beduin remains a highly important symbolic figure, representing the glorious and romantic image of a warrior past. In a society undergoing increasing modernization, however, the reality of the living tribesmen tends to be somewhat less glorious. Foreign observers have noted that people express pride in their beduin ancestry but show contempt of contemporary beduins. Modern-day descendants of the important tribes occupy a variety of positions in the modern sector of society. They attend schools and universities, serve in the government, and a number of tribes own urban properties and extensive farmlands. Both as traditional beduins and as modern citizens, however, the tribes occupy a crucial place in Jordanian life.

The Villages

In settled agricultural communities the principles of organization resemble to a great extent those of the nomadic communities. Villages tend to be organized around kin groups, and the most important elements of social identity are established at birth. Villagers, for example, count as members of their communities natives who live and work in cities or even in foreign countries. Many of these individuals, for their part, return personally or remit money to buy or maintain properties in their village "home."

In many villages the descendants of a common, relatively distant ancestor form the *hamula* (pl. *hamulas*), a word translated by some authors as clan. The *hamula* ordinarily has a corporate identity; it may maintain a guesthouse, its members usually reside in a distinguishable quarter or neighborhood, and it acts in concert in village political affairs. The *hamula*, of course, is the repository of family honor and in most cases is predominantly endogamous.

Below the level of the *hamula* and above that of the individual household various intermediate groups of kinsmen may form, depending on local circumstances. In many cases a group of closely related households, descendants of a relative closer than the founder of the *hamula*, form the *luzum* (pl., *luzums*), a consultation group. This level of organization may be less formal and institutionalized than the *hamula*, but it nevertheless exercises an important influence in social control.

Social control and politics in the village environment traditionally grow out of the interactions of kin groups at the *hamula*, *luzum*, and other levels. Although blood ties between men supply the major outline and primary ideology of kin relations, the numerous ties to other local kin groups through sisters, mothers, daughters, and wives generally provide for most individuals direct or indirect access to most other persons and groups within the community. In cases of conflict, leaders of the appropriate kin sections or persons in intermediate positions between them attempt to mediate the problem through kinship ties.

Villages ordinarily lack nonfamilial institutions strong enough to compete with kin groups for loyalty. Islam is community based rather than congregational, and voluntary clubs and associations have scarcely begun to penetrate village life (see ch. 4). Consequently, loyalty and identity center on a single focus, as does leadership. Observers have suggested that the lack of respected opinion leaders who could appeal to the people on nonfamilial or universalistic grounds contributed significantly to the flight of refugees from West Bank villages after the 1967 war. They hypothesize that, once opinion among individual families leaned in the direction of flight, no countervailing loyalties existed to hold the villagers in place.

Village organization and values, like those of the tribes, emphasize the essential equality of fellow villagers. Traditional stratification distinguished the respected elderly from the subservient young, the admired pious from the mass of humanity, and elevated the senior kinsman whose wisdom and judgment had stood the test of trial. Economic differences, although present, carried less weight. Religious teachings and practices, such as the requirement to give alms at all times and to distribute special gifts at the end of Ramadan and at other festival seasons, emphasized the responsibility of the prosperous for the less fortunate and the inherent right of the latter to enjoy a portion of the community's resources (see ch. 4).

In many cases, however, social change has begun to strain village structure. The uncontested control of the economic resources necessary for contracting marriage, participating in politics, and even earning a livelihood long guaranteed the elder generation a position of authority. A significant land shortage has forced many younger men into other pursuits, however, so that some "agricultural" villages contain a majority of men engaged in other types of work. The army, government service, trade, and industry supply employment to many village residents who earn an income independent of their elders' control and often considerably larger than the older generation could command. In such cases the lines of village authority and prestige no longer follow those of true power and control. Although deeply ingrained traditions often hold custom in place for a time, eventually the imbalance between power and authority shows itself in intergenerational conflict, confusion of values, and ultimately the breakup of kin groups.

A further disruptive element in villages, particularly those near the West Bank, has been the intrusion of Palestinians unrelated to the village families. Traditionally any outsider visiting a village was treated as a guest to be fed and lodged in one of the *hamula* guesthouses at *hamula* expense. As in tribal society, hospitality was not only a virtue but a point of honor. For a visitor even to offer to reimburse his hosts marked him as a boor, an ingrate, and probably an enemy. The continuing influx of Palestinians resulting from decades of turmoil, however, eventually strained some villages beyond their ability to supply traditional hospitality. In some cases commercially operated coffeehouses, which villagers of all family groups may patronize at will and in which each person pays for his own food and drink, have replaced the guesthouses. Abdullah Lutfiyya states, "No longer does the community recognize all outsiders as guests to be provided for at the expense of those who belong to the [guesthouse]. Outsiders are now either looked upon as guests of a specific person or as guests of no one at all."

In some villages outside influence and social change have proceeded to such a degree that the modernists and the traditionalists form distinct groups, living in different sections and following, to some extent, different customs. For the most part, however, the patterns and constraints of traditional life remain the guide for the residents of Jordan's villages.

A Modernizing Element: The City

From very ancient times society in the Middle East depended on the interaction of the tribes and villages with the urban centers. Cities were integral to society and culture even in pre-biblical times; Damascus, for example, has been continuously occupied for at least four millenia. The region's highest achievements in cultural, political, economic, and intellectual life took place in its vibrant cosmopolitan centers. The claims of Arab-Islamic culture to status as one of the world's major civilizations rest largely on products of city populations. In addition, city dwellers have traditionally been both initiators and transmitters of social change.

Except for Jerusalem, however, which the Israelis have held since 1967, no major urban center existed in Jordanian territory until the late 1940s. East Bank towns served as local markets and administrative centers rather than centers of high culture; the territory formed the hinterland of cities outside it. Truncated by external political considerations rather than by internal social or cultural realities, the East Bank consequently lacks the kind of long-established metropolis that has for centuries dominated other parts of the Middle East.

Amman, the major city of the East Bank, has ancient roots but as a modern city is scarcely more than a generation old; it passed the first decades of this century as a provincial trading center and garrison on the margin of the desert. In 1943 it had only 30,000 inhabitants. Its position as capital of the new kingdom impelled it to grow in thirty years into a booming overcrowded metropolitan center. As a result it lacks both the old quarters characteristic of most Middle Eastern cities and an established urban population with a unified cultural outlook and an organic bond to the indigenous society of the area. Its people are a mixture of all the elements of the country; Circassians, Christians, and Palestinians, rather than Transjordanians, set the tone.

The lesser towns of the East Bank, however, retain a good deal of the traditional kin- and quarter-based social organization characteristic of Middle Eastern towns. Each quarter functions relatively independently, according to egalitarian values similar to those found in villages.

In rapidly modernizing or industrializing areas such as Amman, however, the quasi-paternal relationship of the rich to the poor has begun to break down, and the old egalitarian values have begun to give way to class distinctions based on income and style of life. Furthermore, the intrusive Western culture that clothes a good deal of modernization has introduced radically foreign ideas and concepts among the educated that eventually estranged them from the culture of the mass of the people.

As a result the cultural unity that once could have knit a population into an organic whole has given way to confusion, malaise, and conflict. In the words of Ishaq Qutub, "The price of losing tradition is paid without a real understanding of modernization and westernization."

Because of their access to the techniques of industry, finance, and government and in spite of their small numbers, the modernized elements tend to dominate urban society. At the top stands a small wealthy group of large absentee landlords, industrialists, leading financial figures, and members of the important families dominating these fields. Just below them, professionals, army officers, and government officials live a somewhat less grand but still comfortable life. White-collar workers, schoolteachers, and marginal professionals struggle to retain a style of life that separates them socially from the small shopkeepers and artisans below them. At the bottom is a large underemployed proletariat.

Poorly educated and impoverished migrants from rural areas generally inhabit the lowest strata of urban society. A significant land shortage, the attractions of a more exciting and varied city life, and the upheavals of war have sent a steady stream of villagers toward Amman, jamming the city and overtaxing its resources (see ch. 6). It has expanded at the prodigious rate of over 7 percent annually for two decades and in the early 1970s had about 500,000 inhabitants (see ch. 3). It is not at all clear, furthermore, that the city will be able to integrate satisfactorily these uneasy and often unwilling new urbanites. Research has indicated that urban-born persons prove considerably more upwardly mobile than the rural-born after coming to Amman. This tendency has expressed itself in part in the greater upward mobility of Palestinians, exacerbating to some extent the existing hostility between them and the Transjordanians.

Although up-to-date figures were not available in 1973, it was estimated that urban dwellers would constitute close to 50 percent of the
country's population by 1975. It was known that urban areas were
growing almost twice as fast as rural areas in the early 1970s. It seems
likely, therefore, that population will continue to grow not only in
Amman but also in other budding industrial centers, such as Az Zarqa
and Irbid. One might reasonably expect social trends similar to
Amman's to appear in those and other growing centers as city life, only
recently implanted, comes to dominate the society of the East Bank.

The Refugees: A People Without a Country

Alongside the other elements of incoherence and discontinuity in
Jordanian society, the Palestinian refugees persist as a bitter, unassimilated mass. Although hundreds of thousands of refugees have
over the years successfully established themselves as independent
private citizens in various parts of the country, a greater number still
endure a tedious existence in squalid relief camps. Accurate figures on
the size and makeup of the refugee population were unobtainable in
1973; the census does not consider them a separate category, nor do
observers agree on which categories of persons should be classified as
refugees. Nevertheless, estimates placed the total number of refugees
in both banks in 1965 at approximately 637,000, or about one-third of
the population at that time. Of these, 437,000 were camp residents
holding United Nations Relief and Works Agency for Palestine Refugees in the Near East (UNRWA) identity cards (see ch. 6).

The 1967 war produced a new wave of refugees and further complicated the situation. At that time well over 200,000 people fled to the East
Bank, of whom somewhat less than one-half had reportedly also been
refugees from the 1948 conflict.

Of the refugees of the 1967 conflict, only one-third were estimated to
be living in camps in the early 1970s. The remainder had either been
unable to gain entrance to the camps or had attempted with varying
degrees of success to establish themselves in their new surroundings.
In general, those of higher social origins and greater resources tended
to exploit their money or contacts to move to cities or towns. The tent-
camp residents form a distinctly lower class and rural population.

The problems of providing for the material needs of this large and
mainly destitute population have proved small in comparison with the
problem of integrating them socially and politically into the nation.
For most refugees residence in the East Bank is involuntary and dis-
tasteful. They, as well as other Palestinians, consider themselves a
people apart from the Transjordanians and yearn intensely to return
to the native land of which they claim they have been unjustly deprived. Many hold Hussein responsible for their plight, and this bitter-
ness has repeatedly threatened the stability of the government (see
ch. 2; ch. 9).

For the camp population, life is especially bitter. Largely unemployed, living at a bare subsistence level on international relief, they have in many cases lost the will, desire, or ability to earn their own living. Furthermore, an entire generation has grown to adulthood in the idleness and acrimony of camp life.

The camp populations are consequently a highly volatile element in an already unstable nation. They feel themselves to have neither a sympathetic ally in the king nor a political outlet in his country. No camp resident, for example, has ever sat in the cabinet or legislature although the camps formed 25 percent of the pre-1967 population. Four noncamp refugees, on the other hand, served in parliament between 1950 and 1965, and one served in the cabinet.

Political agitation appears to continue unabated among the camp refugees, and the desperate, disinherited youths of the camps form the shock troops of the extremist movements (see ch. 9). Naseer Aruri states, "Because they are unemployed, they have no stake in the country's economy. Their rate of literacy, however, is by no means low, with schools . . . in each camp. Their exposure to the mass media is relatively high. They are not ignorant, but they are idle. Their propensity for political violence is likely to continue as long as their grievances are not redressed."

THE INDIVIDUAL, THE FAMILY, AND THE SEXES

Social life in Jordan centers in the family. The household is composed of kinsmen, and among the tribes family ties ramify into tribal structure. The individual's loyalty to his family overrides most other obligations. Ascribed status often outweighs personal achievements in regulating social relationships. One's honor and dignity are tied to the good repute of his kin group and especially to that of the group's women.

Sexual segregation is basic to Jordanian social life, and sex is one of the most important determinants of social status. Men dominate women in most aspects of life. An observer notes that this segregation lasts even into death; although relatives may often be buried in a common grave, the sexes are never mixed. Although the systematic seclusion of women is not generally practiced, men and women constitute largely separate subsocieties, each with its own values, attitudes, and perceptions of the other. The character of separation varies; it is strictest among the traditional town middle class and most flexible among tribesmen. Nevertheless, all groups observe it to some extent, and the worlds of men and women often intersect only in the home.

Family and Household

Jordanians reckon kinship patrilineally, or through men, and the household is based on blood ties between men. Ideally, it consists of a man, his wife or wives, his married sons with their wives and children, his unmarried sons and daughters, and possibly other relatives, such as a widowed or divorced mother or sister. At the death of the father each married son ideally establishes his own household to begin the cycle again. Because of the centrality of family life, it is assumed that all persons will marry when they reach the appropriate age: many divorced and widowed persons remarry and for the same reason. In most areas adult status is only bestowed on married men and often only on fathers.

Although practiced only in a minority of cases, polygyny and the extended family household remain important cultural ideals, and households are relatively large. A survey of the West Bank village of Baytin in the early 1960s found that 64 percent of village households contained six or more people. A 1960 survey of Amman found the average household size to be 6.5 people. Nevertheless, commentators state that in the former case most households were essentially nuclear, that is, composed of a married couple and their unmarried children, although in many cases additional relatives lived in the home. In the latter case commentators ascribe the high number in part to the acute housing shortage (see ch. 6).

Whatever combination of kinsmen composes it, a household may be viewed as a unit of consumption. Richard Antoun describes it as "a common purse to which all members contribute. This purse . . . is disbursed solely by the oldest male adult who is the head of the family." Within the household a nuclear family is a unit that eats from the same common plate.

Traditionally the individual subordinated his personal interests to those of his family and considered himself a member of a group whose importance outweighed his own. In mid-1972 it was still not common for persons to live apart from a family group. Grown children ordinarily live with parents or relatives until marriage; for a girl of respectable family to do otherwise would be unthinkable. Child-rearing practices train the young to be docile members of a family group rather than independent individualists.

Symbolic of the subservience of the individual to his family is the fact that the traditional Arabic system of names always associates the individual with specific others. Both men and women are known by their own given name and that of their father until the birth of their first child, at which time they adopt a new name within their local community. A man previously called Muhammed ibn Ali, whose wife gives birth to a son Husayn, would become Abu Husayn (father of Husayn), and his wife, Umm Husayn (mother of Husayn). If the first-born child is a girl, parents use her name until the birth of a son.

Marriage is a family rather than a personal affair. Because the sexes ordinarily do not mix socially, young men and women have few or no acquaintances among the opposite sex, although among beduins a limited courtship is permitted. Parents arrange marriages for their children, finding a mate through either their own social contacts or a professional matchmaker. Among both village and tribal populations the preferred marriage partner is the child of the father's brother. In most areas, in fact, a man has a right to forbid his father's brother's daughter from marrying an outsider if he wishes to exercise his right to her hand. If the ideal cousin marriage is not possible, marriage within the partilineal kin group is the next choice. Such endogamous marriages produce several advantages for all parties: the bridewealth payments demanded of the bridegroom's kin tend to be smaller; the family resources are conserved; no danger exists of an unsuitable match; and the bride need not go as a stranger to her husband's house. For these and other reasons endogamous marriage is very common.

In Islam, marriage is a civil contract rather than a sacrament. Consequently, representatives of the bride's interests negotiate a marriage agreement with those of the groom's. Although the future husband and wife must, according to law, give their consent, they usually take no part in the arrangements. At times a young man might suggest to his parents whom he would like to marry; girls usually have no such privileges. The contract establishes the terms of the union and, if they are broken, outlines appropriate recourse. Special provisions inserted into the standard contract become binding on both parties to the union.

Islam gives to the husband far greater discretion and leeway than to the wife. For example, he may take up to four wives at one time, provided he can treat them equally; a woman can have only one husband at a time. A man can divorce his wife by simply repeating "I divorce thee" three times before witnesses; a woman can instigate divorce only with difficulty. Any children of the union belong to the husband's family and stay with him in case of divorce. Although economic factors make divorce rare, the one-sided nature of the law symbolizes the woman's subservient position. Men of course exercise authority in the home. They expect virginity of their brides, but no such expectation exists for bridegrooms.

Men and Women

The social milieu in which the family lives significantly affects the circumstances of the wife. In towns and villages male social life goes on outside the home, usually in coffeehouses where friends meet to chat, where politics is discussed, and where much business is transacted. In the countryside and among the urban poor, however, women fulfill important economic functions without which the family could not exist. Some women of poor urban families work outside the home, and countrywomen help in all kinds of work. As a result, women occupy a position of relative importance and enjoy relative freedom. Although casual social contact between the sexes of the sort common in the West is not known, segregation of the sexes is much less pronounced than in traditional towns. Among the traditional urban bourgeois, on the other hand, women fulfill fewer and less important economic functions.

Artisan and merchant families earn their living from the skills of the men, and women make little contribution. Their responsibilities are often limited to the household.

In such circumstances it is more likely that women are confined to the home and their social contacts and interests limited to an exclusively feminine sphere. The houses of comfortable town families traditionally contain distinct men's and women's areas: the reception room where the man of the family entertains male guests and the women's quarters, from which adult males other than relatives and servants are excluded. Unlike their rural sisters, who move freely in the fields and villages, urban women walk in the street, discreetly avoiding coffeehouses, *suqs*, (bazaars), and other public gathering places, as well as any social contact with men.

Jordanians assume, often explicitly, that men and women are different kinds of creatures. Women are thought to be weaker then men in mind, body, and spirit, more sensual, less disciplined, and in need of protection both from their own impulses and from the excesses of strange men. The honor of the men of a family, which is easily damaged and nearly irreparable, depends on the conduct of their women, particularly of sisters and daughters; consequently women are expected to be circumspect, modest, and decorous and their virtue to be above reproach. The slightest implication of unavenged impropriety, especially if publicly acknowledged, could irreparably destroy the family's honor. Female virginity before marriage and sexual purity afterward are essential to maintain honor. In case they discover a transgression, the men are traditionally bound to punish the offending woman.

Arab societies generally value men more highly than women, and both sexes concur in this estimation. In the words of R.Z. Uzayzi and Joseph Chelhod, men view woman as "a necessary evil. . . . What man expects of her is to perpetuate his line, and what he seeks in her is less the companion of his life than the mother of his children." Their upbringing quickly impresses on girls that they are inferior to men and must cater to them and upon boys that they are entitled to demand the care and solicitude of women. The birth of a boy occasions great celebration, whereas that of a girl does not. Failure to produce sons can be grounds for divorcing a wife or taking a second. Barren women, therefore, are often desperately eager to bear sons and visit shrines of saints to seek fertility (see ch. 4).

Most women, except those of the more sophisticated urban families, marry in their middle teens. Men are usually up to ten years or more older than their wives. Government figures show that in 1969 the most common age for marriage among women is between fifteen and nineteen and among men, twenty to twenty-nine. The young bride goes to the household, village, or neighborhood of the bridegroom's family, where she may be a stranger and where she lives under the constant critical surveillance of her mother-in-law. A great deal of familial friction centers on the difficult relationship between mother-in-law and daughter-in-law.

A women only begins to gain status, security, and satisfaction in her husband's family when she produces boys. Therefore, mothers love and favor their sons, ordinarily nursing them longer than girls. In later life the relationship between mother and son often remains very warm and intimate, while the father is a more distant figure. Observers suggest that women compensate for the emotional lacks in their often rather impersonal marriages and submerged adult lives through their relationships with their sons, who often remain as adults in or near the parental household. The wife who enters such a home finds herself in a distinctly secondary position. Furthermore a girl's own parents are eager for her to marry as soon as she reaches puberty to forestall any mishap to her virginity; she therefore is not encouraged to remain in her own family home.

Changing Values

Relations within the family and between the sexes have, along with all other aspects of Jordanian society, begun to show change, especially among the modern-educated. Modern education often embodies a set of familial and sexual values, attitudes, and customs much different from those traditional in the country. As these ideas have begun to percolate through the society, new perceptions and, to some extent, new practices have begun to appear.

Increased opportunities for mobility, both social and physical, have undermined the old familial ties and the values that subordinated the individual to his kin group. Especially among the educated young, a growing individualism has appeared. Many young people prefer to set up their own household at marriage rather than live with parents, and the modern-educated often view polygyny with scorn. At the same time social security has lessened the dependence of the aged on their children and other relatives (see ch. 6).

Among the most marked changes are those concerning women. Young women, especially in the cities, towns, and more modern villages, have begun to demand greater freedom and equality than in the past, although the guidelines of traditional practice still broadly govern their lives. Women have begun in recent decades to participate more in activities and interests outside the home. In modern-educated families relations between the sexes tend to be more egalitarian and westernized. Observers note for example that women dressed in Western clothes walk abreast of male companions, unlike the traditionally dressed woman who customarily follows a few paces behind. Nor do Western-dressed women carry burdens on their heads, as is the traditional custom.

Despite masculine opposition, a number of women of respectable families have taken jobs in the modern sector. Many of these are poor women who work out of economic necessity, but a growing number come from financially secure families. Small numbers of women hold responsible posts in a number of fields. Nevertheless, most end their careers at marriage; masculine resistance remains strong even in the educated, westernized middle class.

Women enjoy increased opportunities for education, although facilities for advanced study are limited in many country districts (see ch. 6). Observers have noted that educated women tend to convey fewer superstitious folk beliefs to their children and therefore could aid modernization even if they do not enter the work force. They point out, however, that because few countrywomen attend school, a substantial reservoir of these beliefs remains, especially among the poor, which is reinstilled in each generation. The gap between the educational opportunities offered to men and those available to women often produces a significant cultural gap between husband and wife.

City girls who attend school are not as closely chaperoned as formerly, although they rarely go out with friends in the evening. They also tend to marry later, often after working for several years. Some observers also have noted a tendency to want fewer children than was common in the past, paralleling the desire for greater freedom for women.

Other trends among the modern-oriented include the spread of the ideal of the nuclear household and the consequent detachment of the individual from the demands of the extended family. Modern-oriented parents tend to live a more permissive, child-centered life than their tradition-oriented counterparts. Conflict among the generations, which observers believe to be increasing, plagues families in which the young are attempting to adopt standards and behavior different from the time-honored ones of their parents. Urban life, with its greater emphasis on utility and efficiency, tends to undermine the great respect for the wisdom of age and the rightness of tradition found throughout the rural and traditional populations of the Arab world (see ch. 4).

CHAPTER 6

EDUCATION AND LIVING CONDITIONS

In the areas of educational services and standard of living, the turbulent events of the late 1960s and early 1970s as well as continuing tremendous and abnormal social and demographic demands on extremely limited resources sorely taxed the nation's power to maintain or improve the lot of the average citizen (see ch. 2; ch. 9; ch. 11). Governmental good intentions in these areas contended with an inherently poor natural endowment; straitened financial circumstances; physical devastation; the loss of a significant proportion of productive industrial, agricultural, and other facilities to the Israelis; and another of the recurrent influxes of destitute and homeless Palestinian refugees. In addition, significant price inflation coupled with severe unemployment eroded the position of many citizens.

Nevertheless, despite the great obstacles the country has faced since 1967, which differ mainly in degree from those confronting it since independence, significant progress has been made in a number of areas. Progress is especially evident in education, which has been a stated priority of the government for a number of years. Especially at the primary and preparatory levels (the first through the ninth grades), education has become widely available, although some observers have questioned both the quality of the instruction and the appropriateness of the curriculum to the students' life circumstances and the country's economic resources. Recognizing the need to supply training more suited to realistic employment prospects and the country's needs and to improve the level of teacher training, the government has announced its intention to strengthen vocational and technical education and to provide in-service training for its teachers. In view of the difficulties it faces, the educational system has apparently achieved significant success in promoting literacy, especially among the young.

The forces affecting the standard of living and the effects of those forces on the average Jordanian were more difficult to assess in mid-1973. Information was extremely scarce and its reliability open to question. The results of the 1970–71 civil strife were not clear (see ch. 2; ch. 13). It appeared safe to generalize only that living conditions varied considerably according to region, type of settlement, social position, and fortune of war. At the high end of the spectrum, well-to-do city dwellers appeared to enjoy reasonably balanced diets and salubrious surroundings as well as other comforts of modern life. In cities, however, basic public services, such as water, sewerage, and electricity, were insufficient to meet the needs of all residents. Poorer and rural people generally lived in more primitive and less sanitary circumstances. At the bottom were the poorest of the refugees, many living as dependents of international relief services.

Diet was generally reported to be adequate to support life and activity, if not good health. No reports of starvation were found, but nutritional deficiencies of various kinds were reportedly not uncommon. The diet reflected the agricultural limitations of the country and therefore was inadequate in a number of nutrients, especially high-quality protein and certain vitamins. Although epidemic diseases appeared to be under a degree of control, neither the state of health of the average citizen nor the availability of medical facilities was satisfactory.

The continuing presence of the Palestinian (see Glossary) refugees both caused and exacerbated problems in the political and social arenas (see ch. 2; ch. 5; ch. 9). Their needs overwhelmed resources that would have been taxed even without their presence. Although the necessity to assimilate, employ, and control this displaced population fell most heavily on the government, a number of relief organizations, especially the United Nations Relief and Works Agency for Palestine Refugees in the Near East (UNRWA), defrayed a substantial proportion of the cost of their subsistence, supplying food rations, housing, and educational, medical, and other services to eligible persons.

EDUCATION

In 1973, as in previous years, the role of the Jordanian educational system in society at large reflected the severe social dislocation caused by the Arab-Israeli War of 1948 and exacerbated by subsequent developments, particularly the disastrous events of 1967. The necessity to absorb large numbers of Palestinian refugees, increasing urbanization, and the sluggish development of the industrial economy since 1967 have resulted in chronically poor employment prospects for most graduates; in addition, cultural and other factors have inhibited the development of personnel with skills readily usable in the existing labor market. The rapid relative and absolute growth in enrollment since the 1950s coupled with the loss of important revenue sources have severely strained the country's ability to provide the resources, and especially the teaching personnel, necessary to provide mass education of acceptable quality.

In strictly organizational terms, moreover, the 1967 war exacted a toll on education. The Israeli occupation of the West Bank (see Glossary) removed from effective control of the Jordanian government a significant portion of both students and educational resources. In addition, the share of national income devoted to the educational establishment has increased.

Education and Society

Like the nation itself, the educational system resulted from the amalgamation of the quite different resources of the East Bank (see Glossary) and the West Bank and the later addition of institutions designed to serve the refugee population. In 1921, with the establishment of the Amirate of Transjordan, East Bank educational institutions were limited to twenty-five religious schools, which had been established under Turkish rule and which offered tradition-oriented education. The three-year primary schools taught reading, writing, simple arithmetic, and religion; the teaching was in Arabic. Four six-year elementary schools added to those subjects history, geography, geometry, science, and the Turkish language.

Educational modernization began under the Amirate of Transjordan. A modern curriculum was established, including seven years of elementary and four years of secondary schooling. Also, private schools, primarily run by religious groups, were organized. By 1930 the total number of schools had risen to sixty-five.

In Palestine, meanwhile, educational development was quite different. By 1914 a number of foreign missionary groups, including American, English, German, French, Italian, and Russian organizations, had established some 500 elementary schools. In addition, three secondary schools, one of which offered a complete secondary program, existed in that year. By the end of the British Mandate for Palestine in 1948, over 250 public elementary schools were functioning, along with four complete secondary schools. The Palestinians, traditionally far more westernized and town oriented than the Transjordanians (see Glossary), have for generations enjoyed higher standards of education and better educational facilities.

In 1950 the school systems of both areas came under the control of the Ministry of Education of the newly formed Hashemite Kingdom of Jordan. In addition, during the same period UNRWA undertook the education of the children of the Palestinian refugees from the 1948 Arab-Israeli War.

The Jordanian government has for a number of years attempted to use the school system to weld the disparate elements of the society into a cohesive whole. Curriculum and textbook selection has been centrally controlled for both public and private schools, and the national goals of increased literacy and identification with the values of Islam and the monarchy have found expression in school programs. The schools have not been consciously used for manpower planning, however, and programs and facilities available have not produced a body of graduates able either to find appropriate employment or to meet the country's labor needs.

School enrollments are relatively high (see fig. 6). In 1970 nearly 90 percent of the nation's six-to-eleven-year-olds were enrolled in the primary cycle, nearly 65 percent of the twelve-to-fourteen-year-olds

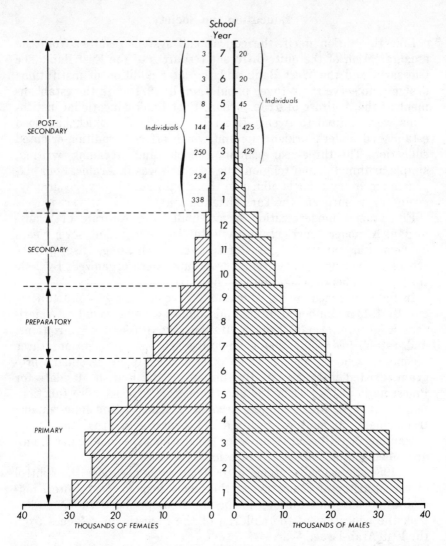

School Year

POST-SECONDARY

Individuals

		Individuals
3	7	20
3	6	20
8	5	45
144	4	425
250	3	429
234	2	
338	1	

SECONDARY

12
11
10

PREPARATORY

9
8
7

PRIMARY

6
5
4
3
2
1

40   30   20   10   0   0   10   20   30   40
THOUSANDS OF FEMALES   THOUSANDS OF MALES

Source: Adapted from Najati al Bukhari, *Education in Jordan*, Amman, 1972, p. 19.

Figure 6. School Enrollment, East Bank, Jordan, 1971/72

were in the preparatory cycle, and 35 percent of the fifteen-to-eighteen-year-olds were in the secondary cycle. Some observers have suggested, however, that, particularly in the secondary and subsequent grades, these high figures represent in many cases a form of hidden unemployment, and in the vast majority of cases graduates of secondary and higher institutions find few opportunities to work in their fields of academic specialization. Progress in literacy, however, has been substantial. By 1970 the government claimed an adult literacy rate of 55 percent, although some observers call this figure too high.

Of secondary students, in 1970 the vast majority were enrolled in academic programs, the graduates of which suffer the worst unemployment rate of any educational group. Very few, on the other hand, were enrolled in the vocational programs, which were unable to meet the national demand for mid-level technicians and skilled workers. This situation results from both cultural and organizational causes. The number of places in vocational schools is inadequate to meet demand, in both absolute and relative terms. Furthermore, cultural values emphasize the prestige of the academic diploma and denigrate manual work of all kinds (see ch. 5). Nevertheless, observers suggest that the success of well-trained technicians in obtaining well-paid employment has begun to enhance the status of these workers. The government plans to increase appreciably the number of places in vocational schools, so that by 1980 this kind of training should account for 30 percent of the secondary enrollment.

Such plans, however, do not solve the problem of the large numbers of educated unemployed, both secondary and university graduates. In addition to those trained in the liberal arts, persons with university-level technical training find few opportunities in the economy. Government is the largest single employer of educated personnel in Jordan, and the country routinely exports educated workers, especially to the neighboring oil-producing countries.

The high enrollment figures result from nearly two decades of rapid growth in numbers of students, teachers, and schools (see fig. 7). The bulk of the growth has taken place in the public system, which enrolled 68 percent of the students in 1970. Growth in enrollment has been especially rapid since a 1964 law made education compulsory through the ninth grade. Growth represents both absolute and relative increases in enrollment in each age group.

In addition to the beneficial effect of extending education to more children, the expansion of enrollment has had the deleterious effect, according to some observers, of causing some erosion of educational standards. Although the number of university graduates far exceeds the nation's needs, the number and annual production of trained teachers fall far short of present and future requirements. The overall ratio of students to teachers was thirty-four to one in 1970; in primary schools it was forty to one, and in secondary schools, twenty-five to one. In 1969 only 22 percent of primary and preparatory teachers had two years of postsecondary training in education; approximately 53 percent had finished secondary only, and 13 percent lacked even this credential.

Along with expanding vocational education, the government intends to establish new teacher training institutions and also has begun an ambitious program of in-service training for existing teachers who lack professional training. Before the 1967 war the country had eight teacher training schools. After the war the government retained control of three; and UNRWA, of an additional one. The three government

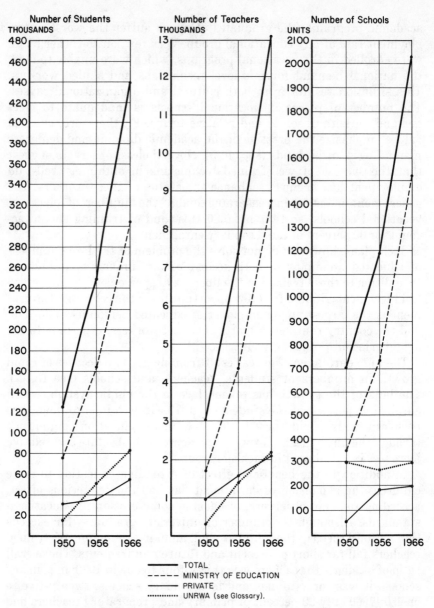

Number of Students
THOUSANDS

Number of Teachers
THOUSANDS

Number of Schools
UNITS

TOTAL
MINISTRY OF EDUCATION
PRIVATE
UNRWA (see Glossary).

Source: Adapted from Najati al Bukhari, *Education in Jordan,* Amman, 1972, pp. 3–4.

Figure 7. Progress in Education, Jordan, 1950–66

schools produce 350 graduates a year, a number inadequate to meet annual demand.

An important impediment to progress in the post-1967 period has been the fact that education has become an increasing financial burden. For the decade before the 1967 war, both educational expenses and gross national product (GNP) rose at an annual real rate of 8 percent or more. During those years education claimed a steady 4.5 percent of GNP. With the 1967 war, however, the situation worsened. Jordan lost both important facilities and sources of revenue. Nevertheless, in 1970 (and possibly in 1973) the government continued to pay salaries to teachers in the West Bank, even though Israel had taken control of education there. Even without the expenses of the West Bank, educational outlays were 6.5 percent of the East Bank GNP. Counting those costs, educational expenses rose to 8.1 percent of the East Bank GNP, or close to twice the prewar percentage.

Administration of Education

Education is both financed and administered by the Ministry of Education. The National Council for Planning Human Resources, chaired by the prime minister, makes broad policy, which the ministry carries out. Curriculum, which is uniform throughout the country in both public and private institutions, is set by the Higher Committee for Curriculum and School Textbooks, which also selects and approves all reading materials used in the classroom. Members of this committee include the minister of education and representatives of the University of Jordan, other higher educational institutions, private nonforeign schools, the Curricula and Textbook Division of the Ministry of Education, professional unions, chambers of commerce, and industry.

The ten directorates that compose the Ministry of Education have responsibility for system-wide functions, such as accounting, auditing, and procurement; preparation of instructional materials; university-level scholarships; relations with foreign states and instrumentalities; school library standards and procurement; research, documentation and statistics; and planning. Under this centralized overall supervision, day-to-day administration takes place largely at the level of the educational district. Of the fifteen educational districts, in 1973 five were located in the East Bank. Functions such as assignment of teachers, selection of principals, local budget planning, local facilities planning, and local inspection were handled at the local level under the authority of a district director.

The bulk of educational funds comes from the Ministry of Education, which in 1967 contributed 56 percent. The remainder comes from other ministries (10 percent), localities (5 percent), UNRWA (19 percent), and private sources (10 percent). Support for the University of Jordan comes from the Ministry of Finance and from a 1-percent tax on imports. Government educational expenditures took close to 20 percent of the government's domestic income in 1970, not counting foreign aid. The bulk of the funds went for teachers' salaries, as more than 60 percent of the classrooms in 1960 were rented. Although some of these rented facilities were poorly equipped for classroom use, their cost was relatively economical. Despite the high proportion of funds devoted to salaries, teachers' incomes are not high. In 1972 the average salary of a primary teacher was JD425 (for value of the Jordanian dinar—see Glossary) a year; of a preparatory teacher, JD500 a year; and a secondary teacher, JD600 a year. Total education expenditures in the country in 1970 equaled the equivalent of about US$12 per capita, a figure that compared not unfavorably with other countries at a similar level of development.

The Educational Career

Unlike previous generations of Jordanians, the youths of the 1970s find attendance at school a common experience. One in four persons in the entire country was a student in 1972, and schools were located throughout the nation, even in rather isolated spots. School attendance has become nearly as common for girls as for boys, despite traditional attitudes about the social role of women (see ch. 5). In 1972 girls constituted 45 percent of primary students, up from 30 percent in 1958. The government intends to equalize the ratio of the sexes in the near future. Although modernization of the economy and society was far from complete, education had begun to assume the role of a significant vehicle of upward mobility. Consequently, many parents, even in rural areas, desired education for their children.

The educational ladder consists of four parts: primary, preparatory, secondary, and postsecondary (see fig. 8). Grades one through nine are compulsory for all, within the limits of the government's ability to provide facilities. Entrance from the compulsory cycle to the more specialized secondary cycles is controlled by state-administered standardized written examination, as is passage from secondary to postsecondary programs.

Between the ages of six and seven a child enters a primary school whose teachers and pupils belong to his own sex. A minority of the children entering first grade have previously attended a kindergarten. Preschool classes, sponsored both by the government and by private groups, accept children from the age of four.

The primary curriculum stresses basic literacy skills. Subjects taught include reading and writing in Arabic; religion (Islam for Muslims and the appropriate religion for non-Muslims); arithmetic; civics and history, with emphasis on the history of the Arabs and the concept of the Arab nation; geography, with emphasis on the Arab countries; science; music; physical education; and drawing for male students and embroidery for females. In the fifth grade English is added to the official curriculum, although many private schools teach it earlier, and some offer French in addition. Within the primary cycle, promotion from grade to grade is required by law to be essentially automatic. Children may be held back only twice in six years, after which they proceed to higher grades regardless of the quality of their work.

The majority of the students proceed to the preparatory cycle, which includes seventh, eighth, and ninth grades. Schools remain segregated by sex. During these years work on academic subjects continues, both to improve the skills of terminal students and to prepare those going on for their secondary studies. In addition, vocational education begins on a limited basis. Each school is required to provide at least one course in a vocational subject for each grade. Boys' schools may offer agricultural, industrial, or commercial studies, and girls' schools offer home economics. In general, each school offers only one of the vocational options, and all students must take that subject for three periods a week for three years. To the academic courses offered in the primary grades, the preparatory curriculum adds geometry, algebra, and social studies.

On completion of the ninth grade, public and private students may sit for the public preparatory examination, the successful passage of which is required for promotion to the noncompulsory secondary level. Of those who took the examination in 1971, approximately 75 percent passed, and 70 percent of those completing preparatory studies proceeded to secondary studies. For those who fail and for those who choose not to continue, education ends at the ninth grade. These individuals therefore enter the labor market at about age sixteen with basic literacy and citizenship skills but without serviceable vocational training.

Secondary education is somewhat selective in enrollment and quite specialized in purpose. Both academic (general) and vocational careers of study exist; the former is designed to prepare students for university-level studies and the latter to train middle-level technical personnel for the working force. Within the academic curriculum, students further specialize in scientific or literary studies. By the tenth grade the proportion of female students has dropped to about one-third of the academic students and students in the commercial track of the vocational schools. Enrollment in the other vocational tracks appears to be exclusively male. Because of the specialized nature and relatively limited number of secondary facilities, however, students are not necessarily segregated by sex into separate schools.

The number of qualified applicants to secondary vocational institutions routinely exceeds the number of available places, and selection to one of these schools is considered desirable because it virtually guarantees reasonably well-paid employment on graduation. In addition to agricultural schools and to commercial schools offering secretarial, accounting, and bookkeeping courses, the system includes industrial schools offering programs in metalwork, auto mechanics, plumbing and air conditioning, electrical work, and building trades such as carpentry. The program includes both theoretical training and practical experience in a given trade, and teachers are themselves vocational school graduates, many of whom have additional training or experience abroad. Of the four industrial schools existing before the 1967 war, two remained under government control, as did two of the three agricultural schools in 1973.

The academic secondary program, which does not prepare students for specific employment opportunities, accounts for over 90 percent of the secondary students. Eighty percent of academic students, or 70 percent of all secondary students, pursue the literary course, which emphasizes courses in literature, history, and social sciences. Female students tend to enroll predominantly in the literary program, whereas males tend to choose the literary and science programs in about equal numbers. The science program emphasizes pure or theoretical science and mathematics rather than more applied studies, which would prepare the student for work as a technician or engineer.

The secondary program culminates in the public secondary education examination, which qualifies students for higher study. A variety of postsecondary institutions exist, including the University of Jordan, which enrolled 2,700 in 1972, and nonuniversity centers of vocational and other training, such as teachers colleges, schools of nursing, social work, and commerce, as well as advanced vocational schools. At the time of the 1967 war 15 percent of the relevant age group was enrolled in universities, 90 percent of them abroad.

University graduates, however, except for well-qualified teachers, medical personnel, and civil and architectural engineers, generally have little success finding work appropriate to their training. Many university-trained scientific personnel, for example, are too highly specialized to be absorbed into the relatively unsophisticated industrial system. Many university-trained Jordanians therefore seek an outlet for their skills abroad, especially in oil-producing nations such as Kuwait and Saudi Arabia, where they find generally higher wages than those available in Jordan. The number of Jordanians who routinely remit a portion of their incomes from abroad is so great that it has a significant effect on the national foreign exchange position (see ch. 11).

Although little information on the social origins of students was available in 1973, observers suggested that the majority of university, and probably of postsecondary, students generally come from the educated, urban-oriented middle and upper middle classes (see ch. 5). Furthermore, graduates tend to gravitate toward urban areas where they seek a style of life more suited to their training than that of the rural communities. Observers have noted, in fact, that modern education generally tends to be associated with a westernizing trend in dress, family relations, religious observance, and other aspects of life.

Refugee Education

The presence of large numbers of Palestinian refugees presents a special and continuing problem to government and society. UNRWA has been active for many years in the field of refugee education, supplying 21 percent of the country's primary and preparatory schools in 1970. In 1972 the UNRWA primary and secondary schools in the East Bank enrolled approximately 69,000 and 17,500 students, respectively. In addition, UNRWA maintained three vocational schools in Jordanian territory, of which one for boys was in the East Bank and one for each sex was in the West Bank. The East Bank schools enrolled approximately 750 students in 1972. Both secondary and postsecondary courses were available in UNRWA schools in such occupations as upholstery; building trades; automobile and diesel mechanics; pipe fitting; radio and television repair; telephonic communications; electrical work; and metalwork for boys and needle trades, child nursing, secretarial work, home economics, and hairdressing for girls. In January 1972 two new vocational schools, one for each sex, opened near Amman. UNRWA placement service figures indicated that in general approximately half their graduates find work in Jordan, and the rest find work primarily in Saudi Arabia and Iraq.

LIVING CONDITIONS

It appears probable that the turbulent conditions of the late 1960s and early 1970s had a deleterious effect on the standard of living of substantial numbers of Jordanians, and it was not clear in mid-1973 whether the reestablishment of relative stability had permitted conditions to improve. After a period of relatively stable prices, the cost of living began to climb steeply following the 1967 war and continued to climb well into 1972, although it leveled off somewhat in the latter part of that year. The cost of food rose especially quickly (see fig. 9). Housing and related services were in short supply, especially in urban areas, as large numbers of people, both refugees and others, crowded into the cities.

Environmental Health

In mid-1973 housing, water supply, and related facilities were inadequate to supply most residents with comfortable accommodations. Although some high-quality housing was available, especially in cities, the bulk of residential buildings was comparatively primitive. A small percentage of the population lives the nomadic life of the beduin, residing in the traditional black tents.

Since the 1967 war with Israel the shortage of housing had become increasingly severe, although it was not possible in 1973 to state the shortage in numerical terms. Even before the refugee crisis, however, urban housing was not plentiful; a 1960 survey of Amman, for example, disclosed that one-half the population was living one family to a room. Although some construction was taking place in the early 1970s, government sources stated that a disproportionate share of new housing was in the luxury price class. Amman has seen a decided

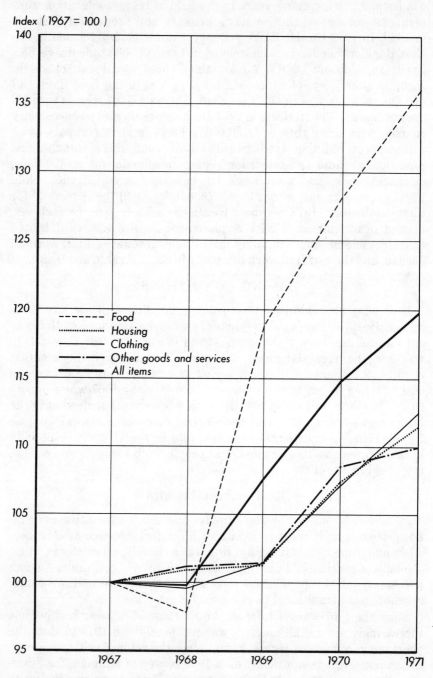

Index (1967 = 100)

Food
Housing
Clothing
Other goods and services
All items

Source: Adapted from *Quarterly Economic Review: Saudi Arabia, Jordan, Annual Sup-plement, 1972*, London, 1972, p. 19.

Figure 9. Cost of Living Index, Amman, Jordan, 1967–71

shift from multifamily tenements to detached houses. Observers note, however, that new housing units based on Western patterns are in several respects less suited to climatic conditions and social practices than are older structures of more traditional design.

Perhaps of even greater importance to health and comfort than the housing shortage is a fact that dominates many aspects of Jordanian life, the chronic and severe water shortage. The country has few significant sources of surface water and must depend largely on groundwater. As a consequence, water supply is insufficient for adequate sanitation, and per capita consumption is quite low; city people consume thirty-seven quarts per capita daily for all uses; and rural people, thirteen quarts per capita daily. In comparable Middle Eastern cities, Damascus and Istanbul, 1972 consumption was 118 quarts per capita daily and ninety-eight quarts per capita daily, respectively. Urban areas tend to have access to piped water, as do refugee camps, although in the camps service may be only through a public tap. A 1966 survey of Amman indicated that 82 percent of the houses had inside water taps.

Within the piped water systems, however, both quality and supply are said to be unreliable. Water frequently is contaminated at the source or may become polluted in the system or in the rooftop storage tanks used by many householders to regularize flow. It also appears that a number of illegal hookups exist; in Amman over 40 percent of the water in the municipal system may be unaccounted for annually because of illegal hookups, leakage, faulty meters, and overflow. A further problem is the irregularity of supply. Especially during the summer, water is piped to the various sectors of the city on a periodic basis in order to divide an inadequate supply.

The water shortage seriously complicates sanitation and waste disposal. A sewage treatment plant and sanitary and storm sewers were completed in Amman in 1969, but by 1972 only 1,500 houses had been hooked onto the system, although its capacity was 300,000 people. As a result, cesspools are in common use there and throughout the country, in both urban and rural areas. In many places the septic capacity of the ground has been severely overtaxed by close placement of many cesspools, and both groundwater and the ground have become contaminated. Because of the extreme scarcity of wells and streams, however, people commonly use contaminated water supplies and use streams for a number of conflicting purposes, such as drinking, washing, waste disposal, irrigation, and watering of animals. The shortage of moisture is such that in some areas untreated sewage is used for irrigation, even of vegetables for human consumption.

Environmental conditions create other health and sanitation problems. Twice each year, in spring and fall, a scorching wind from the desert, *khamsin,* sweeps over the country carrying quantities of sand, dust, and dirt into populated areas, which generally have no greenbelt or other windbreak protection against it. At such times, respiratory and eye problems—which are common throughout the year because of the extremely hot, dusty, dry conditions—become particularly widespread. At other times of the year, flash floods resulting from rain falling on parched ground unable to absorb it sweep over inhabited areas contaminating wells and other water supplies. Furthermore, the village and tribal custom of living in close proximity to domestic animals, which often occupy the lower portions of houses to provide heat during the winter, encourages the spread of disease.

A number of diseases related to poor sanitation and climatic conditions are common. Enteric diseases such as typhoid, paratyphoid, salmonella, hepatitis, and dysentery, both amoebic and bacillary, are endemic. Intestinal parasites such as roundworm, whipworm, and hookworm are common, as is the pork tapeworm among Christians, the only pork-eating group. Eye diseases are extremely widespread, especially in desert areas and after the windstorms. A 1967 survey found trachoma among 75 percent of the persons surveyed; 50 percent of those in Amman suffered from it as did 90 percent of those in the province of Al Karak. Conjunctivitis is epidemic in the wake of a windstorm and is widespread at other times as well. Ophthalmia is widely found among children.

The extremely dusty conditions may also be responsible in part for the prevalence of respiratory diseases, of which tuberculosis is one of the more common, and of skin infections. Insect-borne diseases, such as typhus, encephalitis, sandfly fever, leishmaniasis, and relapsing fever, have been reported, although malaria appears to be under control, because of World Health Organization projects. Of other vector-borne diseases, schistosomiasis, which depends on fresh water, has not traditionally been common in Jordan; since the completion of the East Ghor Canal, however, observers have noted an increasing incidence. Bejel, or nonvenereal syphilis, an acute inflammation of the skin and mucous membrane, is reportedly widespread in the southern desert, where 50 percent of some tribes are said to be afflicted. Observers have suggested that the customary method of eating with the hands from common bowls probably facilitates the spread of this infection.

Diet

The diet of most of the people is not seriously deficient in calories and proteins; the average adult consumes from 2,300 to 2,800 calories daily, of which close to 50 percent may come from bread. In 1962 a study of low-income workers found that many infants and small children suffer from lack of vitamins such as vitamin A and vitamin B complex, especially riboflavin. Malnutrition is most severe among infants and occasionally results in eye diseases and general growth retardation. This is especially true among refugees. Nevertheless, starvation is rare. Basic food rations provided to the refugee population by UNRWA contain 1,500 calories per day in summer and 1,600 calories per day in winter. The refugee diet is nutritionally equivalent to that of most citizens, and supplementary feeding and milk distribution programs benefit children and pregnant women.

The diet of the nomads has little variety, consisting mainly of camel's milk and dried dates and supplemented with boiled wheat or rice. On special occasions a beduin feast may include trays of boiled mutton, rice, and pine nuts. These foods are often taken with *leben* (semisolid curdled milk), which is rolled into balls of edible size. Wild succulent plants and roasted locusts are also eaten.

Villagers subsist on a diet of bread, *leben*, olives and olive oil, cheese, onions, and seasonal fruits. Bread made from wheat is eaten with all meals. A villager's breakfast often consists of bread dipped first into olive oil and then into a dish of powdered wild thyme. Lentils and chick-peas are dried for storage, then cooked before eating. Lentil soup is one of the few hot meals served in village homes. In some villages, especially in the irrigated regions, additional vegetables may include tomatoes, beans, okra, squash, and eggplant. Clarified butter, called *samin*, is kept in jars and used throughout the year. It is eaten with bread or used for frying. Meat is scarce, and beef is seldom consumed because cattle are considered too useful as work animals to slaughter. Tea is the popular beverage among the majority of Jordanians.

Town and city dwellers have a more varied diet and consume more fruits, vegetables, and meats than the rest of the population. Popular dishes include rolled grape leaves filled with rice and ground meat, or small, tender squash stuffed with the rice and meat filling. A commonly served side dish known as *hummus* consists of crushed chick-peas, mixed with sesame seed oil.

The people show a marked preference for lamb, mutton, and goat meat. Beef is scarce, and pork, because of the Muslim religious proscription, is eaten only by the Christian community. Camel meat is consumed by the beduins but in decreasing quantities. During the mid-1960s annual meat consumption was estimated at about twelve pounds per person.

Medical Facilities

Medical facilities are inadequate throughout most of the country (see fig. 10). Among the twenty-six hospital facilities in 1971, there were general institutions as well as institutions specializing in tuberculosis treatment; maternal and pediatric care; infectious and contagious diseases; leprosy; and eye, ear, and nose ailments. Other specialized medical units include a mental health clinic, public health laboratories, and radiology centers. Many hospitals and clinics are operated by religious and charitable organizations and by UNRWA.

The introduction of modern medicine and the growth of health

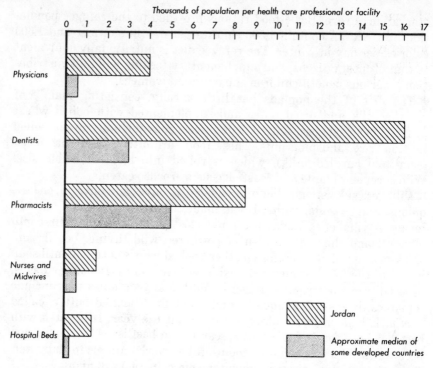

Source: Adapted from World Health Organization, Regional Office for the Eastern Mediterranean, *Annual Report of the Director, 1969–70*, Alexandria, 1971, pp. 21, 23.

Figure 10. Health Care, Jordan and Some Developed Countries, 1970

services have freed the country from the large-scale epidemics that once afflicted it. During the late 1960s a national public health organization engaged in programs of increasing scope and effectiveness. Private medical care was also available. There was, however, a great shortage of medical personnel and facilities, particularly in the rural areas.

A shortage of doctors has aggravated the nation's poor health conditions. All professional medical personnel are foreign trained and generally prefer to practice in the urban centers rather than in the small towns and villages, where medical aid is critically needed. The opening of the medical faculty of the University of Jordan in 1972 promised an increased supply of physicians.

Welfare and Refugee Services

Public welfare in Jordanian society has been traditionally provided by the family and religious institutions. The religious duties of every Muslim include the obligation to aid all needy family members and other poor individuals. The government, however, has replaced almsgiving, the *zakat*, with a modern social welfare tax. Funds obtained through this tax system are distributed to the poor and are used for the maintenance of mosques and for the salaries of religious teachers and prayer leaders.

The consitution contains various welfare provisions and states that the well-being of all Jordanians is one of the government's major aims. Legislation has been enacted condemning child labor, permitting foster parenthood, and providing for workmen's compensation and vacation benefits. On the national level the Ministry of Labor and Social Affairs has responsibility for community development, family welfare and protection, youth leadership development, and rehabilitation of the handicapped. In addition, approximately 140 philanthropic organizations provided a variety of services.

Since 1948 UNRWA has conducted large-scale welfare projects, which include food and clothing distribution; the establishment of housing facilities; and the operation of health, sanitation, education, and rehabilitation programs. Eligible for UNRWA services are refugees of the 1948 conflict, their children, and their grandchildren. The extremely low reported death rate among holders of UNRWA cards has led observers to the conclusion that a black market exists for these documents. Other international organizations, such as the Lutheran World Federation, the International Red Cross, and the World Council of Churches, aid the refugees either directly or through UNRWA. The Jordanian government has also provided aid for the refugees, whose numbers increased after the June 1967 conflict (see ch. 3).

CHAPTER 7

MASS COMMUNICATIONS
AND THE ARTS

In mid-1973 communications media and cultural activities were either controlled or closely monitored by the government. The government-owned radio and television and an official daily newspaper were utilized to foster national solidarity; to instill various concepts of modernity among the rural population; and to solicit public support for official policies, particularly foreign policies, both in Jordan and in other Arab countries. Cultural policies were designed to stimulate creativity in literature, drama, and the visual arts; to foster native crafts and folklore; and to stimulate interest, both domestic and foreign, in the country's archaeological and architectural relics.

Nearly constant warfare since the 1940s and related massive demographic, economic, and political dislocations have relegated contemporary artistic and intellectual endeavors to a secondary place. In the early 1960s an indigenous cultural movement, sponsored by the Ministry of Culture and Information, was beginning to make headway. Interrupted by the Arab-Israeli War of June 1967, the movement began to gather strength near the end of that decade, finding expression mostly in literature and painting, featuring themes drawn from the Palestinian resistance movements and Arab nationalism. In 1973 artistic life was still loosely organized; writers and visual artists had relatively little social influence and little formal contact with each other.

Radio was the best developed technically of the communications media and was available to virtually every segment of the population. Battery-powered sets were widely used in the rural regions that lacked electricity. Television, started only in 1968, was fast becoming the most popular of the media, its growth limited only by the cost of sets. In 1973 television facilities were undergoing extensive modernization to improve reception in some areas and to enhance Jordan's potentiality in a cooperative area-wide effort to coordinate Arab television programs. Televised courses helped to upgrade science and language teaching in secondary schools, and televised newscasts were preferred by educated urban audiences to radio news.

The press appealed to a relatively limited, mostly urban readership.

Developed largely by Palestinians (see Glossary) who had come to the East Bank (see Glossary) after 1948, the press was an important forum of Palestinian opposition to government policies during the 1950s and 1960s. It has since diminished greatly in scope and was limited by a stringent press code and by close government surveillance.

Despite its wide range, government-sponsored information was of limited effectiveness. Palestinians, for example, who account for perhaps 40 percent of the population of the East Bank, were wary of information transmitted by the government-owned media and of information available in the private press, which they considered to be largely under government influence. The Palestinians relied mostly on radio, television, and press reports from other Arab countries and consulted the domestic media primarily to evaluate the current government position on major issues and to obtain local news.

THE COMMUNICATIONS MEDIA

The Press

Press activity during the Amirate of Transjordan (1921–46) was minimal. In the presence of a traditionalist, mostly nomadic, and largely illiterate population, there was little official or private interest in forming public opinion. Because of the country's late start as a political entity, the stage was not yet set for a party press. Two weekly newspapers, *Al Urdun* and *Al Nasr*, were nevertheless published in Amman, catering to a handful of educated readers.

The development of a national press began after the annexation of a portion of Palestine, including most of the city of Jerusalem, at the end of the Arab-Israeli War of 1948 and the subsequent large-scale entry of Palestinian Arabs. Bringing with them the tradition of a well-developed press, the Palestinians stimulated the establishment of newspapers and set the tone for a polemical, irredentist journalism that became dominant in the Jordanian press after 1948 for the next decade.

Jordan's first dailies, *Filastin* and *Al Difaa*, appeared in Jerusalem in 1949. Originally published in Jaffa (later renamed Yafo), both newspapers enjoyed high prestige before their publishers were forced to flee that city when it became part of the newly created state of Israel. The 1950s ushered in an era of vigorous journalism reflecting the growing opposition of the Jerusalem newspapers to the government's relatively cautious position on the Palestine question. After some outspoken critics of the government were elected to the National Assembly in April 1950, criticism directed against official policies was also forthcoming from Amman newspapers, including *Al Urdun*, which had become a daily in 1948.

Weeklies and periodicals appeared in the capital, supported by parties and interest groups representing a wide range of political views or started as commercial ventures; many of these were short lived because of financial difficulties or the lack of interest of their sponsors. Jerusalem, however, remained the center of press activity. New publications appeared during the late 1950s and early 1960s, including two Arabic-language dailies, *Al Jihad* and *Al Manar*, the latter supported by the conservative Muslim Brotherhood; two English-language dailies, the *Jerusalem Star* and the *Jerusalem Times;* and most of the weeklies that survived into the 1970s.

Freedom of the press was governed by the constitutional provision of free speech "within the limits of the law" and by specific codes defining those limits. According to the press code of 1955, still in force in mid-1973, newspapers are required to be licensed by the Ministry of Culture and Information, which is also empowered to confiscate publications for attacking religion or national dignity, disturbing public order, or offending public morality. Moreover, newspapers were forbidden to print news about military operations or about the king unless such news originated with the government.

In criticizing the government, newspapers were usually careful to observe the legal limitations of press freedom and were receptive to official guidelines indicating the limits of official tolerance of press criticism directed against certain subjects. In the exigent and sensitive issues of foreign relations, notably the Israeli question and relations with other Arab countries, the press was opposed to the government's position. Refraining from overt criticism, the press expressed its opposition by not commenting or reporting on these issues at all. The newspapers' policy of passive resistance became a major source of embarrassment to the government during the early and mid-1960s; Jordan came under increasing attack by the media of countries representing radical Arab nationalism and demanding a more militant posture against Israel. These foreign attacks were denied through the government-owned radio, but the private press steadfastly refused to espouse and to support the government's position. During the crisis that followed an Israeli reprisal attack on a Jordanian village in November 1966, the Jordanian press joined newspapers of other Arab countries in bitterly censuring the government and the army.

Unable to make itself heard through the domestic press, the government drafted a new press code, promulgated by executive order in March 1967, that strengthened official controls over the private newspapers. Under the law all newspapers had to apply for new licenses. Specifically, the law provided for the merger of the four Arabic-language dailies in Jerusalem and called for one daily each in Amman and in Jerusalem. The government was authorized to assign senior editors to each newspaper and to own shares in the companies that published them. Thus, a new daily, *Al Dustur*, was published in Amman by the editorial personnel of *Filastin* and *Al Manar*. Because of the war with Israel in June 1967, plans for the other daily in

Jerusalem did not materialize. In 1968, however, the editor of *Al Difaa* started a new daily by the same name in Amman. The venerable *Al Urdun*, which had been appearing only irregularly and had a much lower circulation than the other dailies, was not required to apply for a new license.

In the struggle for political control between the government and the Palestinian guerrillas, known as the fedayeen, in 1970, the stringent official controls over the press proved largely ineffective. As the guerrilla organizations established increasing influence over the country's internal affairs, newspapers began to print more and more of the guerrillas' news and commentary, partly expressing their own long-restrained sympathies, partly deferring to the guerrillas' growing power. The guerrillas independently published a number of militantly antigovernment magazines, pamphlets, and the daily *Al Fatah*. In June 1970, at which time the armed conflict between the government and the guerrillas was expanding dangerously, both Amman dailies, *Al Dustur* and *Al Difaa*, featured a strongly worded guerrilla antigovernment communiqué. Both newspapers were closed down but were allowed to reopen two weeks later to break the near monopoly of *Al Fatah* which, in the absence of competition, had increased its sales spectacularly. After governmental control was generally restored late in September 1970, the fedayeen press disappeared, and the publishing license of *Al Difaa*, which had been the most vocal in supporting the guerrilla movement, was canceled. Convinced more than ever of the need for a newspaper that represented its point of view, the government in 1971 launched *Al Rai*, the country's first official daily.

A less spirited and less diversified press emerged after the 1970–71 civil war, reflecting the weakening of political opposition and the wearying of the fourth estate, which resulted from futile efforts to influence the government (see ch. 9). There was no prepublication censorship, but in order to avoid government interference, newspapers refrained from criticizing the pronounced features of official policies, especially those that concerned foreign relations. The Palestine question was still of major interest to the press, but its treatment in most newspapers was more compatible with the government's view than in the past.

Various public officials also showed growing sensitivity to press criticism, and in 1973 a bill was introduced in the National Assembly calling for prepublication censorship, removing the publishers' recourse to the courts. The proposed legislation, however, met with government opposition and as of late 1973 had not been passed.

In response to these threats to freedom of the press, newspapers appeared to be less inclined to take up politically divisive issues, focusing instead on the problems of economic development and social reconstruction. Many leading journalists, moreover, became discouraged with the diminishing influence of Jordanian newspapers and moved to other countries, many of them to Kuwait and Lebanon.

In mid-1973 three dailies were published in Amman. The government-sponsored *Al Rai*, which had an estimated circulation of about 8,000, supported official policies although it was at times mildly critical of official administrative measures and bureaucratic practices. The minister of culture and information was a member of the newspaper's board of directors, and many of its editors were recruited from the various ministries. *Al Dustur*, a semi-independent daily with a circulation of about 12,000, was more in demand than its government-sponsored counterpart. Staffed by trained journalists, the newspaper often dealt with economic and social problems of public concern, such as the water shortage and high prices; such social issues were usually avoided by *Al Rai*. On questions of foreign policy, *Al Dustur* generally upheld the government's viewpoint although it was guardedly pessimistic on the Arab-Israeli question. The third and oldest daily, *Al Urdun*, lost much of its readership to its two competitors and in 1973 had a circulation of about 1,000; it has consequently faced financial difficulties and depended mostly on radio monitoring for its news. Despite its generally progovernment stand, the newspaper often candidly criticized some aspects of government policy, but because of its long tradition there is greater official tolerance for such candor than in the case of other newspapers.

In addition, there were seven fairly important weekly newspapers. *Al Sabah* was the most popular because it regularly featured news from Israeli-occupied territories. *Al Osbu* featured political and social commentary; *Al Hawadith* specialized in tabloid-style presentation of popular topics. All three newspapers were published by Palestinians. *Amman Al Masa* was the only evening newspaper. *Al Liwa*, temporarily banned from December 1971 until June 1973, supported the Muslim Brotherhood; *Al Suhufi* was published under private auspices. *Al Aqsa*, with a circulation of 20,000, was distributed free by the army to the Jordanian military. All other weeklies had low circulations ranging from 500 to 4,000 and were heavily dependent on commercial advertisements for financial survival.

Few periodicals were published; those that were, catered to intellectual interests and were published by the various ministries. *Al Afkar*, a publication of the Ministry of Culture and Information, featured literary and cultural articles. *Tammiya*, published by the same ministry, reported on economic development. The Ministry of Education published *Risalat al Muallin*, a monthly magazine for teachers. *Al Majalleh* and *Al Askariyah* were technical-military magazines sponsored by the army. *Al Shabab* was an organ of the government's Jordan Youth Organization.

Radio

Broadcasting from Jordan began during the Arab-Israeli War of

1948 from studios in Jerusalem's old city; British-built transmitters were located in Ram Allah, about nine miles north of Jerusalem. The Jerusalem studios were taken over by Israel after 1948, but Jordan continued to use the Ram Allah transmitting facilities. The signals from that facility, however, were not effectively received in Amman, and another transmitter was built near the capital in 1956. This transmitter and another that was added later provided the new technical base of operations for the government-owned and -operated Hashemite Jordan Broadcasting Service, founded in 1959. The Ram Allah facilities came under Israeli control after June 1967.

In mid-1973 the Hashemite Jordan Broadcasting Service used two mediumwave transmitters ranging in power from twenty to 100 kilowatts and five shortwave transmitters ranging from five to 100 kilowatts. The Arabic-language domestic service broadcast about nineteen hours a day, and an English-language program was on the air four hours a day. The Arabic-language program was typically broadcast from 3:30 A.M. to 11:00 P.M., featuring music, drama, cultural programs, Quranic readings, and religious services. There were about twelve newscasts during the broadcasting day, in addition to editorial comment, official speeches and interviews, agricultural information, and special programs for members of the armed forces and for residents of the West Bank (see Glossary). Western music, political programs, commentary, and news were featured on the English-language program, broadcast from 5:00 A.M. to 6:00 A.M., 11:00 A.M. to 1:00 P.M., and 4:30 P.M. to 5:30 P.M.

The international program broadcast over ten hours weekly. Daily half-hour programs were broadcast to the Middle East in French and Hebrew and to Latin America in Arabic and Spanish.

Radio communication facilities have been undergoing constant expansion and improvement. During the early 1970s modernization of broadcasting equipment was mainly aimed at improving Jordan's radio broadcasts to other Arab countries. A new radio station was in the process of construction near Amman in 1972, utilizing two 1,200-kilowatt mediumwave transmitters; a 1,500-kilowatt mediumwave transmitter was being built in early 1973.

The number of licensed radio receivers totaled about 1 million in early 1972 and the estimated audience, 1.5 million. Most receivers were in urban areas, but transistor sets have become increasingly popular throughout the country, including the beduin camps. Audience reaction to the different types of programs varies widely. Educated groups including Palestinian refugees were generally wary of government-controlled news broadcasts, except those concerning local events and economic conditions. Rural residents tended to be uninterested in national and international affairs, but they appreciated agricultural information and market news. In general the effect of information programs in the rural areas tended to be limited. Many rural Jordanians were unable to understand either literary Arabic or the Western terms that have been incorporated into the Arabic language to discuss technical and political topics (see ch. 5). As a source of entertainment, on the other hand, the radio is popular with most Jordanians. Educated urban listeners enjoy broadcasts of Western popular and classical music; Arabic music, Quranic reading, and religious chants are preferred in the countryside.

Television

Television was introduced in 1968 under government sponsorship. In early 1973 programs were telecast from the central studio in Amman over two channels for an average of six hours daily. Reception of domestic programs has been inadequate in some parts of the country, especially in the south. According to press reports in late 1972, Al Aqaba and its vicinity were dominated by Israeli television signals because of poor reception of domestic programs. Telecasts from Egypt, Syria, and Lebanon were received in some localities.

Government plans in 1972 called for the expansion and modernization of television facilities. Several new relay stations were under construction in the provinces. A relay transmitter located in Irbid was to be replaced by a new, high-powered facility that would improve reception throughout the area, particularly near the borders of Syria and Lebanon. Foreign experts were invited to design a modern subsystem that would connect the Al Aqaba relay transmitter by microwave links to the central studio in Amman. The government has also used its earth satellite ground station, inaugurated in early 1972, to receive and relay television programs from other countries; the first exchange of programs (with Morocco) took place in November of that year. Programs have also been relayed from Malta, Cyprus, and Italy. The use of satellite ground stations to exchange television programs received further attention at the Arab World Conference on Telecommunication via Satellite Relay held in Amman in September 1972.

There were an estimated 60,000 television sets in 1972. Programs included Arabic-language features and videotaped films from the United States, Great Britain, and the Federal Republic of Germany (West Germany). Educational programs were introduced with British assistance. Under the sponsorship of the British Council, Jordanian personnel were trained in Great Britain in the production of secondary school programs in science and English. In 1968 the first televised courses in physics, mathematics, and English were offered three times a week in forty secondary schools.

Films

In 1972 there were thirty-five film theaters with a total seating capacity of about 15,400. Films are a popular form of recreation with educated urban groups; however, they have only gradually gained acceptance with villagers and beduins. According to the latest official statistics available in 1973, fewer than 2 million people attended film performances in 1971 compared to almost 5 million in 1968. This decline apparently was related to the rising popularity of television and the increased price of film theater tickets.

The government produces a few films for tourist information, but otherwise the country has no facilities for film production. Almost half of the films shown are imported from the United States. The rest come mostly from Arab countries, Italy, Great Britain, and France. In 1971 the majority of Jordanians who attended motion pictures saw films produced in non-Arab countries. American films were the most popular, followed by those made in Italy and France.

Films from communist countries were rarely shown except during an annual weeklong festival sponsored by the embassy and the cultural center of the Soviet Union. The government, through its Film Censorship Board, screens foreign films and bans those that may offend Muslim religious sensibilities and those that contain scenes and dialogues considered discrediting to the Arabs.

Foreign Information

Foreign broadcasts are the most popular source of information from other countries. Broadcasts in Arabic are received from various Western networks. The British Broadcasting Corporation broadcast seventy hours weekly; the French Office de Radiodiffusion-Télévision Française, over twelve hours weekly; and the West German network, twenty-eight hours weekly. The Voice of America broadcast six hours daily in Arabic from mediumwave transmitters in Rhodes.

According to information available in mid-1973, communist countries in 1972 broadcast a weekly total of 248 hours in Arabic to the Middle East. Of this total, the East European countries broadcast 143 hours; the Soviet Union, sixty-seven hours; Cuba, sixteen hours; the People's Republic of China (PRC), fourteen hours; and other communist countries of Asia, seven hours.

Many Jordanians also listened to broadcasts from other Arab countries, including Egypt's Voice of the Arabs program, Libya's broadcasts to the Gaza Strip and other Israeli-occupied areas, and Arabic-language programs from Cyprus, Iran, and Israel.

Foreign information, mostly of a cultural nature, was available to urban, educated Jordanians through foreign missions. The United States Information Service (USIS) had a 5,000-volume library, motion picture shows, and English-language courses. USIS also offered a program of seminars on timely topics, published one Arabic- and one English-language magazine, and operated a film lending program. Other informational and cultural programs under Western auspices included those of the British Council and the West German Goethe Institute. There are also Spanish and Turkish cultural centers. Information from the Soviet Union was disseminated by the Soviet Cultural Center, which was opened in 1971.

Informal Channels

Informal communication, still important in the present day, is carried on chiefly in the local coffeehouses, the market, and beduin camps. The traveling merchant is usually the source of news from the city. In the villages the contents of newspapers are passed on by literate residents to those who cannot read. In the coffeehouses men discuss politics or listen to the radio, particularly in the event of a political crisis or a government speech. Women exchange news and rumors in the home, at the marketplace, or at the village well.

The landlord and members of the ulama (see Glossary) are traditional opinion leaders although their influence has somewhat declined in the cities. The imam, however, has remained a respected source of information and a source of communication between the ruling elite and the tradition-oriented masses. The imam, moreover, plays an important role in familiarizing the people with official objectives by relating these objectives to the themes of religious sermons. Because sermons are subject to prior official approval, the government has control over this type of information.

Book Publishing and Libraries

Domestic publishing activities are limited. In 1970, 114 new titles were published, mostly in the social sciences, the natural sciences, and the arts. Many books are imported, mainly from Egypt, Lebanon, and Syria. The principal distributor of domestic and foreign books and periodicals is the Jordanian Press and Publishing Company, a semiofficial agency.

The government sponsors the general public libraries and the collections maintained by the various ministries and government organizations. A few learned societies and educational institutions have specialized libraries; the best known is the 30,000-volume library of the Jordanian Archaeological Museum. The largest collection, over 100,000 volumes, is that of the University of Jordan Library. The combined holdings of the country's six public libraries total about 45,000 volumes; there are also nineteen specialized libraries with some 52,000 volumes.

Research Facilities

Museums and specialized libraries are the main research facilities available to the public and to visiting scholars for the study of archaeology, local history, and Islamic culture. The Islamic Museum in Amman has manuscripts and specialized collections valuable to students of Islam.

Learned societies and research institutes include the Department of Agricultural and Scientific Research and Extension, founded in

1958 in Amman. The institution engages in agricultural investigations, data gathering, and extension work. The Royal Scientific Society, founded in 1970, has research projects in education, engineering, economics, and managerial sciences. Library science is fostered by the Jordan Library Association, which was founded in 1963.

THE ARTS

Role of Government

The Ministry of Culture and Information is the principal agency involved in the implementation of cultural policies. The Department of Arts and Culture under this ministry operates through six divisions, each representing a field of artistic endeavor. The Division of Folklore, dedicated to the revival of traditional crafts, fosters research projects and arranges folklore festivals. The Division of Dramatic Arts has a training program for actors, subsidizes playwrights, and sponsors the production of plays. The Division of Painting and Sculpture offers scholarships to talented painters and sculptors and arranges exhibitions. The Division of Music sponsors a music teaching institute, the country's only public facility for the training of musicians.

The ministry also sponsors the Jordanian Folklore Dancers, dedicated to the revival of traditional dances, and arranges folklore festivals in Jordan and in other Arab countries. The Ministry of Tourism and Antiquities is responsible for the preservation of the country's archaeological and architectural relics and for disseminating material on the country's cultural accomplishments to tourists and visiting scholars.

Literature

Jordanians share with other Arabs a rich heritage of poetry, speech, and formal prose and esteem literature above all other creative forms. Classical literature, especially poetry, remains a source of intellectual enjoyment for many Jordanians, but modern adaptations of classical Arab forms and Western literary models have gained acceptance especially with educated urban groups. Palestine was in the mainstream of the Arab literary movement and was an important center of literary development. Traditional forms of oral literature survived in the relative isolation and predominantly rural society of Transjordan, but there was little formal literary activity.

Poetry

Among the oldest and most dynamic types of Arabic poetry is folk verse, an oral literature that continues to flourish. Sagas and recited verse, sometimes accompanied by traditional musical instruments, have wide appeal and strong emotional impact, especially in the rural regions. Preservation of this material is officially encouraged, and much of it has been taped by scholars. Much of this early poetry shows beduin influences in its praise of the beduin ideals of courage, independence, and simplicity.

Nimr al Adwan was an exponent of traditional poetry during the 1930s and 1940s. A poet of beduin origin, he recited traditional poems at festivals and in the tents of tribal shaykhs (see Glossary). Mustafa Wahbi al Tal (may be translitered as el Tell), once private secretary to the amir, became known for his work in rendering beduin and gypsy love songs into literary Arabic. Although eventually an outspoken critic of the amir and his administration, Tal was nevertheless liked by Amir Abdullah and admired by his countrymen.

In classical Arab literature the poem was written according to rigid rules including the use, throughout a poem, of a single rhyme sound and one of several traditional meters. Poems written in this tradition excelled in structural beauty and power of description but lacked specific themes or meaning. The classical style prevailed until approximately the first quarter of the twentieth century, when Arab poets, mainly in Syria and Iraq, sought to express contemporary themes related to the political and social issues affecting the Arab world.

The reform of classical poetry began with the introduction of thematic unity and relaxation of some of the classical rules of rhyme and rhythm and culminated after World War II in the rise of a completely modern style of free verse and innovative imagery. Strongly imbued with national feelings, the new poetry recalled events of the Arab-Islamic past and the struggle against foreign domination. Nationalist verse was already an important literary form before World War II in Palestine, being directed against both British rule and Zionism. Among the most popular nationalist poets of the period was the late Ibrahim Tuqan of Nabulus. He influenced his sister Fawda Tuqan, who later became one of the country's outstanding poets.

The modern trend in poetry has found ready acceptance among Jordanian educated groups. It has been encouraged, moreover, by prominent Lebanese literary magazines, including *Shiir* and *Al Adaab*, each of which is read extensively and is contributed to by a small circle of Jordanian intellectuals. The most popular poets with this circle were Jabra Ibrahim Jabra, a Palestinian who left Jerusalem for Iraq in 1948, and Tewfiq Sayegh, who emigrated to Lebanon at the same time.

Nationalist sentiments of modern Arab poetry were given added impetus by the Arab-Israeli conflict, the Palestine guerrilla resistance, and the plight of refugees from Palestine. Among the country's most popular contemporary poets is Fawda Tuqan, daughter of an intellectual but conservative Muslim family. Known mainly for her lyrical, nationalist verse about Palestine, she also was one of the first women in the Arab world to write and publish romantic love poetry. After the Arab-Israeli War of 1948, while still in her teens, she first gained recognition for a eulogy she composed in memory of her brother. Since the war of 1967 she has composed many poems with a resistance theme, such as "Forever Palestine," which expresses sorrow but also faith that a new life will emerge from the suffering.

Kamal Nasir, a native of Jaffa, who has resided in Jordan since 1968, composes revolutionary poems about the determination of refugees to return to their homeland. One of the first Jordanians to gain recognition in the modernist Arab literary movement was Salma al Jayussi, daughter of the Palestinian nationalist Subhi al Kahadra. Her poetry deals with the Arab-Israeli conflict and with problems of Arab identity. Comparable to her works are the poems of Thurayya Malha, residing in Lebanon, who is also a short story writer.

An outstanding young, less widely known Jordanian modernist poet is Fayez Suyyagh. His deep knowledge of traditional Arab poetry enriches the power of his modern verse. Blending lyricism and realism, he often draws upon Arab mythology to convey a contemporary poetic vision of struggle, suffering, and social ideals. His powerful imagery conveys the spirit of the desert in both a literal and symbolic sense, and many of his lyric works are written in the purest form of traditional Arab love songs. Abdul Rahim Umar, a modernist poet and literary critic, suggests contemporary messages through symbolic or allegorical use of ancient myths and familiar religious stories. Among the other contemporary Jordanian poets is Abdul Munim Rifai, minister of foreign affairs in 1968, who is credited with writing the Jordanian national anthem.

Prose

Modern prose writing in the form of novels and short stories was introduced relatively recently as a result of Western literary influences that reached the country mainly through Egypt and Lebanon. The short story has been especially favored by young writers and is frequently published in literary magazines.

Issa Nauri was among the first post-World War II novelists. A refugee who has resided in Jordan since the 1948 war, Nauri writes about his homeland and countrymen. His published fiction includes several short story collections and a recently completed novel on Israel, revised during the course of its writing to incorporate events relating to the 1967 war.

One of the country's most popular writers is Ibrahim Abu Naab, novelist, poet, journalist, and political and social columnist. He is most widely known for his serialized fiction in the press, but his short stories and poems have also appeared in local periodicals and in the Lebanese literary magazine *Al Adaab.*

Among the leading women writers in the Arab world until her premature death was Samira Azzam, also known throughout Jordan for her radio programs on various aspects of Arab culture. Characterized by conventional plots with a deep sense of social commitment, her stories focus upon the glories and hardships of her native Palestine.

Among the most promising and talented young modernist writers is Jamal Abu Hamdan, a lawyer by profession. His fiction explores themes of the individual's integrity and worth, of human communication, and of the quest of his people for identity in both an individual and a communal sense. In addition to fiction, Abu Hamdan has written a play, *The Locusts*, and has shown an increasing interest in writing for the theater.

In 1968 two Jordanian novelists shared first prize in a fiction contest sponsored by *Shiir* magazine of Beirut. One of the novels, *Al Kaabus* (The Nightmare) by Ameen Shunnar, is a lyrical and symbolic work reflecting the impact of the 1967 war. In addition to his prize-winning novel, Shunnar's writings include newspaper articles and columns on political and social issues and two published collections of poetry. The second prize-winning novel, *Anta Munthu al Yaum* (You as From Today) by Tayseer Sboul, was written after the 1967 war in a poetical style that confronts the present on an artistic rather than on a journalistic plane.

Biography, History, and Literary Studies

A contributor to the field of political biography was the country's first ruler, King Abdullah, whose *Memoirs* were translated into English. In addition to his unpublished poetry, the king also wrote *Political Reminiscences* and a work entitled *Who Am I*, which was intended to stimulate the national and religious zeal of Jordanian students. Abdullah's grandson, King Hussein, also wrote an autobiography, *Uneasy Lies the Head*.

Another historian, Sleiman Moussa, who has held numerous positions in the Jordanian government, wrote *A Modern History of Jordan* and a work on T.E. Lawrence from an Arab viewpoint. This latter book, completed in the early 1960s, was subsequently published in an English edition by Oxford University Press. Aref el Aref, who also held many government posts under the British mandate as well as since 1950, has produced voluminous historical writings in article and book form.

In literary analysis Issa Boullata, the elder brother of Jordan's modernist painter, is best known for *Romanticism in Arab Literature*, which has received little attention in Jordan but claimed substantial recognition in Lebanon as a university textbook. He also translated into Arabic two books on major American poets and contributed articles on contemporary Arabic literation to the government-sponsored literary magazine.

Theater

Although dramatic expression finds primitive precedent in Middle Eastern mimicry, passion plays, and shadow plays, theater is not an indigenous Arab art. It was introduced as an imitation of the European theater in the mid-nineteenth century and has since combined foreign influence with elements and themes drawn from the native culture.

During the British mandate amateur Palestinian troupes performed in Jerusalem, but they preferred translations and adaptations of European plays to the works of native playwrights, such as Nasril Jauzi and Jamil Bahri. Visiting Egyptian theatrical troupes supplemented local theater performances.

The Arab-Israeli War of 1948 stimulated the theatrical performances of political plays and sketches such as *The Tragedy of Palestine*. These performances, however, had limited appeal because of the lack of theatrical tradition among the predominantly rural East Bank population and the preference of educated Jordanians for English-language plays.

During the 1950s Western diplomatic personnel and other foreigners residing in Jerusalem and Amman organized amateur theatrical groups and patronized their performances. Among the oldest and most representative of these groups was the Jerusalem Players, whose initial membership included only a few native Jordanians. By the early 1960s, however, the Jerusalem Players consisted primarily of Arabs. Despite a predominantly Arab composition, the group continued to present only English-language performances, consequently limiting audiences to the English-speaking Arabs and to the foreign community of the area.

A talented and promising contributor to theater until his suicide in the mid-1960s was Samir Farah, a Christian Arab from Jerusalem, who was trained in drama, cinema, and television in the United States, London, and Beirut. Perhaps the first Jordanian to dedicate his life to the theater in a fully professional sense, Farah organized a student theatrical group in Beirut that often performed in Ram Allah, Jerusalem, and Amman.

Since the mid-1960s the Division of Dramatic Arts of the Ministry of Culture and Information has supported an Amman theatrical group. Each year it performs Arabic translations of works by Anton Chekhov, Oscar Wilde, George Bernard Shaw, Eugene Ionesco, and other well-known Western playwrights. The Amman group has attracted enthusiastic viewers from outside the capital, but admission costs restrict popular attendance.

Radio has brought the theater to a wide audience and provided channels for presenting works by aspiring native playwrights. Serial plays, dealing with social problems and current events, delivered in a modified form of the classical language, are popular radio entertainment. Television also serves as a major vehicle for theatrical productions.

Painting

Despite the Sunni Islamic tradition against depicting animals or the human form in art, representational painting was never entirely absent in what is now Jordan. Soon after the founding of Islam, a form of secular court art emerged, the earliest known examples of which are found in east Jordan. The finely designed murals depicting dancers, musicians, royalty, hunting scenes, and other human and animal forms decorate the walls of Qusar Amrah, a small desert castle about forty miles east of Amman, probably built about A.D. 715.

The most characteristic forms of Islamic art over the centuries, however, were ornamental designs derived from geometric and floral figures and from the Arabic script. A frieze from the eighth century Jordanian palace at Al Mushatta (presented as a gift to the German emperor just before World War I and still in the Berlin Museum) is an example of this geometric ornamentation.

Calligraphy has been highly esteemed by Muslims from the earliest times. Arabic inscriptions adorn manuscripts, buildings, and art objects. Although no longer preeminent in Islamic art, calligraphy is still practiced by many contemporary Jordanian artists. Calligraphy has also inspired modern Arab abstract art, such as the painting of Kamal Boullata.

Modern painting developed after World War II, largely under the influence of European schools. By the 1960s several promising artists had adopted an original style employing representational and abstract elements to portray themes that reflect a strong attachment to their cultural heritage.

Among the first artists to stimulate interest in painting was George Aleef, a White Russian artist who resided in Amman and instructed aspiring young painters. Ismail Shammout, a refugee after the 1948 war, is noted throughout the Middle East for his stark, realistic portrayals of the refugees' plight. His works have been exhibited throughout the Middle East, as well as in the United States, the Soviet Union, and Eastern Europe. Mohanna Durra of Amman, a former director of the Division of Painting and Sculpture of the Ministry of Culture and Information, is popular for his paintings of daily life of the region.

Art shows and exhibitions gradually gained popularity during the late 1960s, but the interest was confined to urban educated groups. The Ministry of Culture and Information encourages painters and sculptors through its Division of Painting and Sculpture by offering scholarships to gifted artists to study abroad and by organizing local exhibitions.

Music

Music performed in Jordan during the early 1970s included traditional Arabic styles, contemporary compositions treating Arabic themes in Western musical modes, and Western classical and popular music. Arab folk music has been popularized through radio and television and through government-sponsored folk festivals.

Jordanians have retained their attachment to traditional Arab music. Many still prefer the five-note scale to Western musical forms. Traditional music, moreover, is closely interwoven with poetry; in the villages, poets and musicians improvise songs at local celebrations and holidays. Unlike Western music, most of which is composed according to fairly explicit formal rules, Arabic music is based on a modal framework within which the performer is free to improvise. In the absence of a system of musical notation, the musician or singer learns his art by ear and transmits it through his performance.

The performance itself represents an interplay between the singer and the instrumentalists in which the latter render an embellished version of a basic melody. Because vocal elements tend to be ascendant over instrumental components, Arab ensembles accompany singers rather than perform solely instrumental works. The most commonly used instruments in classical Arabic music include the oud, a plucked stringed instrument with nine to eleven strings; the kemancha, a bowed instrument comparable to the violin; the *qanuun*, another plucked stringed instrument; and the nay, which resembles a flute.

The *takht*, a popular modern variant of the traditional instrumental ensemble, includes traditional instruments as well as a few Western ones. Each radio station has its own *takht*, which may accompany singers or interpret native classical works.

Folk music includes traditional songs, some passed down by beduin tribes, as well as popular contemporary compositions based on Arab folklore. Stimulated by well-known vocalists such as Lebanon's Fairuz, contemporary folk music has gained increasing popularity in Jordan. In the 1960s the Ministry of Culture and Information sponsored folk festival performances in Jordan and engaged Lebanese folk singers and dancers to train local performers. Native folk music and dance festivals were held in Ram Allah and Jericho in the mid-1960s but have not been held since the 1967 war.

Among the country's leading composers of folk music are Tawfiq Nimri and Jamil il Aas, both of whom began their careers as radio station employees and singers. Female vocalists, including Samira Tawfiq, Souas Hashem, and a singer known as Salwa, are also known outside Jordan.

Western classical music and works composed by native musicians in Western musical style appeal to a limited urban audience. Western classical music received greater emphasis during the mid-1960s when the Ministry of Culture and Information sponsored a symphony orchestra that performed briefly before the 1967 war. The war caused the cancellation of the country's first art festival in July 1967, scheduled to include performances by the Royal Liverpool Philharmonic Orchestra and the London Festival Ballet at the Roman Theater in Jarash.

128

An award recipient in international piano competitions, Ibrahim Sus, has performed Western classical music and his own works not only in the Arab world, but in London, Paris, and Italy. His compositions, reminiscent of Igor Stravinsky in their modern character and style, include a work entitled "1948." Yusef Khashu, classical musician and composer, assisted in the organizing and training of the ministry-sponsored symphony orchestra in the mid-1960s. Among those modern Arab composers who have sought to incorporate native melodies and themes into music of a Western classical style, Khashu won acclaim for a work described as Jordan's first symphony, whose theme is the 1967 war.

Facilities for musical education are limited. The Ministry of Culture and Information sponsors a musical education program, and private lessons are available in Amman.

Handicrafts

Handicrafts, traditionally predominant over other art forms, still constitute a major form of native artistic expression. Embroidered articles incorporate designs native to individual villages, and religious articles of olivewood, silver, and mother-of-pearl combine the heritage of Palestine with a contemporary response to tourism.

The weaving of silk, linen, and other fibers became a highly developed art in Palestine during Greek and Roman domination. In modern Jordan beduin carpets reveal the native culture; primitive designs, handed down from generation to generation, have become associated with particular tribes. Woven on rustic handlooms using wool, goat, or camel hair, beduin carpets are used for floor coverings, sacks, blankets, and camel saddlebags. Mass production methods are now being employed in weaving and in the making of tapestries, but the rich shades characteristic of handmade tapestries have not been successfully reproduced.

Embroidery designs derive from traditional native dresses, whose patterns sometimes date back to early Muslim textiles of the seventh and eighth centuries or to Coptic tapestries of the fourth and fifth centuries. Patterns are often associated with specific villages and thus identify one's place of residence. Embroidered products portray religious motifs, flowers, leaves, and mosaic patterns. The influence of European medieval culture and of contemporary Holy Land tourism upon Jordanian folk art is illustrated by two other embroidered products, crusaders' capes and jackets. Originally of a southern European design, the capes were introduced to the area by the Crusaders and subsequently modified with embroidery patterns by native villagers.

Pottery making in Jordan dates back to the Neolithic population of about 5000 B.C., and by 2100 to 1500 B.C. Palestinian craftsmen were using the potter's wheel. Around 300 B.C. the Nabataeans were producing open pottery bowls, decorated with delicate painted designs and characterized by a porcelain-like fineness extremely difficult to achieve on a potter's wheel. The craft was revived as a tourist and a small export industry after World War I with the establishment of Jerusalem's Palestine Pottery Factory in 1919.

Metalwork originated with gold jewelry from 1600 B.C. The principal product of contemporary Jordanian metalworkers is handmade silver jewelry. Centered at Jerusalem, this important domestic craft produces such traditional ornamental designs as the ancient diamond-shaped Semitic symbol, the olive leaf, and the Jerusalem Cross.

Having originated in the Middle East in prehistoric times, the art of glassblowing has been practiced for centuries in the town of Hebron, now under Israeli occupation. Hebron glass appears in the windows of Jerusalem's Al Aqsa Mosque, in the windows of the Dome of the Rock, and in chandeliers and decorative glass items in a number of public buildings throughout the country.

Centered in the Bethlehem region, also under Israeli occupation, inlaid mother-of-pearl work constituted one of the principal craft industries of pre-1967 Jordan. The craft may have been introduced by caravans transporting precious materials.

SECTION II. POLITICAL

CHAPTER 8

THE GOVERNMENTAL SYSTEM

In late 1973 the government, under the firm command and leadership of King Hussein, continued to hold in uneasy equilibrium the two distinct elements of the population, the Transjordanians (see Glossary) and the Palestinians (see Glossary). The situation was complicated by the fact that the West Bank (see Glossary) remained under Israeli occupation (see ch. 2). The residents of the West Bank were Jordanian citizens in name only, inasmuch as they were subject to neither the protection nor the demands of the Jordanian government. Within the Israeli-occupied Territory local government, the courts, the police, and related governmental activities were under the de facto control of Israel. No attempt has been made to describe the system of government or other activities in the occupied territory (see fig. 1).

The Constitution of 1952 provides for a bicameral parliament to which in theory significant power is delegated, but the constitution reserves to the king broad and almost unlimited power over all branches of government. Since assuming full monarchical control in 1953, Hussein has on several occasions invoked royal powers that suspend the rights and freedoms of the citizenry. In 1957, for example, after the discovery of a planned coup d'etat by forces that sought to overthrow the monarchy, the king suspended the constitution; disbanded all political parties; and expelled from the government many Palestinians, Arab nationalists, and advocates of a republic.

The king's ability to rule is based not so much on the constitution, which is of marginal significance to most Jordanians, as on the continuing allegiance to him of the beduins and the beduin-dominated armed forces (see ch. 9). The beduins continue to revere and support Hussein as a direct descendant of the Prophet Muhammad, and with the support of the beduins Hussein has weathered several coup (and assassination) attempts as well as defeat in the Arab-Israeli War of 1967, and he emerged victorious from the civil war of 1970 and 1971 between Palestinian guerrillas and the army (see ch. 2; ch. 4; ch. 13).

THE CONSTITUTION

Jordan's constitution was promulgated in January 1952 during

131

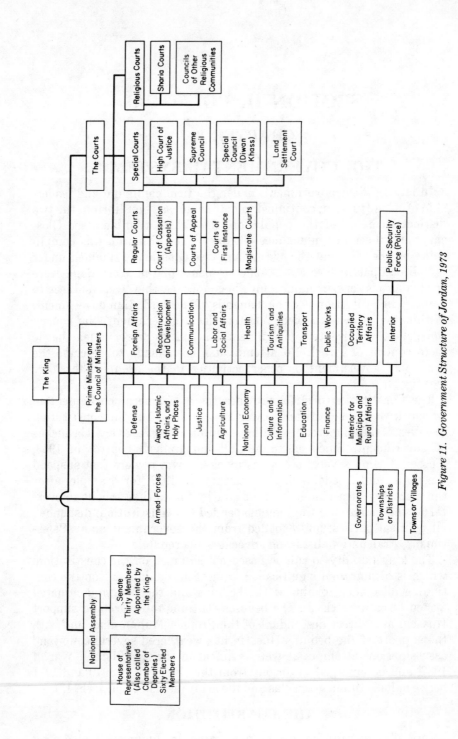

Figure 11. Government Structure of Jordan, 1973

the brief reign of King Talal (see ch. 2). The constitution declares Jordan a hereditary monarchy and reserves ultimate control over the executive, legislative, and judicial branches of government to the king (see fig. 11). Nevertheless, the constitution recognizes the principle of cabinet responsibility to the parliament, and the House of Representatives is empowered to force the resignation of the cabinet by an absolute majority vote of no-confidence. Moreover, a two-thirds majority of both houses (the Senate and the House) possesses the power to override a veto by the king.

The constitution also declares the people to be the source of all power and defines in detail the civil and religious rights of the citizens. In so doing the constitution implies separate sources of legitimacy— one in the sovereign, the other in the people.

The constitution is divided into nine chapters. Chapter I describes the kingdom and specifies its government. The kingdom of Jordan is an independent, indivisible sovereign state forming part of the Arab nation (see ch. 2; ch. 9). Islam is the state religion, and Arabic is the official language.

Chapter II specifies in detail the rights and duties of the Jordanian citizen. Citizenship is defined by law, and personal freedoms are safe-guarded. Citizens are assured freedom from forced labor or loans, and no citizen may be discriminated against for reasons of race, religion, or language. Arrest, imprisonment, exile, forced residence, and the expropriation of property may be imposed only under due process of law. Freedom of opinion and press and the right of peaceful assembly are ensured within the limits of the law, which permits censorship in periods of martial law or when a state of national emergency exists. The right of petition is guaranteed, and citizens are free to form political parties and associations provided their objectives are lawful. The constitution further states that elementary education is compulsory and free in government schools. Every Jordanian is declared eligible for appointment to public posts, subject only to the candidate's merit and qualifications. The constitution declares work to be the right of every citizen, outlines various principles of labor legislation, and directs the government to promote work and to protect labor.

Chapter III, titled "Authorities," outlines the powers of the state. The people are declared the source of all authority. Article 25 vests legislative power in the king and the bicameral National Assembly. The king and his ministers are granted executive authority, and judicial powers are given to courts. Chapters IV, V, and VI elaborate the powers of the three branches.

The remaining chapters deal with finances, general provisions, and the enforcement of laws and appeals. Chapter VIII contains four important articles: the procedure for interpreting the constitutionality of laws (Article 123), the definition of the Defense Law (Article 124), an emergency clause enabling suspension of constitutional law by the

133

king (Article 125), and the procedure for amending the constitution (Article 126).

Amendment of the constitution requires the affirmative vote of two-thirds of the members of each house and the approval of the king. An amendment to the constitution relating to the rights of the king and his heirs cannot be adopted during a period of regency.

Although the government has sought the conscientious implementation of the constitution in both letter and spirit, constitutional guarantees have been suspended during various periods of crisis involving either the continuing Arab-Israeli conflict or the internal conflict between the Transjordanians and the Palestinians. The king's alternatives in periods of emergency have been to dissolve the House of Representatives; to invoke emergency powers under the Defense Law; or, in the extreme, to declare martial law and assume full decree powers. The last two of these measures legally suspend the citizens' rights and freedoms.

In general, constitutionalism remains less important to the average Jordanian than the personality of his leaders or the traditional concept of law based on Islam (see ch. 4). The constitution, the parliamentary form of government, and the state itself are comparatively recent creations. They have still to prove themselves necessary and desirable to many of the population whose known lineages predate the national boundaries by hundreds of years. The spirit of nationalism and respect for the central government have risen with the increase in urbanization and education, but they compete with the ideologies of regionalism and supranationalism which, representing different interests and objectives, often clash with the monarchy, especially with respect to the handling of the Palestine problem. Under such conditions it is difficult for the government to create public confidence in constitutional procedures as the key to political viability for itself or to social betterment for the nation (see ch. 9).

STRUCTURE AND FUNCTION OF NATIONAL GOVERNMENT

The King

Executive power is vested in the king and the cabinet. The monarch appoints the prime minister and appoints or dismisses members of the cabinet at the recommendation of the prime minister. The king also appoints the members of the Senate, designates its president, and is empowered to dissolve the House of Representatives. The king signs and promulgates laws and holds veto power that can only be overriden by a two-thirds vote of each house. He may issue royal decrees (*iradah*) but only with the consent of the prime minister and four members of the cabinet. The king appoints and may dismiss all judges by decree, approves amendments to the constitution, declares war, and commands the armed forces. Cabinet decisions, court judgments, and the national currency are issued in his name, and he is immune from all liability for his acts.

Because of the critical importance of the monarchical institution, the constitution makes careful provision for royal succession. Basically, the throne "devolves by inheritance in the dynasty of King Abdullah Ibn al Hussein in direct line through his male heirs," but exceptions to the procedure of primogeniture are possible (see ch. 2). Succession flows from the eldest son but, should a reigning king die without a direct male heir, the deceased king's eldest brother would have first claim, followed by the claim of the eldest son of the eldest brother. Should there be no suitable direct heir, the National Assembly would select a new king "from among the descendants of the founder of the Arab Revolt, the late King Hussein Ibn Ali" (see ch. 2). The constitution also states that a successor to the throne must "be sane, a Muslim, the son of Muslim parents, and born of a lawful wife."

A reigning monarch may alter the succession, however, by means of a royal decree. In 1965 Hussein used this method to exclude from the line of succession his two sons by his Muslim, but English, second wife (Princess Muna) (see ch. 9). He also issued a royal decree that excluded from succession his next younger brother, Muhammad, and designated a second brother, Hasan, as crown prince and heir apparent. In 1972 Hussein married an Arab, Muslim woman; even if she should bear a son, a clarifying royal decree would be necessary for him to supersede Hassan as crown prince.

The constitution also includes explicit instructions for the designation of a regent, or a regency council, to rule during a king's minority. There are also provisions for the delegation of authority and responsibility should the king be incapacitated or absent from the kingdom for more than four months. In all instances the Council of Ministers is empowered to make the necessary appointments in the absence of an operative royal decree.

The Council of Ministers

The Council of Ministers, consisting of the prime minister and his ministers, conducts all affairs of state, both internal and external. Although the members serve at the pleasure of the king, the Council of Ministers is collectively responsible to the House of Representatives for matters of general policy. Every new cabinet is required to present its program to the House for approval by the affirmative vote of two-thirds of the deputies. If the House votes no-confidence, the Council of Ministers must resign.

Ministers are allowed to present their points of view in either house and, should they be members of one of the legislative chambers, they may also vote in that body. Ministers are not allowed to have any interest in a commercial company or to take part in any financial

135

act of trade. The House of Representatives has the power to impeach ministers and may also impeach its own members. The prime minister and four other ministers (two of whom must be the ministers of interior and justice) must approve a royal decree before it can become law.

Each member of the cabinet heads and is responsible for the functioning of his ministry. In 1973 the functioning ministries were interior; defense; justice; reconstruction and development; foreign affairs; agriculture; health; interior for municipal and rural affairs; culture and information; communication; education; *awqaf* (Islamic charitable foundations), Islamic affairs, and holy places; tourism and antiquities; labor and social affairs; national economy; public works; finance; transport; and occupied territory affairs.

The Legislature

Legislative power is vested in the king and the bicameral National Assembly. The size of the Senate cannot be more than half that of the House of Representatives (sometimes cited as the Chamber of Deputies). In 1973 there were thirty senators and sixty representatives (deputies). Senators are appointed by the king for renewable terms of four years; they are chosen from present and past ministers, ambassadors, judges, generals, veteran politicians, religious authorities, or other notables. They must be over forty years of age and, according to the constitution, must "enjoy the confidence and trust of the people for their services to the nation and country."

The members of the House are elected to four-year terms by direct male suffrage. On April 1, 1973, the cabinet decided, upon the recommendation of the king, to amend the electoral law to give women the right to vote and to sit in the House of Representatives. The electoral law of 1960 requires the minorities—Christians, Circassians, and beduins—to be accorded representation in the National Assembly. Candidates must be over thirty years of age and have Jordanian citizenship. Individuals representing foreign interests or having material interests in any government contract are excluded.

The prime minister submits legislative proposals to the House of Representatives, which can accept, amend, or reject a proposal. If accepted or amended, the proposed legislation is forwarded to the Senate. If accepted by both houses, the proposal is sent to the king for confirmation and promulgation. If one of the two chambers twice rejects a bill that has been accepted by the other, a joint session of both chambers is called to discuss the disputed clauses; two-thirds of the members present at the joint meeting may adopt the bill. If the bill is rejected, it cannot be resubmitted during the same session.

The joint session of the two houses provides another opportunity for the manifestation of the king's latent power. The thirty members of the Senate, constituting one-third of the maximum of ninety votes, are appointed by the king and serve at his pleasure. With the help of only one vote from the House, they can block any legislation that the king dislikes but which he does not wish to veto. Conversely, the senators plus one more than half of the House members can pass legislation that the king wants.

Every proposal passed by the Senate and House must be submitted to the king for approval. The king may veto a bill and return it within six months to the legislature, where a two-thirds majority of each of the legislative chambers voting separately is required to override the veto. When the legislature is not in session, the king may rule temporarily by emergency decree. Such decrees must be enacted in the normal manner at the next session, or they are repealed automatically. Laws become effective thirty days after their publication in the *Official Gazette.*

In contrast to the generally harmonious atmosphere pervading the sessions of the appointed "elitist" Senate, political views expressed in the elected and therefore more representative House range from pan-Arabism and socialism to the provincialism and quasi-feudalism of landholders and tribal shaykhs (see Glossary). Anti-Zionist Palestinian representatives also constitute a strong pressure group (see ch. 9).

National Assembly members enjoy immunity from arrest when the chambers are in session. Freedom of speech in the legislature is guaranteed, and no member may be condemned for opinions expressed during meetings or relieved of his position except by a majority action of the chamber to which he belongs. The legislature convenes annually on October 1 and remains in session for four months. The king may convene, adjourn, prorogue, or dissolve the House of Representatives by royal decree. A general election must follow the dissolution of the lower chamber. If an election has not been concluded at the end of four months, the full constitutional powers of the House are automatically restored.

In practice, therefore, the king constitutes a strong check upon the representative lower house, which in turn can pose only limited restraint upon him. His right of dissolution, his decree power during eight months of the year, and his indirect veto through the appointed upper house insulate him from legislation contrary to his approval. Nevertheless, the lower house does, by the letter of the constitution, represent an authority potentially as powerful as his own—that of the people.

The Judiciary

The legal system of Jordan has two basic sources: Islamic law, or the sharia (see Glossary), and those laws of European origin stemming from the period of the British Mandate for Palestine (1922–48) (see ch. 2; ch. 4). The laws of the mandate period were the source for the constitution and the enabling legislation for the civil court system. In 1973 the civil and religious jurisdictions were separate and generally noncompetitive.

The origins of Jordanian law correspond to two concepts of law—the revealed order of Islam and laws formulated by men. Rather than place these concepts in opposition, the framers of the constitution separated their jurisdictions. In 1973 a Muslim Jordanian was subject to religious law in matters of personal status and to civil law in all other matters. Both Islamic and constitutional law may be interpreted, the former by religious authorities and the latter by special legal organs.

The constitution and the Court Establishment Law of 1951 grant judicial power to an independent court system subject to the law itself and to the king's power of dismissal and appointment. Three categories of courts are outlined in the constitution: regular civil courts, religious courts, and special courts. The civil court system has jurisdiction in all civil and criminal cases not expressly reserved to the jurisdiction of religious or special courts. The three categories are mutually exclusive and function harmoniously in administering various types of law to various segments of the population.

The civil court system consists of a four-tiered regular court system and three extraordinary bodies. The system includes magistrate courts, courts of first instance, courts of appeal, and the Court of Cassation (Appeals). The three special organs are the High Court of Justice, which hears habeas corpus and mandamus petitions and issues injunctions involving public servants charged with acting illegally in performance of state functions; the Supreme Council (or High Council), which interprets the constitution at the request of the prime minister or of either chamber of the National Assembly; and the Special Council (Diwan Khass), which judges the constitutionality of laws at the request of the prime minister.

The religious courts are divided into sharia, or Islamic courts, and councils of religious communities for adherents of non-Muslim faiths. Their functions are similar. Each religious court system handles matters of personal status and communal endowment among its believers. For the sharia courts this includes the application of interpreted Quranic law and the settlement of blood money in cases of manslaughter. Greek Orthodox, Roman Catholic, Armenian Catholic, and Greek Catholic communities have religious councils to serve their needs (see ch. 4).

The special courts include the three special civil courts, tribal courts that administer tribal law to the beduin, and the Land Settlement Court (see ch. 13). Trials are public except where closed proceedings are requested in the interest of public morals. Judgments are issued in the name of the king, and amnesty and pardon rights also rest with the king.

ELECTORAL SYSTEM

The elected positions in the central government are the sixty deputies in the House of Representatives. According to the laws in force in late 1973, representation was semiproportional on religious and ethnic grounds in that a fixed number of seats were reserved for Christian, beduin, and Circassian minorities (see ch. 5).

The electoral law of June 1960 extended suffrage to all males, including Palestinian refugees who adopt Jordanian citizenship. Voters must be at least twenty years of age, in possession of full civil rights, and registered within their voting precinct.

Jordan is divided into seventeen electoral districts, of which three are beduin zones and fourteen are districts in the usual sense. For the purpose of filling the three beduin seats, all of Jordan is divided into northern, middle, and southern zones, in each of which specified tribes may elect one beduin representative. Seats in the other fourteen districts are apportioned according to population and ethnoreligious factors. Amman, for example, being the most heavily populated district has eight seats, two of which are reserved for Christians; the other six are for Muslims, one of whom must be a Circassian. Jerusalem, the second largest city, had five seats in the 1967 elections. Of the fourteen regular districts, seven were on the West Bank.

According to the legislation that was still in effect in late 1973, half of the regular House membership came from the seven regular districts on the West Bank and half from the seven districts on the East Bank (see Glossary). This ratio was maintained in 1973 through the legally questionable tactic of having the sitting members of the House act as an electoral college to fill the West Bank seats.

Candidates for election to the House must be at least thirty years old, have no record of convictions for proscribed offenses, possess full civil rights, hold no interests of profit connected with government contracts, and have no blood ties with the monarch within a proscribed degree of relationship. Candidates wishing to place themselves in nomination must submit a declaration of intention to the appropriate governor and deposit JD75 (for value of the Jordanian dinar—see Glossary).

The conduct of elections is marked by several interesting features. The Ministry of Interior draws up the final list of candidates for each district and posts it for public challenge. Voters are registered by precinct. On election day the voter has his name checked off the registration list and is given a ballot for each electoral list. He retires to "an isolated place," where he marks names on the list he is supporting. He then places his ballot in the box and discards the unused lists. Winners are decided by majority or plurality. If there is a tie between two or more candidates for a plurality, the final decision is made by a lottery carried out in their presence. Repetition of an election is not permitted.

Jordanian elections have a reputation for honesty as far as the mechanics of voting and counting are concerned. Disputes over the validity of an election are infrequent. Political parties are banned, and candidates therefore run as independents. The Ministry of Interior has the power to qualify or disqualify candidates in its role as determiner of the lists. Manipulation of elections, therefore, tends to occur at the nominating level rather than at the balloting level. Street disturbances caused by opposition groups threatened to disrupt Jerusalem on Easter 1967; however, five candidates were declared winners of uncontested elections.

CIVIL SERVICE AND PERSONNEL

The government recognizes the need for a capable civil service and has taken steps to modernize and upgrade the system. Recruitment aims at the educated youth. Selection is by competitive examination but, as the number who qualify in this manner exceeds the number required by the state, political and social criteria are a factor in determining who is accepted. Training is carried out at a school of public administration in Amman. Until 1967 there was also a school near Jerusalem but, because it was in Israeli-occupied Territory the school has not since been available to the Jordanians.

The civil service serves the king, who is a constant in the political and governmental structure, rather than the parliamentary government, which is changeable. Policy is determined at cabinet level and immediately below, well within the range of appointed positions. Promotion at lower levels is more formal, but political factors are operative throughout the system. Partly for this reason but partly also because their general attitude echoes the British tradition of public service, civil servants enjoy public confidence and esteem. Recruits appear to be drawn to it for honorable motives, not for personal gain at public expense. Civil servants are not unionized.

In the aftermaths of the abortive coup of 1957 and the civil war of 1970 and 1971, a large but unknown number of civil servants were forced to resign. Most if not all of those forced out were former Palestinians, reflecting the fact that the civil service was heavily Palestinian because of their generally higher level of education in comparison with the beduins, who formed the majority in the armed forces.

LOCAL GOVERNMENT

Local government—regional, municipal, and village—is under the supervision and control of the Ministry of Interior for Municipal and Rural Affairs. The kingdom is divided into eight provinces (governorates), three of which—Al Khalil, Al Quds, and Nabulus—are in the Israeli-occupied Territory (see fig. 1).

The provincial governors are appointed, transferred, and dismissed

140

by the king either on his own initiative or on the recommendation of the Ministry of Interior. According to observers, the most important attribute or qualification of a governor tends to be his proven loyalty to the throne. The powers and responsibilities of a governor and his civil service assistants are more extensive and more meaningful to the public than those of an elected mayor and town council. A governor, for example, has the power to declare null and void the election of a mayor whom the governor does not want.

Nevertheless, the basic administrative unit is the village or town and its elected council and mayor. Although most social and welfare measures are instituted and controlled by central government ministries, the town council does have various responsibilities for markets, law and order, sanitation, and related functions. To execute its duties, the town council has limited, but apparently adequate, powers of taxation.

CHAPTER 9

POLITICAL DYNAMICS

In mid-1973 King Hussein I, supported by his beduin-dominated army, remained the central policymaker and executive authority in Jordan. To a large extent he personally conducted the foreign relations and defense of the realm and maintained tight control over key ministries, such as information, justice, and interior, that dealt with internal security matters (see ch. 13). Crown Prince Hasan, the king's younger brother, had become increasingly responsible for economic and administrative matters.

Hussein's palace staff was predominantly Transjordanian (see Glossary) and, although the cabinet in July 1973 included nine Palestinians (see Glossary), the ministries of foreign affairs, defense, justice, and interior were headed by individuals of Transjordanian background. Since the autumn of 1971, Hussein has also appointed more of his loyal supporters to the Senate. With the exception of the Jordanian National Union, the sole authorized political organization, political parties were not legal, although they continued to function clandestinely, particularly after the 1967 war. Elections to the National Assembly, half of whose members represent the West Bank, were held in April 1967 but, because of the Israeli occupation of the West Bank, no subsequent elections had taken place by late 1973.

During the late 1960s various Palestinian guerrilla groups, such as Al Fatah, the Popular Front for the Liberation of Palestine (PFLP), and the Palestine Liberation Organization (PLO), increasingly used Jordan as a staging area for terrorist attacks against Israel. By mid-1970 these guerrilla organizations had taken on the characteristics of a state within a state, and at least some of the organizations openly attempted to overthrow the monarchy (see ch. 2). In the aftermath of the ensuing civil war (1970–71) during which the Jordan army effectively crushed the guerrilla movement in Jordan, the government ousted a number of Palestinian radicals from key positions within the civil service, and it reinforced the senior officer corps of the army with individuals of beduin background (see ch. 13).

In conformity with Hussein's stated policy never to allow the guerrillas to reestablish their positions in Jordan, the intelligence service of the Ministry of Interior maintained tight surveillance over individuals suspected of belonging to the guerrilla movement. The government did not allow fedayeen (see Glossary) propaganda agencies to operate within the country, and roadblocks and spot checks were numerous, particularly between the Syrian border and Amman. Although only a few of the guerrillas captured during the civil war were executed, several hundred of them who belonged to radical organizations remained in detention until their release, under a general amnesty, on September 18, 1973.

Between September 1971 and mid-1973 Hussein had taken a series of bold steps to reassert his authority. In addition to strict law-and-order legislation and the filling of key positions in the administration with Transjordanians, he had also created the Jordanian National Union, a pseudo-political party to bring the people into closer participation with the government; established an intertribal council to maintain control over tribal affairs; formulated an imaginative economic development program, including the regional development of the Jordan River valley; and formulated a plan for a federation to be called the United Arab Kingdom that would accord semiautonomy to the Palestinians on the West Bank (see ch. 10; ch. 11).

POLITICAL SETTING

Two Peoples—the Transjordanians and the Palestinians

As a result of the Arab-Israeli War of 1948 and the annexation of the West Bank in 1950, Jordan acquired 400,000 West Bank Palestinians and 460,000 Palestinian refugees. Whereas the Transjordanians were largely tribal and kinship oriented and traditional in outlook, the Palestinians were generally better educated and politically more sophisticated. In Palestine they had engaged in agricultural and commercial occupations, had developed a commercial middle class, and many of them had acquired administrative expertise as employees of the Palestine Civil Service. The Palestinians had produced a highly politicized element within their ranks and, whereas the Transjordanians gave their allegiance to the Hashemite monarchy, the Palestinians opposed monarchical absolutism and wished to gain access to political power by democratic means.

After 1950 the Palestinians began to move to the East Bank and to assume positions in the government and its bureaucracy. They brought with them their expectations for equality and proportional participation in the governmental process. In response to this pressure the government adopted in 1952 a more progressive constitution, which accorded the legislature some checks over the executive.

Through the years, however, the Palestinians' interests clashed with and threatened those of the monarchy. The Palestinians opposed the conservative character of the monarchy and its pro-Western policies. They distrusted Jordan's military and economic dependence first upon the British and then upon the United States—the country they considered Israel's major ally. They identified with the nationalist and socialist policies of the regimes in Egypt and Syria and distrusted the government's handling of the Israeli problem. They never lost their attachment to their old homeland, Palestine, and their paramount objective was the creation of a political atmosphere conducive to the restoration of that homeland.

The nationalistic Palestinians also felt their aspirations frustrated by the monarchical power structure. They accused the government of blocking their full and effective participation in the political process by barring them from influential positions of authority in the cabinet, Senate, armed forces, and administrative apparatus; by not allowing them a proportionate voice in the National Assembly; and by banning political parties (see ch. 2).

The tension between the government and the nationalist Palestinians created by this atmosphere led to the development and growth, particularly after June 1967, of the Palestinian guerrilla movement. At first Hussein sought to accommodate and compromise with the estimated 15,000 commandos operating from the East Bank, mainly because the preponderant Palestinian population of approximately 900,000 favored such accommodation. The king felt his throne threatened when the various guerrilla groups began increasingly to disregard Jordanian laws and to enforce their own policies, particularly in Amman and in the northern towns where they enjoyed particular popularity. The guerrillas literally became a state within a state. They set up roadblocks, levied taxes upon the population, and appeared armed and uniformed in the main cities, often clashing with the Jordanian police and army. Thus during the mid-1967 to mid-1971 period the central political issue revolved around the battle for political power between the guerrillas and the monarchy (see Political Events: 1970-73, this ch.).

King Hussein

Since his accession to the throne in 1953, Hussein has weathered various abortive coups and assassination attempts, two Arab-Israeli wars, and the 1970-71 civil war (see ch. 2). He has emerged as the central power figure in Jordan and has been able to assert and maintain his authority in a society where the personality of the ruler has overshadowed governmental institutions. Hussein has been supported throughout his reign by the original Transjordanian population, particularly by the beduin tribes, who revere him as a descendant of the Prophet Muhammad and as a ruler imbued with those qualities of leadership—courage, independence, valor, and honesty—most valued by them. The beduins, forming a prominent segment within the army, have helped Hussein through a number of his crises and have thereby served as a strong stabilizing force within the country.

To counter a persistent Palestinian threat to his throne, Hussein has made use of various political means at his disposal. He has maintained tight control over Jordan's key and nonelective institutions, such as the cabinet, Senate, army, and civil service, by filling many of their main posts with individuals of Transjordanian background who have proved their loyalty to the throne. This practice was facilitated when, as a result of his dissolution of political parties in 1957, the king was no longer compelled to appoint the leaders of the most popular parties to the government.

Furthermore, the king has been able to check the adoption of unfavorable legislation by the National Assembly, the country's only popularly elected body, through the use of his constitutional power to legislate by decree during the eight-month parliamentary recess; through his access to an indirect legislative veto made possible by the generally concurring votes of his thirty-member appointed Senate; and ultimately through his power to dissolve the National Assembly. As a result the king has preempted the power of the National Assembly, and its deputies, representing equally the East Bank and the West Bank, have in practice been able to wield little influence in the government.

During the more severe periods of crisis Hussein has either invoked emergency powers under the defense law or declared martial law and assumed full decree powers (see ch. 8). Crisis situations have usually erupted in Jordan at the end of periods during which Hussein has attempted to make concessions to his main opponents, who have usually taken advantage of the royal concessions by attempting to overthrow Hussein and to assume power.

In the twenty years between April 1950 and September 1970, Jordan had thirty-eight cabinets. The longest lasting of these cabinets remained in office for twenty-two months, and the shortest for five days. The majority of the ministers were supporters of the monarchy and thus shared more or less the same political outlook; yet the cabinets were frequently changed. According to foreign observers, the changes were made to give credence to the myth that the cabinet was the policy-making organ that had to be dismissed for unpopular policies or for ineffective administration.

The king usually chose his ministers from one of the following groups: members of the royal family, the palace staff, and former army officers; representatives of the old East Bank tribes and clans, such as the Fayiz and Majali families; and scions of traditional and aristocratic Palestinian families who were known for their Hashemite sympathies, for example, the Nashashibi, Tuqan, Dajani, Khatib, and Rifai families. Members of these Palestinian families had, under the British mandate, been enemies of Haj Amin al Husseini, the former mufti of Jerusalem, and many members had served in the Palestine Civil Service.

In the overwhelming majority of the thirty-eight cabinets, Transjordanians outnumbered Palestinians by at least two ministers, despite the fact that until the 1967 war the Palestinians formed two-thirds of

Jordan's population. This practice resulted primarily from the fact that East Bank ministers had proved to be more loyal to the king than those from the West Bank, who were always subject to the accusation of selling out on Palestinian interests. In accordance with a precedent set by King Abdullah during the mandatory period, almost every Jordanian cabinet included one Circassian and one Christian.

Political Interest Groups

The Military

The Jordan Arab Army, known as the Arab Legion before July 1956, was formed in 1923 by F.G. Peake, a British officer, mainly for the purpose of pacifying the rebellious beduins (see ch. 13). With the annexation of the West Bank in 1950, Palestinians entered the armed forces, particularly the lower ranks and the technical branches. Until the ouster of Lieutenant General Sir John Bagot Glubb, better known as Glubb Pasha, in 1956, the army remained the exclusive instrument of the monarchy. In 1956 Hussein, bowing to nationalist pressures, dismissed Glubb, who had not carried out the king's request for more promotions and training of Jordanian officers as part of the plan to jordanize the army. With Glubb's departure the army became embroiled in nationalist politics and ceased for a time to serve as the backbone and supporter of the monarchy (see ch. 2).

In 1957 a small group of nationalist officers challenged the monarchy in a coup attempt staged by Ali Abu Nuwar, the chief of staff, in cooperation with Prime Minister Suleiman Nabulsi (see ch. 2). Loyalist army units, composed mostly of beduin officers and men, enabled Hussein to crush this coup attempt, and Hussein subsequently reinforced his beduin units and appointed to sensitive command positions officers related to the royal house or those beduins or Circassians whose loyalty had been proved.

After the 1957 crisis the army emerged as the main support of the monarchy and succeeded during the 1970–71 civil war in thoroughly defeating the Palestinian guerrilla forces in Jordan. After the civil war the government further strengthened beduin dominance within the senior echelons of the army (see ch. 13). In 1973 Habis al Majali remained the commander in chief of the armed forces, and a cousin of the king was the chief of staff.

Guerrilla Organizations

Although guerrilla organizations such as the Palestine Liberation Organization (PLO) and Al Fatah began to develop in the early 1960s, the overwhelming defeat suffered by the Arab states in the June 1967 war brought to the various guerrilla groups the support and impetus they needed. In the aftermath of the war the guerrillas became a symbol of self-respect for the Palestinians and for many other Jordanians who became disillusioned with the failure of the Arab nations to defeat Israel.

The guerrilla groups consequently drew much of their manpower from the refugees who, after having lived in a state of misery much of their lives, felt themselves to be surrounded by a world largely hostile and indifferent to their cause. These people were fatalistic on the one hand, yet desperately eager for an effective political and military organization on the other.

Although the various guerrilla organizations differed in ideology and tactics, they all agreed on one objective—destruction of the state of Israel. They furthermore opposed Hussein's pro-Western foreign policy, particularly his ties with the United States, which they felt had tacitly approved and even encouraged Israel's expansion beyond the borders of the 1947 United Nations (UN) partition plan. Al Fatah and the PLO, the two largest groups, have generally avoided specific ideologies such as socialism versus capitalism, and prior to the 1970-71 civil war they had not demanded the overthrow of the monarchy. The more radical groups, such as the Popular Front for the Liberation of Palestine (PFLP) and the Popular Democratic Front for the Liberation of Palestine (PDF or PDFLP), have advocated the revolutionary and socialist programs of Marxist-Leninism, however, and have on this basis demanded the overthrow of the conservative Arab regimes, such as the Jordanian monarchy.

Because of their nonideological stance and pledge not to interfere in the domestic affairs of other Arab nations, Al Fatah and PLO have been financed by several Arab governments, ranging from Saudi Arabia, Kuwait, and Abu Dhabi to Libya, Syria, and Egypt. The more doctrinaire and radical groups, such as the PFLP, PDF, and Al Saiqah, have usually remained dependent upon one country, such as Syria or Iraq, for their financial support. The People's Republic of China (PRC), the Soviet Union, and various Eastern European communist governments reportedly have also provided a few of these groups with military equipment (see table 3).

The leaders of the guerrilla groups claim to have studied the insurgency strategies of Mao Tse-tung, Ernesto (Che) Guevara, Ho Chi Minh, and the Zionist revolutionaries who fought the British during the mandatory period. They have rejected any compromise political settlements, such as the UN Security Council resolution of November 1967, and they considered the battle with Israel to be one of protracted struggle that might last for generations (see ch. 10).

The internal structure of most guerrilla organizations is similar to that of Al Fatah. Regional Al Fatah committees, which include political information and military bureaus, exist in every Palestinian community of any size outside the territories occupied by Israel and, since 1971, also outside Jordan. Smaller cells exist within the universities, refugee camps, or places of work and keep in close contact with the appropriate regional committee. The regional committees constitute the central committee of Al Fatah, which is topped by its executive branch.

148

The PLO and its military arm, the Palestine Liberation Army (PLA), coordinate the activities of the various guerrilla groups. The PLO's Central Committee represents Al Fatah, the PFLP, Al Saiqah, and the PDF. In the early 1970s the PLO maintained offices in all Arab countries as well as in many others, such as the PRC, France, the United States, Yugoslavia, and Switzerland.

After its ouster from Jordan in July 1971 the guerrilla movement, badly fragmented and divided over ideology and tactics, settled in Lebanon and Syria. In response to actual or threatened massive Israeli reprisals those countries have also tried to prevent the guerrillas from carrying on their armed attacks against Israel (see ch. 10).

POLITICAL EVENTS: 1970-73

When as a consequence of the Arab-Israeli War of 1967 the Palestinian guerrilla movement in Jordan grew in popularity and strength, it soon threatened to undermine Hussein's authority. Whereas the only objective of a few of the guerrilla groups, such as Al Fatah and the PLO, was the liberation of former Palestine, other more radical groups, such as the PFLP and the PDF, also insisted upon the ouster of Hussein and upon the liberation of Jordan from what they considered to be a conservative and anachronistic regime. Furthermore, the more radical guerrillas opposed any plans for a negotiated compromise settlement with Israel and took it upon themselves to carry on the armed battle against Israel, using Jordanian soil as their main base of operations.

The threat to his authority and the heavy Israeli reprisals against Jordanian territory that followed such guerrilla attacks on Israel became a matter of grave concern to Hussein. As a result of tension between Hussein, whose loyal beduin army sought to eliminate the guerrilla raids, and the Palestinian guerrilla movement, sporadic outbursts of fighting occurred during the first half of 1970. In June 1970 an Arab mediation committee found it necessary to intervene in order to put a halt to two weeks of serious fighting between the two sides.

On June 28, 1970, Hussein designated Abdul Munim Rifai to head a cabinet of "reconciliation," which included more opposition elements than any other government since that of Nabulsi in 1957 (see ch. 2). Although the composition of the cabinet maintained a traditional balance between the East Bank and the West Bank, it included a majority of guerrilla sympathizers, particularly in the key portfolios of foreign affairs, interior, and defense. The king's action did not reflect a new domestic policy but rather indicated Hussein's desire for the support of a nationalist cabinet for any peace negotiations that might have resulted from the projected peace mission by Gunnar Jarring on behalf of the UN (see ch. 10).

On July 10, 1970, an agreement conciliatory to the guerrillas was signed between Rifai and Yasir Arafat, head of Al Fatah and chairman of the Central Committee of the PLO, which at the time claimed to

Table 3. Jordan, Principal Palestinian Guerrilla Groups, 1973

Names, Acronyms, and Ideology	Estimated Fighting Strength	Main Leaders	Arms Sources	Income Sources
Al Fatah Liberation of Palestine through armed struggle and creation of democratic, secular Palestinian state	15,000	Yasir Arafat Salah Khalif Khalid al Hasan Hanni al Hasan Zuhayr al Alami	China open market, captured Israeli arms, rockets of own manufacture	Mainly Palestinian private individuals channeling payments through governments of Saudi Arabia, Kuwait, Libya, Abu Dhabi
Palestine Liberation Organization (PLO); Palestine Liberation Army (PLA); Popular Liberation Forces (PLF) Ideology same as Al Fatah	10,000	Yasir Arafat Brigadier Abdul Razzaq Yahya Shafiq al Howt Abu Mahmud	Same as Al Fatah, Eastern Europe, and Arab governments	Same as Al Fatah, plus Arab government subsidies decided by Arab League
Popular Front for the Liberation of Palestine (PFLP) Marxist-Leninist	4,000	George Habbash Ahmad al Yamani Haytam Ayubi	Eastern Europe, Iraq, open market, captured Israeli arms	Iraq; private

Organization	Number	Leaders	Arms source	Financial support
Popular Democratic Front for the Liberation of Palestine (PDF) Trotskyist; committed to total revolution in Arab politics and society	1,000	Nayef Hawatmeh Salah Raafat Adib abd Rabu Bilaad al Hasan	Syria, Eastern Europe, open market, captured Israeli arms	Eastern Europe; private
Popular Front for the Liberation of Palestine—General Command	500	Ahmad Jabril Fadil Chrorou	Miscellaneous................	Miscellaneous
Al Saiqah Baathist (Syrian branch)	7,000	Zuhayr Muhsin Dafi Jamani Ahmad Shahabi Yusuf al Berji	Syria, Soviet Union, open market, captured Israeli arms	Syria
Arab Liberation Front (ALF) Baathist (Iraqi branch)	3,000	Zayd Haydar Munif al Razzaz	Iraq................	Iraq
Popular Struggle Front (PSF)	200	Bajat abu Gharbiya	Private................	Private
Black September Terrorist activities	n.a.	n.a................	n.a................	Libya (?)

n.a.—not available.

Source: Adapted from Abid A. Al-Marayati, et al., *The Middle East: Its Governments and Politics*, Belmont, California, 1972, pp. 473–474.

represent all of the most influential guerrilla groups. According to the provisions of the agreement, the government allowed the commandos freedom of movement within Jordan, agreed to refrain from anti-guerrilla action, and expressed its support for the guerrillas in the battle against Israel. In return the commandos pledged to remove their bases from Amman and other major cities, to withdraw their army units from Amman, and to respect law and order within Jordanian cities.

Small-scale clashes continued throughout the summer of 1970, however, and by early September the guerrilla groups were in control of several strategic positions in Jordan, including the oil refinery near Az Zarqa. The guerrillas were also at this time calling for a general strike among the Jordanian population and were organizing a civil disobedience campaign.

The internal situation in Jordan became explosive when, as part of a guerrilla campaign to undermine the Jarring peace talks to which the United Arab Republic (UAR), Israel, and Jordan had agreed, the radical PFLP on September 6, 1970, hijacked three commercial airliners belonging to British, Swiss, and American companies and subsequently destroyed the aircraft after releasing the 400 hostages.

Hussein, encouraged by his army, decided to curb the guerrillas. On September 16, 1970, the king proclaimed martial law and appointed Brigadier Mohammad Daoud to head a cabinet that was composed entirely of army officers. At the same time the king appointed Field Marshal Habis al Majali, a fiercely proroyalist beduin, commander in chief of the armed forces and also military governor of Jordan. Majali was given full powers to implement the martial law regulations and to quell the guerrillas. On the same day Arafat became supreme commander of the PLA, the regular military force of the Palestinian national movement. The new government immediately ordered the guerrillas to lay down their arms and to evacuate the cities.

During a civil war that lasted ten days, Syria sent tanks to aid the guerrillas, and Iraq kept its 12,000-man force stationed near Az Zarqa. The United States dispatched its Sixth Fleet to the eastern Mediterranean, and Israel undertook "precautionary military deployments" to aid Hussein, if necessary, against the guerrilla forces (see ch. 13). Under attack from the Jordanian army and in response to outside pressures, the Syrian forces began to withdraw on September 23 and 24; the Iraqi forces on September 17 and 18 had begun to withdraw from Jordan. On September 25 the guerrillas found themselves in a defensive position throughout Jordan and agreed to a cease-fire, which at the urging of ten Arab heads-of-state was signed by Hussein and Arafat in Cairo on September 27, 1970.

The agreement called for rapid withdrawal of the guerrilla forces from Jordanian cities and towns to positions "appropriate" for continuing the battle with Israel and for the release of prisoners by both sides; the agreement also provided for a supreme supervisory committee to implement the provisions of the agreement. Tunisian Premier Bahai Ladgham was designated to head this committee.

On October 13 in Amman, Hussein and Arafat signed a further, agreement, similar to the one signed in Cairo. Under its terms the guerrillas were to recognize the king's sovereignty and authority, to withdraw their armed forces from towns and villages, and to refrain from carrying arms in inhabited areas. In return the government agreed to grant amnesty to the guerrillas for incidents that had occurred during the civil war.

With the end of the civil war, which had caused great destruction and several thousand casualties, Hussein on September 26 appointed Ahmad Tuqan to head a new half-military, half-civilian cabinet to replace the previous all-military cabinet of Daoud. Army officers continued to head the key defense and interior ministries, however, and Field Marshal Majali retained his special powers as military governor until October 16.

In spite of the September and October agreements fighting continued, particularly in Amman, Irbid, and Jarash, where guerrilla forces had their main bases. On October 28 Hussein appointed Wasfi al Tal as his new prime minister and defense minister to head a cabinet of fifteen civilian and two military members. The cabinet also included seven Palestinians. Tal, known to be a staunch opponent of the guerrilla movement, was directed by Hussein to comply with the cease-fire agreements; furthermore, according to Hussein's written directive, the government's policy was to be based upon "the restoration of confidence between the Jordanian authorities and the Palestinian resistance movement, cooperation with the Arab States, the strengthening of national unity, striking with an iron hand at all persons spreading destructive rumors, paying special attention to the armed forces and the freeing of the Arab lands occupied by Israel in the war of June 1967." The closing months of 1970, as well as the first six months of 1971, were marked by a series of broken agreements and by continued battles between the guerrilla forces and the Jordanian army, which was attempting to establish its authority throughout the country and to oust the guerrillas from the populated areas.

As a result of continued and persistent pressure by the army, the fedayeen withdrew from Amman in April 1971. At that time Al Fatah, feeling its existence threatened, abandoned its earlier posture of noninvolvement in the internal affairs of an Arab state and issued a statement demanding the overthrow of the Jordanian "puppet separatist authority", and in a subsequent statement of early May it called for "national rule" in Jordan. Against this background of threats to his authority, Hussein decided to oust the remaining guerrilla forces from Jordan.

In response to rumors that the PLO was planning to form a

government-in-exile, Hussein in early June directed Tal to "deal conclusively and without hesitation with the plotters who want to establish a separate Palestinian state and destroy the unity of the Jordanian and Palestinian people." On July 13 the Jordanian army undertook a strong offensive against guerrilla bases in the area between Jarash and Ajlun—the guerrillas' last stronghold. Tal announced at that time that the Cairo and Amman agreements, which had regulated relations between the guerrillas and the Jordanian governments, were no longer operative or binding.

On July 19, 1971, the government announced in Amman that the remainder of the bases in northern Jordan had been destroyed and that 2,300 of the 2,500 Palestinian guerrillas had been arrested. A few days later many of the captured Palestinians were released either to leave for other Arab countries or to return to a peaceful life in Jordan. On September 18, 1973, King Hussein granted a general amnesty to the several hundred guerrillas who had been imprisoned in Jordan since the 1970–71 civil war or since their capture in early 1973 (see ch. 13).

Thus by July 1971 the army had virtually eliminated the guerrilla forces from the country. As a consequence of its defeat the guerrilla movement became even more fragmented, and a few thousand fedayeen established headquarters in Syria and Lebanon, where they remained dependent upon the goodwill of those governments. Hussein became virtually isolated from the rest of the Arab world, which accused him of harsh treatment of the Palestinian guerrillas and denounced him for his responsibility for the deaths of many civilian Palestinians who were caught in the cross fire (see ch. 10).

After his victory over the guerrillas, Hussein succeeded in reestablishing his authority throughout the country, particularly through the formulation and implementation of confident and aggressive policies in domestic and international affairs. One such activity was the formation on September 7, 1971, of the Jordanian National Union, which was open to all the people of Jordan (see Political Setting, this ch.). Hussein also arranged for the formulation of a far-ranging economic development plan and of a plan for a federation to be called the United Arab Kingdom that would accord the Palestinians of the West Bank a good measure of autonomy (see ch. 10; ch. 11). To strengthen his control over the beduin tribes throughout Jordan, Hussein also announced in August 1971 the formation of a tribal council to be responsible for tribal affairs. This council was composed of shaykhs and notables appointed by the king and was until April 1973 headed by Crown Prince Hasan.

On November 28, 1971, members of the Black September terrorist group seeking to avenge the deaths of fellow resistance fighters assassinated Prime Minister Tal in Cairo. On November 29 the king designated Ahmad Lawzi as the new prime minister and minister of defense. Ministers of the previous government retained their posts, with the exception of a reshuffle in the leadership of the ministries of finance and transport. On December 15, 1971, members of the Black September group again struck out against Hussein in an unsuccessful attempt on the life of Zaid Rifai, Jordanian ambassador to Great Britain.

On November 27, 1972, in an interview with the Beirut newspaper *Al Nahar*, Hussein revealed that the Palestinian guerrilla movement, in complicity with Libya's Colonel Muammar Qadhafi, had engaged in a plot to overthrow the monarchy and the government. The projected coup was to have been led by an acting commander of an armored unit who had links with the guerrilla movement.

On March 4, 1973, the government announced death sentences for seventeen Black September guerrillas charged with plotting to kidnap the prime minister and other cabinet ministers and to hold them hostage in exchange for the release of a few hundred guerrillas captured during the civil war. On March 14, 1973, Hussein commuted the death sentences to life imprisonment "for humanitarian reasons" and in response to outside pressures; the king later released the prisoners, including their leader Muhammad Daud Auda (also known as Abu Daud), under the general amnesty on September 18, 1973.

After a partial rearrangement of the cabinet in late 1971 and another on August 21, 1972, Hussein on May 26, 1973, appointed Zaid Rifai prime minister after the resignation, for reasons of health, of Ahmad Lawzi. Rifai, the king's closest political adviser, was reputed to hold antiguerrilla views. Rifai's nineteen-man cabinet included nine Palestinians, but Rifai retained the ministries of defense and foreign affairs, and other key ministries such as interior were held by men of East Bank origin.

POLITICAL PARTICIPATION

In 1973 popular participation in the political process was with minor exceptions limited either to membership in the Jordanian National Union, which by definition was a creature of the king, or to some clandestine activity in one of the illegal political parties. Elections for the members of the lower house of the National Assembly are scheduled at four-year intervals, but the election that would usually have been held in 1971 was indefinitely postponed, and in late 1973 there were no public plans for a new election.

Political parties have been banned since 1957. The Ministry of Interior makes up the lists of candidates in each electoral district and possesses the power to disqualify candidates (see ch. 8). It sometimes occurs that there is but one candidate for a seat, in which event that candidate may be installed without the actual casting of ballots. In 1963 twenty-one of the sixty seats were claimed by uncontested candidates, and there were exactly seventy-eight candidates for the remaining thirty-nine seats.

During the election of 1967 seven of the sixty seats were claimed by uncontested candidates. During that election the government relaxed its ban on political parties somewhat by allowing candidates from the Muslim Brotherhood to stand for five of the seven single candidate contests. The leader of the Muslim Brotherhood, Haj Amin al Husseini, a former mufti of Jerusalem, had for a long time been considered an enemy by the king because of Husseini's alleged involvement in the assassination of King Abdullah, but Husseini had won the king's favor by publicly opposing the PLO a few months before the election.

The Jordanian National Union

In September 1971 Hussein announced the establishment of the Jordanian National Union to serve as the nation's sole authorized political organization, representing—at least in theory—both banks of the Jordan. The union was not a political party in the traditional sense but would, according to the king, serve "as a melting pot for the Jordanian people." With the exception of Communists, Marxists, and "other advocates of imported ideologies," all citizens were eligible for membership within the union, which would "provide constructive opposition from within its own ranks."

According to the draft charter of the union, Jordan was an "indivisible part of the Arab nation." The provisions of the charter favored a continuation of the struggle to retrieve territories seized by Israel during the 1967 war and opposed any separation or division of the East and West banks of Jordan; advocated peaceful solutions to international problems; encouraged cooperation with other Arab states; and promised all citizens freedom of opinion and expression "within the framework of democratic practices."

On November 25, 1971, the Constituent Congress of the union elected Hussein as its president and Crown Prince Hasan as its vice president. Hussein then appointed a provisional executive committee of thirty-six members, and on August 30, 1972, elections were held for 240 members of the 360-member Jordanian National Congress, intended to represent the various sections of the population. The guerrilla movement rejected the union as "an attempt to deviate from the path of the Arab nation."

Banned Political Parties

Before Transjordan's union with the West Bank, King Abdullah discouraged the formation of independent political parties and created his own parties from above. Independence (Istiqlal) was the most significant independent party at that period, although the Communist Party and the Baath Party (Arab Socialist Resurrection Party) also had a measure of support. As a result of the 1948 Arab-Israeli War, the existing parties in Transjordan and Palestine either were completely transformed or disappeared altogether.

After the union in 1950 political parties attained more significance in Jordan's political life. The new Constitution of 1952 accorded the people the right to form political parties; it furthermore recognized cabinet responsibility to the legislature and thus laid the groundwork for the emergence of representative government and for a meaningful electoral process.

Even during this period, however, party development suffered from restrictive governmental laws and also from the people's inexperience in partisan politics. According to a 1953 law governing the establishment of political parties, a party had to be licensed by the Ministry of Interior, and the ministry would grant a license only if it were persuaded that the party's tenets did not foster internal dissension or oppose Arab unity. In practice, only the conservative and moderate groups received licenses to operate. Furthermore, additional laws issued in 1954 gave the cabinet the authority to dissolve existing parties and to withhold licenses from new ones.

The several parties that emerged between 1950 and 1957 were ideological and sectarian, appealing to limited regions and social classes. Most were centered on the West Bank and appealed to the displaced Palestinian Arabs. Four kinds of parties developed: the unionist, or pan-Arab, parties, such as the Arab Revival, Baath, Liberal, National Socialist, and Arab Nationalist parties; the status quo parties, such as the National Bloc, the Constitutional Bloc, and the Nation (Ummah); the Marxist parties, represented by the Communist and National Front; and the religiopolitical parties, such as the Muslim Brotherhood and the Islamic Liberation Movement. These parties, with the exception of the fourth group, were anticolonialist and advocated the emancipation of Jordan from what they described as British domination. Some parties supported the monarchy, but many others favored republicanism. At first only the Communist Party supported violent and forceful change.

As a result of the 1956 election—the only free national election ever held in Jordan—the National Socialist Party of Nabulsi won the largest number of seats (twelve) in the National Assembly. On October 29, 1956, Nabulsi formed a liberal coalition cabinet of seven National Socialists, one Baathist, one Communist, and two independent nationalists. In response to the new cabinet's demands and in the aftermath of the Anglo-French invasion of Egypt, Hussein abrogated Jordan's longstanding treaty of alliance with Great Britain on February 13, 1957.

The king resisted, however, when the Nabulsi government next pressed for the rejection of the Eisenhower Doctrine, for an economic union with Syria, and for the dismissal of pro-Western government officials. On April 10, 1957, Hussein dismissed Nabulsi after an abortive coup by a group of Baathist and pro-Egypt officers who were alleged to have staged the plan in cooperation with Nabulsi and Ali Abu Nuwar, the army chief of staff (see ch. 2). With the support of his beduin army and traditional authorities, the king furthermore suspended the constitution, dissolved all political parties, and removed a number of Palestinian Arab nationalists and liberals from the government.

The parties have continued to function in secrecy, however, and in 1973 their ideologies remained influential among various sections of the population. Moral and financial support from the surrounding Arab states has helped the parties survive the ban. Most of the internationalist groups, including the Baathists, Communists, and Arab Nationalists, have branches that speak for them through local organs in Beirut, Damascus, and Cairo. Radio propaganda from the Arab Republic of Egypt and from Syria was obviously untouched by the ban and remained a powerful influence upon Jordanian public opinion in 1973 (see ch. 7). Broadcasts reflecting the views of the outlawed parties easily reach Jordan and cannot be successfully countered.

Government response to illegal party activity has taken three forms: arrest and prosecution of party leaders under the 1957 ban; curfews and similar ad hoc legal measures in times of unrest; and police or military action to repress drastic breaches of the peace. In the absence of public disturbances, application of the 1957 ruling has been selective, aiming at key party leaders and potential conspiracies rather than at the rank-and-file membership.

The ban on political party activity weakened not only the parties but also the legislature, which was deprived of the service that parties render in aggregating disciplined support for or against proposed legislation. The lower house ceased to represent a center from which influence could be wielded to modify government policies. Hence the overall attractiveness of conventional party activity diminished, the reason for interparty competition ceased, and the penchant for unconventional activities against the government, such as guerrilla tactics, increased.

Because of their clandestine nature, details of the structure, internal dynamics, and political alliances of the various parties were virtually nonexistent in 1973 for the period between 1957 and mid-1973. The various parties' programs and objectives were not believed to have changed in essence since their dissolution in 1957, however.

The National Socialist Party, founded in 1950, emerged as the dominant political organization in the elections of 1956. Basically an anti-British and Arab nationalist movement, it denounced the Baghdad Pact and the Anglo-Jordanian agreement of 1948 in favor of cooperation with Egypt and Syria. Originally it had advocated union with Iraq. On the subject of internal reforms its socialism was moderate but clearly implied a reduction of monarchical prerogatives and East Bank influence in the government and an expanded role for the West Bank in determining policy. The National Socialists were still functioning in 1973, but not as a formal party.

The Arab Constitutional Party, founded in 1956 to represent the urban elite, typified the parochialism that characterizes Jordan's political spectrum. Based in Amman and a few of the larger cities, the party spurned popular support, relying instead on the prestige of its leaders, most of whom were ultraconservative landowners. Its program was secular and moderate rather than reactionary. As the only party to advocate both the monarchy and the independence of Jordan, it benefited from the king's approval and won the second largest number of seats in the 1956 legislature.

The Arab Nationalist Party originated in Syria and Lebanon and was established in Jordan on the eve of the elections of 1956 by some graduates of the American University of Beirut. Sponsored by the former mufti of Jerusalem, the Arab Nationalists centered their foreign policy program on the recovery of Palestine and the liquidation of the British presence in Jordan. Intensely pan-Arab, they recognized Syrian primacy in the drive for Arab unification. Internally they emphasized social justice instead of socialism but were staunchly anti-Hashemite. The Arab Nationalists were active in demonstrations against the Baghdad Pact in 1955 and campaigned in opposition to the monarchy in 1956. In 1973 they were reported to be administratively centered in Beirut.

The Muslim Brotherhood and a subsidiary called the Islamic Liberation Movement constituted the reactionary wing of the political spectrum, differing from the other conservative parties by being religious rather than secular. Founded in Egypt in 1929 and established in Jerusalem in 1946, the Muslim Brotherhood is an international movement based on a return to the social and political order of early Islam. The party appeared in Jordan in the 1956 elections, in which it won four seats, and has since then had continuous representation in the National Assembly.

An especially durable force in Middle East politics is the Arab Baath Party, the oldest and ideologically the most doctrinaire of the Arab socialist movements. The indigenous Jordanian Baathists trace their origins to the Socialist Resurrection Party of 1949, two branches of which were founded in Palestine and Transjordan independently of the larger Syrian Baath movement. With the union of West and East banks in 1950, the two branches merged and associated themselves with the Syrian party. The Baath program is imbued with missionary fervor, declaring that all Arabs constitute a single nation having the right to exist as one state and the mission to regenerate and reform human existence. It advocates revolutionary means toward implementing this renaissance. Its conception of state administration is socialistic, involving land reform, nationalization of key industries and natural resources such as oil, redistribution of capital, and only limited free enterprise. Politics, information, and education are to be so guided as to produce a secular and authoritarian state culture based on the party's three watchwords—freedom, unity, and socialism.

To the left of the Baath Party is a small but active Communist Party

concentrated among former residents of the West Bank and identify-
itself with their twin political touchstones, anti-Zionism and opposition to the Hashemite monarchy. Alternatively ignored and repressed
by successive Jordanian governments between 1949 and 1953, the Communists worked within a front organization, the National Socialist
Front (also called the National Democratic Front), to elect candidates
running as nominal independents in 1954. Unsuccessful in that
attempt, they allied themselves with the pan-Arab and pan-Islamic
opponents of the Baghdad Pact in 1955 and reappeared in the elections
of 1956 as the National Front. They elected three candidates and became the third party, with the Baathists, in the National Socialist
coalition government.

After the 1957 ban the Communist Party continued to operate underground in cooperation with Communists in other states, expressing
itself mainly through the Lebanese party organ *Al Akhbar*. Two former
members were elected to the legislature as nominal independents in
1961. In October 1968 the party published a manifesto in a Beirut newspaper denouncing governmental suppression of national movements
as detrimental to the national interest and calling for a government
of national unity as essential to the task of placing the whole country
on a combat footing.

Government enforcement of the ban has been strict in the case of
known leftist parties. Official amnesties were granted to fifty Baath
Party and Communist Party prisoners in April 1964 and to 1,700 prisoners in political prisons in April 1965; but in April 1966, 100 individuals were arrested for alleged membership in the Baath, Communist,
and Arab Nationalist parties, and in August of the same year three
men received sentences of five years at hard labor for having been
found guilty of holding offices in the Communist Party.

On April 19, 1968, the leaders of five of the proscribed parties announced the formation of a national front. The Communists, Baathists,
National Socialists, a party called the Independent Socialists, and
the Muslim Brotherhood reportedly issued a "charter for transition"
stressing the need for national unity during the period of Israeli occupation of the West Bank. Calling for the repeal of laws restricting
civil liberties in general and the ban on political parties in particular,
it also urged strengthening of the armed forces through the acceptance
of arms from any country willing to supply them.

CHAPTER 10

FOREIGN RELATIONS

In 1973 the government's overall foreign policy objectives were the preservation of the monarchy; the maintenance of the political independence of the state; the recovery of the West Bank (see Glossary), which was occupied by the Israelis in the June 1967 war; and the continuation of extensive foreign economic and military aid. The government was prepared to coordinate its political and military policies with other Arab states but was not willing to be pulled into a new war with Israel unless the development of Arab military superiority indicated a good chance for victory. Jordan supported the United Nations (UN) Security Council Resolution 242 of November 22, 1967, which called upon Israel to withdraw from the territories occupied during the 1967 war in return for the recognition by the Arab states of Israel's right to exist within secure and recognized borders. Jordan continued to rely upon the West, particularly upon the United States, for military and economic assistance. At the same time it sought diplomatic support from all channels and was slowly expanding its trade and cultural relations with the Soviet Union and with other East European states.

King Hussein I was the chief formulator of foreign policy and frequently was the chief negotiator and representative. The most important and prestigious diplomatic posts were staffed by men whose personal, and frequently family, loyalty to Hussein had been repeatedly demonstrated.

Although Hussein has publicly espoused Arab unity, his government's relations with most Arab states have been notable for acrimony, tension, and frequent ruptures of diplomatic relations. In late 1973, however, Hussein had apparently reestablished good working relations with two important neighbors, the Arab Republic of Egypt and Syria. There were indications that the seeming rapprochement had been strongly supported—if not in fact engineered—by King Faisal of Saudi Arabia, who for some years had been a backer of Hussein's monarchy.

THE FOREIGN MINISTRY AND THE FOREIGN SERVICE

The Ministry of Foreign Affairs, which is largely modeled on the British system, includes six major divisions: political (further divided into sections focused on particular regions or countries); protocol; legal and treaties; international organizations; communications and reference; and consular. The Consular Division deals with documents and authentications other than individual passports, which are handled by the separate Passport Department. The Administration and Finance Department supports the ministry and foreign service.

At the top of the structure is the minister of foreign affairs, selected by the prime minister, appointed by the king and, with the rest of the cabinet, approved by a vote of confidence in the House of Representatives (see ch. 8). In late 1973 Prime Minister Zaid Rifai continued to hold the foreign ministry portfolio himself. He was formerly senior political adviser to Hussein and Jordanian ambassador in London.

Next after the minister of foreign affairs is the minister of state for foreign affairs. The office of minister of state, used for a number of other functional areas besides foreign affairs, is a survival from British practice. In the foreign ministry this appointed official makes decisions on routine matters of an operational nature, screening incoming requirements to determine those on which he can take action and those requiring the personal attention of the minister. The third ranking official in the ministry is the permanent under secretary, who supervises the internal administration of the system and provides long-term executive continuity.

The career employees who man the Ministry of Foreign Affairs and the foreign service are classified, under the country's civil service, in ten grades. Personnel are further classed as administrative or political staff. New administrative staff officials enter at the lowest grade and usually remain in administration and at the ministry, with little service abroad. Political officers enter at an advanced grade and, after a year or two, are usually promoted to a rank associated with the position of third secretary in an embassy. Political officers constitute most of the officers serving abroad. Their total number in 1973 was about 200.

Recruiting for foreign service officers is accomplished by the ministry through public notice. All applicants must be citizens of Jordan. Each applicant must be a university graduate; must be able to speak, read, and write either English or French with fluency; and must pass written and oral examinations.

A selected applicant works in the ministry for one to two years before being sent on his first tour of foreign service. The approximate pattern for service thereafter is alternately four years out of the country and two years back with the ministry, although these periods often vary in length. In 1973 Jordan had diplomatic relations with about forty-five countries and maintained representation in about thirty, some stations having multiple accreditation.

RELATIONS IN THE MIDDLE EAST AND NORTH AFRICA

The Arab States

Relations with other Arab states are of particular importance to

Jordan both in short-range tactics and in long-range strategy in foreign affairs. Because of a deep-seated, although not quantifiable, sense of pan-Arabism and because a high percentage of the Palestinians, who form nearly half of the East Bank population and almost all of the West Bank population, are sympathetic to the forms of government in effect in some other Arab states, foreign relations have unusually strong internal implications, and in practice external and internal affairs are almost always interacting.

Jordan (then Transjordan) became one of the charter members of the League of Arab States, or Arab League, at its formation in 1945. From the outset, however, King Abdullah did not hesitate to follow courses of action that diverged from those of the Arab League (see ch. 2). As a result Jordan from time to time found itself politically isolated from some of its Arab neighbors, especially Egypt, Syria, and Iraq. These same characteristics of independence and recurring periods of political isolation in the Arab world have continued throughout Jordan's history under both Abdullah and Hussein, the monarchy being able to survive largely because of the special relationship with Great Britain until early 1957 and after that because of extensive United States aid.

A rapprochement among all Arab states was attained at the Cairo Conference of January 1964 but, between Jordan on the one hand and the United Arab Republic (UAR) and Syria on the other, broke down in polemical disarray by late 1966. Jordan nevertheless entered the war of 1967 against Israel along with the UAR, Syria, and Iraq. Although the Arab forces were defeated with heavy losses, relations between President Gamal Abdul Nasser of the UAR and Hussein became cordial during and after this shared experience, and both benefited from the recurring financial subsidies paid by Saudi Arabia, Kuwait, and Libya after the Khartoum Conference of September 1, 1967. Jordan's relationship with Syria was not greatly improved after the war but continued erratically, on and off, for the next four years.

The next major stage in Jordanian inter-Arab relations came about in the conflict between the government and the Palestine Liberation Organization (PLO) and its loosely associated guerrilla bands between 1967 and 1970 (see ch. 2; ch. 9). During the 1970-71 civil war the guerrillas were defeated and driven from Jordan, and Hussein's government emerged securely in control—but again generally isolated in the Arab world. Syria broke relations with Jordan in July 1971 after the defeat of the guerrillas; Libya and Kuwait had terminated their subsidies in the fall of 1970, and Libya had severed diplomatic ties.

Relations with Egypt became tenuous, especially after an Egyptian court released the Palestinian terrorists who had assassinated the Jordanian prime minister, Wasfi al Tal, in Cairo on November 28, 1971. Egypt broke connections with Jordan in April 1972 because of Hussein's independent announcement the previous month of his proposed United Arab Kingdom, intended to include the Jordanian East Bank and the old West Bank territories under a federal monarchy (see ch. 9). Nothing concrete came of this proposal, since it obviously required but did not have Israeli concurrence, but it evoked almost total opposition throughout the Arab world. The opposition of the remnants of the PLO was, as expected, categorical and polemical. A counterproposal in September 1972 by President Anwar al Sadat of Egypt for a Palestinian government-in-exile was rejected by Jordan. Hussein and his ministers officially disclaimed on a number of occasions any Jordanian intent to make a separate settlement with Israel, but in late 1971 and most of 1972 the word most frequently applied to Jordan's posture in the Arab world was isolation.

This description was by no means applicable to Jordan's relations with all Arab states, however. From 1964 onward Jordan had gradually improved its connections with Saudi Arabia, a landmark development being the amicable and definitive delimitation of Jordanian-Saudi Arabian boundaries signed at Amman in August 1965 (see ch. 3). Saudi Arabia did not terminate its subsidies to Jordan in 1970, and King Faisal worked actively to restore and improve Jordan's relations not only with Egypt and Syria but also with the Palestinian guerrilla movement. Saudi Arabian army units of about brigade strength had entered Jordan at the time of the 1967 war. Although they did not arrive in time to become engaged, they remained in southern Jordan and were still there in late 1973 as a token of King Faisal's support of Hussein.

During 1972, although Jordan did not withdraw the plan for the United Arab Kingdom, the government sought to mend its fences among the estranged Arab neighbors. By the end of the year Egyptian spokesmen had given hints that a resumption of relations with Jordan might be in the offing, and trade with Jordan had been resumed by Egypt, Syria, and Iraq. Observers assigned much of the credit for the breakup of Jordan's isolation to the quiet diplomacy of King Faisal working behind the scenes. By early 1973 it appeared that Jordan had returned to the mainstream of Arab political interchange, although not all problems had been removed.

The secretary general of the Arab League visited Amman in June 1973; at about the same time the new Jordanian prime minister, Zaid Rifai, visited Damascus for talks that would not have been possible two years earlier. As the Jordanian restoration in Arab councils moved ahead, much interest was aroused in Arab capitals by indications of United States intentions to undertake new steps toward solution of the chronic Middle Eastern question. In particular, it was noted with some apprehension by the Arab press that in their joint communiqué of June 26 President Richard M. Nixon and General Secretary Leonid Brezhnev of the Soviet Union affirmed the need for a Middle Eastern settlement that "should take into due account the legitimate interests of the Palestinian peoples."

Late in June 1973 President Habib Bourguiba of Tunisia entered the situation in a speech in which he proposed negotiations between Israel and the Palestinians; he followed this up on July 6 with a statement to the Lebanese press that Hussein should disestablish his government to make way for a Palestinian state. Hussein and his government took umbrage at this and, after verifying that Bourguiba had made the statement and stood by it, Jordan severed relations with Tunisia on July 17, 1973.

Earlier Jordanian relations with Tunisia had been good, but they had become strained in the aftermath of the Jordanian civil war with the guerrillas. Elsewhere in North Africa Hussein has always had cordial relations with his fellow beleaguered monarch, King Hasan of Morocco. The Algerian government remained ideologically far removed from Jordan, and relations were suspended but not broken in late 1970. The Libyan revolutionary regime of Colonel Muammar Qadhafi not only cut off financial aid and diplomatic relations with Jordan in September 1970 but also, as of late 1973, maintained a posture of unremitting hostility toward Hussein and his government.

The rapprochement in the central Middle East, however, continued during the summer and early fall of 1973. The Syrian defense minister visited Amman and was cordially welcomed; an envoy from Egypt also visited Amman for intensive discussions; and definite cleavages were revealed between Egypt and the Palestinian guerrilla leaders, reportedly because of the latter's insistence on abolition of the Jordanian monarchy. At the same time the Arab League secretary general publicly proposed the convening of a new Arab summit conference to establish unified Arab goals and actions and to consider the new initiatives toward a Middle Eastern peace settlement that seemed to be under formation by the UN and the great powers.

As a further indication of a new phase of diplomatic developments, United Nations Secretary General Kurt Waldheim visited a number of Middle Eastern countries, including Israel, in early September 1973 to inform himself at first hand as to the current situation. He visited Jordan and met with Hussein and government officials as the last stop on his trip before calling at the Fourth Conference of Nonaligned Nations, held at Algiers on September 5 to 9, 1973. At this conference, attended by some seventy-six participating countries, Jordan was represented by a delegation headed by a former prime minister, Abdul Munim Rifai.

Immediately after conclusion of the international conclave in Algiers it was announced that Hussein, Sadat of Egypt, and President Hafiz al Asad of Syria would meet in Cairo commencing September 10. Simultaneously, but separately, a conference of Arab foreign ministers opened in Cairo under the aegis of the Arab League.

After two days of talks among the three leaders, it was announced that diplomatic relations between Egypt and Jordan had been resumed, with Abdul Munim Rifai as the new Jordanian ambassador at Cairo. The formal resumption of Jordanian-Syrian relations followed in October 1973. Jordanian Prime Minister Zaid Rifai described the talks as highly successful. Details were not immediately revealed, but Jordanian sources stated that the three countries had agreed to take a common stand on Middle Eastern political issues at the UN in regard to any new Middle Eastern proposals. Observers commented that this kind of common stand by the three Arab states, if firmly implemented, would initiate a new stage in Middle Eastern affairs. Many previous and similar efforts at unity had failed, however.

Other possibilities, not spelled out, included the reactivation of the Arab Eastern Front Command against Israel, which was disestablished during the Jordanian civil war. Analysts believed, however, that Jordan would seek operational control of all Arab forces stationed in Jordan, though possibly allowing for an overall central Arab command in Cairo. Press observations widely hypothesized that the time of individual Arab initiatives was past and that both Egypt and Jordan might now withdraw their separate proposals for a Palestinian government or federated entity.

Commentators also raised the possibility of a reconciliation between Jordan and the Palestinian guerrillas, and on September 18 Hussein granted amnesty to guerrilla leader Muhammad Daud Auda (also known as Abu Daud), and other political prisoners in Jordan (see ch. 13). Yasir Arafat and Al Fatah, however, consistently rejected reconciliation and continued to call for the overthrow of Hussein and the monarchy. The already shattered power position of the guerrilla movements had been further damaged by the three-power agreement in Cairo. Syria promptly closed down a guerrilla radio station for broadcasting against the agreement; the rapprochement was also seen as a rebuff to Libyan hostility toward Jordan.

In late September 1973, therefore, Jordan's position among its Arab neighbors had apparently been dramatically strengthened. Whether this would prove to be a long-term condition or simply a new Jordanian high point in the cycle of up-and-down Arab relations could not be stated with certainty. Behind the Jordanian-Egyptian-Syrian rapprochement of September 1973, however, many observers again pointed out the encouragement and influence of King Faisal of Saudi Arabia, who was assuming an increasingly significant role.

Other Muslim States

Jordan's relations with the non-Arab but Muslim states in the Middle East and elsewhere continued to be satisfactory or better in 1973. Close and cordial connections prevailed particularly between Jordan and Iran, an atmosphere of amity having long been maintained between the two monarchs. Relations with Pakistan and Turkey were also close; technical and military aid missions have been periodically exchanged with Pakistan since about 1958.

Jordan has supported pan-Islamic movements and conferences, such as the Islamic summit held in Rabat, Morocco, in September 1969 at the urging of the Iranian, Moroccan, and Saudi Arabian monarchs. Specific political developments of note, however, have not resulted from these activities, and Jordanian foreign policy is not made or carried out in an avowed Islamic context, although its principles would be held to be compatible with Islam.

Israel

Jordan's relations with Israel between 1948 and 1973 were marked by three wars: the war of 1948 by which the state of Israel was established and through which Jordan acquired the West Bank; the Suez clash of 1956; and the Arab-Israeli War of 1967 by which Jordan lost the West Bank, including Jerusalem. The intervening periods remained tense and potentially explosive as a result of border attacks and counter-attacks, incidents of terrorism, and shrill counteraccusations of agression that were often filed by either side as formal protests with the UN Security Council.

In 1973 Jordan as well as the other Arab states continued to refuse either to recognize or to engage publicly in direct negotiation with Israel. Until June 5, 1967, Israeli-Jordanian relations were conducted within the framework of the General Armistice Agreement, reached under the aegis of the UN in April 1949. These relations were limited to participation in the joint Israeli-Jordanian Armistice Commission. Soon after the cessation of hostilities in June 1967, Israel denounced the General Armistice Agreement as being inimical to the establishment of peace. The Israeli government maintained that only direct contacts could bring about meaningful negotiations between Israel and the Arab states.

In the aftermath of the June 1967 war battles between Israel and Jordan continued, consisting primarily of attacks by Jordan-based guerrillas upon Israeli territory and of ensuing Israeli retaliatory attacks, such as those launched upon Palestinian guerrilla bases in Karameh on September 15, 1968, and in As Salt on March 26, 1969. On January 1, 1970, during an Israeli reprisal raid upon guerrilla bases in Irbid, the East Ghor Canal, irrigating the east Jordan valley, was badly damaged. At the end of July 1970 Jordan, Israel, and the UAR agreed to a cease-fire under UN auspices. The cease-fire agreement helped trigger the 1970–71 Jordanian civil war between guerrilla groups and government forces (see ch. 2).

Throughout the post-1967-war period, Hussein has publicly denied that he would enter into a unilateral peace agreement with Israel and insisted that he would only accept a general settlement agreed to by the other Arab states involved in the conflict. Although he publicly and frequently rejected reports that he had had direct negotiations with Israel, rumors of secret meetings between Hussein and Israeli leaders, allegedly held since September 1968, appeared with some frequency in the world press.

Hussein has consistently supported the implementation of the UN Security Council Resolution 242 of November 1967. In an April 1969 speech before the National Press Club in Washington Hussein, who stated that he was also speaking on behalf of President Nasser, proposed a six-point peace plan. The plan called for an "end of all belligerency; respect for and acknowledgment of the sovereignty, territorial integrity, and political independence of all States in the area; recognition of the rights of all to live in peace within secure and recognized boundaries; . . . guarantees for all of freedom of navigation through the Gulf of Aqaba and the Suez Canal; guarantees of the territorial inviolability of all States in the area through whatever measures are necessary, including the establishment of demilitarized zones; and a just settlement of the refugee problem." In return the Arab states asked for an Israeli withdrawal from all territories occupied during the 1967 war and for Israel's implementation of all other provisions of the Security Council resolution, which stressed that acquisition of territory by force of war was inadmissible. The king proposed in March 1972 that Israel and Jordan share the administration of Jerusalem as an "open" city under a general peace agreement.

Also in March 1972 the king publicly announced his proposal for the establishment of a federated kingdom wherein the Palestinians of the West Bank would be accorded semiautonomy. The proposed United Arab Kingdom would be composed of a federation of two politically equal states, the East and West banks of Jordan. The new state would be established only upon withdrawal from the occupied territories by Israel and with the consent of the residents of the West Bank who, according to Hussein, would at the appropriate time be free to choose either to enter into a federation with Jordan or to establish a separate state. The king also extended an invitation to other areas under Israeli control, primarily Gaza, to join the proposed federation.

Under the Hussein plan Amman would serve as the capital of the federation and also as the capital of the Region of Jordan, and Jerusalem would be the capital of the Region of Palestine. A people's council, elected by direct secret ballot, would constitute the legislative organ of each region. A governor general, elected by the people's council of each region, would serve as the executive authority of the region and would be assisted by a regional council of ministers. The king as head of state, together with his Council of Ministers, would hold the central executive authority of the kingdom, however, and would be responsible for "matters relating to the kingdom as a sovereign international entity ensuring the safety of the union, its stability and development." The National Assembly and the king would together constitute the central legislative authority of the new state.

The king has consistently condemned any Palestinian guerrilla attacks against innocent targets, such as world passenger aircraft or unarmed civilians. He denounced as a horrible crime the Black September group's massacre of the eleven-member Israeli Olympic team in Munich in September 1972, and termed the murder by the Popular Front for the Liberation of Palestine (PFLP) of twenty passengers in the lounge of Tel Aviv's Lod Airport on May 30, 1972, a "sick crime committed by sick people and planned by sick minds."

Israeli-Jordanian relations in 1973 continued to be marked by uncertainty, although tensions between the two countries had eased since the defeat of the guerrillas in Jordan in 1970 and 1971. Beneath their twenty-five-year antagonism, Israel and Jordan shared fundamental interests in resolving the refugee problem; in ensuring their mutual security; and in developing, on a cooperative basis, the entire region, including its water and mineral resources (see ch. 11).

THE UNITED KINGDOM, THE UNITED STATES, AND THE WEST

Since independence in 1948 Jordan has followed generally a pro-Western foreign policy, supporting the United States and the West in the UN and wherever else possible in the international arena. Although Jordan joined none of the Western alliances such as the Central Treaty Organization (CENTO), it nevertheless maintained its pro-Western orientation and continued to receive from the West an essential allocation of budgetary, economic, and military aid (see ch. 11; ch. 13).

Even after independence in 1948 Jordan had remained in a special treaty relationship with the United Kingdom until March 13, 1957, when the agreement was terminated. The United Kingdom during this period continued to provide financial subsidies and other aid, as it had with varying degrees of direct and indirect control since the formation of the Amirate of Transjordan under British sponsorship in 1922. The historical connection between Jordan and the United Kingdom has thus been particularly close (see ch. 2; ch. 11). In 1973 the United Kingdom continued to be a source of development loans and military purchases.

Diplomatic relations between Jordan and the United States were first established in 1949, and United States assistance, on a relatively small scale, began in 1951 under what was popularly known as the Point Four program. In the decade after 1957 the United States became the principal source of foreign aid and support, in effect replacing the United Kingdom in this role but with very different methods and without treaty engagements. By mid-1967 development in Jordan had progressed to such a level that United States budgetary and military aid was being terminated.

After the 1967 war the United States disapproved of the Israeli annexation of East Jerusalem (the "old city"), seized during the war, and by late 1973 did not recognize this status. United States policy in this regard was, in fact, simply a continuation of its adherence to the UN General Assembly resolution of November 29, 1947, pursuant to which Jerusalem was to have been internationalized. In late 1973 United States policy had not changed from support of the 1947 resolution.

The United States also supported Security Council Resolution 242 of November 22, 1967, in which principles for the settlement of the 1967 war were laid down. This resolution, in brief, declared the inadmissibility of the acquisition of territory by war; called upon Israel to withdraw from "territories of recent conflict"; stated that all belligerency in the area should cease and that the independence within "secure and recognized boundaries" of all states in the area should be acknowledged; affirmed the necessity for freedom of navigation in international waterways in the area and for a "just settlement of the refugee problem"; and requested the secretary general to name a special representative (Gunnar Jarring of Sweden was later designated) to maintain contacts with the states concerned in order to promote the purposes of the resolution.

Because Jordan had accepted Resolution 242 and, in fact, had made it the basis of Jordanian policy for settlement of the 1967 war, United States advocacy of the resolution was greatly useful to Jordan and strengthened relations between the two countries.

United States-Jordanian relations, however, have not been entirely unmarked by differences. In late 1969, as it became clear that a political settlement of the 1967 war could not be quickly engineered by the great powers, Hussein became openly critical of United States policy, and during the next year Jordan actively considered (but in the end rejected) acceptance of military aid from the Soviet Union.

Anti-United States demonstrations by Palestinians in Amman in mid-April 1970 prompted the United States to cancel a scheduled visit by a United States assistant secretary of state. Hussein, annoyed at the implication of inability to provide adequate security for the visitor, required the transfer of the incumbent United States ambassador. On July 26, 1970, however, Hussein accepted the proposals made the previous month by the United States secretary of state for a cease-fire and reevaluation in the Middle East. Hussein's acceptance occasioned more anti-United States demonstrations by Palestinians in Amman.

Substantial United States budgetary and military aid were reinstituted in 1970 after the Jordanian defeat of the Palestinian guerrillas (see ch. 13). Hussein maintained his close alignment with the United States, and reports in July 1973 indicated that United States budgetary aid during the ensuing fiscal year would equal about US$65 million, an increase of some US$15 million over the previous year. In August 1973 the United States government announced that its economic and military aid to Jordan during the 1952–72 period totaled US$887 million and stated that the aid had been instrumental in maintaining a moderate government in Jordan.

In mid-1973, consequently, United States-Jordanian relations were extremely close. Among the Palestinians in Jordan, however, anti-United States sentiment continued and was exacerbated by the United States veto of July 25, 1973, on grounds of imbalance, of a Security Council draft resolution deploring Israel's failure to relinquish the Arab territories occupied in 1967. The effect within Jordan of this veto was offset to some extent by the participation by the United States in a unanimous Security Council resolution of August 15, 1973, condemning Israel for air piracy; the Israeli air force on August 10 had intercepted an Arab airliner within Lebanese air space and had forced it to land in Israel.

With other Western states, Jordanian relations in 1973 were good to excellent and without serious standing problems. Ties with the Federal Republic of Germany (West Germany), a source of development and technical assistance, were strengthened after 1970 when they were resumed after a five-year severance in which Jordan had joined a number of other Arab states in protesting West Germany's recognition of Israel in 1965. The West German foreign minister paid a successful official visit to Jordan in May 1973 and expressed hopes for even closer relations in the future.

THE SOVIET UNION AND OTHER COMMUNIST STATES

Jordan established diplomatic relations with the Soviet Union in August 1963. In the wake of the 1967 war, Hussein made his first visit to Moscow in recognition of the Soviet Union's support of the Arab countries vis-à-vis Israel and also as a signal to the West, particularly to the United States, to increase its overall support of the Arab nations in their attempt to recover the territories lost in the 1967 war. During Hussein's visit Jordan and the Soviet Union signed an agreement for cultural and scientific cooperation that paved the way for further such agreements, as well as for agreements of cooperation in the scientific, technical, and trade fields. These expanded contacts also led to Soviet economic assistance for various Jordanian development projects. Communism remains inimical to the Jordanian monarchy, however, and Hussein has thus far rejected pressures to become a Soviet military client and has refused any Soviet offers of military assistance.

After the 1967 war Jordan also expanded its diplomatic and commercial contacts with other communist states of Eastern Europe. In November 1968 Jordan and Romania signed three agreements providing for cooperation in the economic, trade, technical, and oil exploration fields. In 1969 and 1970 Jordan also improved diplomatic and commercial relations with the German Democratic Republic (East Germany), Yugoslavia, and Czechoslovakia.

In January 1969 Jordan concluded a 60,000-ton phosphate agreement with the People's Republic of China (PRC). In September 1970, however, the PRC denounced the Jordanian government for its aggressive battle with the Palestinian guerrilla forces and referred to the monarchy as a reactionary force in Middle Eastern affairs. In late 1973 Jordan continued to cultivate good relations with the Republic of China (Nationalist China).

THE UNITED NATIONS AND WORLD ORGANIZATIONS

Jordan was granted admission to the United Nations (UN) in December 1955, after previous applications for membership, dating from 1947, had been vetoed by the Soviet Union. Before its admission, however, Jordan had participated in the activities of various specialized agencies of the UN, including the International Monetary Fund, the International Bank for Reconstruction and Development, the Food and Agriculture Organization, the World Health Organization, and the United Nations Educational, Scientific and Cultural Organization (UNESCO). The United Nations Relief and Works Agency for Palestine Refugees in the Near East (UNRWA), of which Jordan is a member, has been a key source of aid to the Palestinian Arab refugees.

Jordan's relations with the UN have been cooperative in spite of the UN role in the creation of Israel and the vicissitudes of Arab-Israeli relations since 1948. Jordan has on several occasions asked for UN condemnation of aggressive acts taken against it. Before the 1967 war the Security Council had at times supported Jordan, for example by condemning the British-French-Israeli action in Suez in 1956 and by condemning Israel for a transborder raid of November 1966.

On June 26, 1967, in the wake of the Arab-Israeli War of 1967, Hussein personally presented the Arab case before an emergency meeting of the General Assembly. After extensive debate on the subject the Security Council on November 22, 1967, adopted a British resolution outlining the basic terms for an Arab-Israeli peace settlement. At the same time the Security Council designated the Gunnar Jarring mission to explore means for ending the Middle Eastern deadlock. A war of attrition continued between the two sides until July 1970, when Jordan, the UAR, and Israel accepted a cease-fire agreement based upon the provisions of the 1967 Security Council resolution and Gunnar Jarring, the UN special envoy to the Middle East, reactivated his peace mission. Nevertheless, as of late 1973 a general peace agreement had not been reached.

Since the 1967 war the Security Council and the General Assembly have adopted several resolutions that supported the Arab position versus Israel, particularly on the issue of Israel's gradual de facto annexation of the occupied territories in the West Bank, including East Jerusalem. For example, in July 1967 the General Assembly adopted two resolutions declaring the unilateral reunification of Jerusalem by Israel to be invalid. In April 1968 the Security Council condemned Israel for its reprisal raid against guerrilla bases in Karameh. On September 25, 1971, the Security Council adopted a resolution that urgently called upon Israel to "rescind all previous measures and actions" in Jerusalem and not to take further steps that would "purport to change the status of the city or which would prejudice the rights of the inhabitants and the interests of the international community or a just and lasting peace." On December 8, 1972, the General Assembly adopted a resolution calling upon member states to refrain from giving Israel any aid that would help it to consolidate control in the occupied territories. On July 25, 1973, the United States vetoed a Security Council resolution, supported by the thirteen other council members, that in part "strongly deplored Israel's occupation of the territories occupied as a result of the 1967 conflict"and encouraged the special UN envoy to continue his peace mission.

SECTION III. ECONOMIC

CHAPTER 11

CHARACTER AND STRUCTURE OF THE ECONOMY

The economy of Jordan remained in 1973 a basically agricultural one that depended for its viability upon unpredictable rainfall and unpredictable budget and balance-of-payments support from abroad. In the years before 1967 per capita income had an average annual growth rate of 5 percent or more in spite of a high rate of population increase. This high rate of income growth reflected high levels of foreign support and public and private investment and a growing efficiency of infrastructure and logistics.

Nevertheless, Jordan had consistently lived beyond its income as embodied in its gross national product (GNP). It was able to do this through the willingness of the United Kingdom, the United States, and various Arab petroleum exporting countries to finance the country's supplementary requirements, in large part by means of grants-in-aid. Throughout the period a major policy objective of the government was to minimize dependence on foreign assistance as far as the government's current operations were concerned, and from 1954 to 1966 it made steady progress in this respect.

This favorable trend was interrupted by the Arab-Israeli War of 1967 and the civil disturbances that followed it. In 1973 the economy was still recovering from the sequence of events set in motion by the war. From the viewpoint of the economy, the most important of these events were the closing of the Suez Canal, the civil war of 1970 and 1971, and the closure of the Syrian border between July 1971 and December 1972 (see ch. 2). These events not only interrupted the momentum of the earlier decade of economic development, they also left the economy truncated and the rhythm of its development distorted both by the loss of the West Bank and by the influx of several scores of thousands of new Palestinian (see Glossary) refugees (see ch. 3).

For practical purposes the results, in short-term planning and in administrative and financial terms, included the writing off of the West Bank, a diminution of the country's and the government's resources, and a breakdown of economic and social development strategy. They also meant an aggravation and indefinite extension of the country's already heavy dependence on support from abroad.

In 1973 the government introduced a Three Year Program (1973-75) of economic and social development. The new program was designed to increase the level of domestic and perhaps also external investment and to help recapture the earlier trend of economic progress. But it was not foreseen that the country would be able in the immediate future to forego the assistance it had been receiving from abroad. This was especially the case in regard to investment, without which economic development would be exceedingly difficult, if not impossible.

RESOURCES

In natural resources Jordan in 1973 had one of the least well endowed economies in the Middle East. Most of its resources consisted of 1 million to 1.5 million acres of cultivable land, chiefly in the Jordan valley, of which an estimated 150,000 to 160,000 acres were either irrigated or suited for irrigation. In the Jordan valley proper (north of the Dead Sea) the combination of water and climate created agricultural conditions that placed Jordan in an advantageous position in comparison with its neighbors in regard to the growing of fruits and vegetables for export. Elsewhere in the country the rainfall, and hence the supply of water for agriculture, was exceedingly unpredictable, making the bulk of the country's agriculture precarious—in terms both of employment and of output—and placing the economy under the constant threat of having to import large portions of its staple foodstuffs. In some considerable part, agricultural output was susceptible to improvement, both in quality and in quantity, by the introduction of improved inputs—better seeds, more fertilizers, and better methods; but in the short run this required a sizable expansion in the available credit facilities and in the long run, the development of a more literate peasantry (see ch. 12).

The economy had little else to show in the way of natural resources. As of late 1973 it had no petroleum and no metallic minerals in commercial quantities. Deposits of high-quality phosphates provided a helpful source of exports but were not available in sufficient quantities at low enough prices to finance a sizable industrial development.

Industry for the most part consisted of small artisanal firms. According to the government's 1967 industrial census, 90 percent of manufacturing establishments employed fewer than ten people each, accounted for less than 40 percent of total employment in manufacturing, and produced about 20 percent of the manufacturing sector's total contribution to the gross domestic product (GDP). This tendency was accentuated by the influx of refugees from the West Bank after the 1967 war.

Before the 1967 war tourism had traditionally been a mainstay of the economy, and its growth had been expected to quadruple between 1964 and 1970. To a large extent the size and dependability of this sector was undermined by the loss of the West Bank. Although the East Bank contained a number of important historical and architectural monuments dating from antiquity and the medieval period, these sites do not approach in tourist value the attraction of the religious monuments of the West Bank, particularly those in and around Jerusalem (see ch. 4). Nevertheless, the government proposed to give priority to the development of the transportation, housing, and other logistics necessary to make the most of the tourist attraction of the East Bank monuments and potential resort areas. Included in these efforts would be development of Al Aqaba as a major tourist resort.

ECONOMIC DEVELOPMENTS: 1967-73

The major economic fact of the 1967 war was that it deprived the country of the West Bank. Although little of the country's basic large-scale industry was located there, well over one-third of the best agricultural land was. Overall, the loss of the West Bank was estimated to represent a loss of some 35 to 40 percent of the domestic output. The West Bank not only had been a major source of supply to the East Bank but also had constituted a major part of the market for East Bank production, and its loss called for a major shift in marketing strategy. With respect to the budget and the balance of payments, the loss of the West Bank was a severe blow that only escaped being catastrophic through prompt and large-scale budgetary assistance from Saudi Arabia, Kuwait, Libya and, in 1970, when Kuwait and Libya terminated their aid, the United States (see ch. 10).

In the international perspective, one of the most important results of the 1967 war was the closing of the Suez Canal. For Jordan this meant a rerouting of phosphate exports destined for countries in the eastern Mediterranean from the canal to overland routes by way of Syria and Lebanon. This involved a fundamental reorientation of export transportation facilities, an increase in costs, and a constraint on the increase of exports because of the limited capacity of the land routes. It also meant a reappraisal of the development of Al Aqaba as a major export-import terminus in the absence of the canal.

In 1968, 1969, and 1970 various guerrilla organizations used the upper reaches of the Jordan valley as a staging area for terrorist attacks against Israel; the Israelis in turn directed many of their reprisal attacks against this region. Also, many of the battles between the guerrillas and the Jordanian military in 1970 and 1971 were fought in this region (see ch. 13). These activities inhibited the use of the irrigated areas of the northern part of the Jordan valley and forced the relocation of some farmers to other parts of the country. After the civil war the Syrian border was in greater or lesser degree closed to Jordanian exports and imports for almost eighteen months. This resulted in a sharp decline in economic activities based on exports to the Mediterranean and on raw materials from Western Europe and the Americas. Increased emphasis was placed on the export of phosphates to South Asia and the Far East and on resumption of the efforts to develop and intensify the use of the port facilities at Al Aqaba.

By 1973 much of the economic impact of the 1967 war had been absorbed. The West Bank had for short-term planning purposes been written off and the inflow of refugees reduced and in some fashion accommodated. The 1971 crop year was a bountiful one, owing to abundant and timely rainfall, which restored agricultural incomes simultaneously with the government's establishment of control over the guerrillas. The year 1972 brought a complete relaxation of the Syrian border closure and resumption of free movement of exports and imports through Syria and Lebanon. The result was a sustained impetus to trade and commerce, both internal and external, and to increased confidence on the part of the private sector in construction and other forms of investment.

By 1973, moreover, the ad hoc improvisation of economic policy that had been necessary through the period of the civil disturbances and the series of international monetary crises had given way to a reversion to forward planning and programming for development. At the start of the new year the government introduced a new three-year economic and social development program.

The program had the support of the members of the Organization for Economic Cooperation and Development (OECD)—mainly North America, Japan, and the countries of the European Economic Community (EEC, known as the Common Market)—and of the international financial institutions. The government hoped to be able to enlist the active participation of the domestic private sector in the program. Other things being equal, for the short term at least, the country hoped to be able to resume its efforts to achieve a greater measure of economic independence through development of its own limited resources.

ROLE OF THE GOVERNMENT

The government's relation to the economy appears basically to have been one of laissez-faire. This attitude is, however, unavoidably qualified on the one hand by the government's desire for economic development and on the other hand by the comparative poverty of the private sector; the smallness of the market; the shortage of water; and the heavy investments required to provide effective irrigation, transport, and power.

The central government owns or exercises effective control over the transport, communications, and electric power systems and the petroleum refinery. The government also controls the country's large-scale (400 employees or more) mining and manufacturing industries, such as phosphates, cement, paper and paperboard, and the tourist sector. It furthermore participates in most of the other important manufacturing enterprises. It appears not to intervene directly in the small-scale (artisan) manufacturing sector, nor has it competed with the private sector as a landlord in the agricultural sector, where its active intervention has in the main been limited to overseeing the use of irrigation water and attempting to assure an improvement in the amount and quality of inputs, such as irrigation, seeds, credit, and extension services (see ch. 12).

Although there exists some government intervention in the pricing and marketing systems, the intervention appears neither to be unduly burdensome nor to reflect a pervasive desire to invade the private sector in the fields of domestic trade and marketing. In the foreign trade area the government maintains exchange control and export-import licensing mechanisms, but these also seem not to have been a major hindrance. In recent years the government has made increasing efforts to provide incentives to both domestic and foreign private capital to participate actively in the country's economic development, especially in the form of joint domestic-foreign ventures that would bring expertise to the country and provide built-in markets abroad for the ventures' exports. Apparently at no time has the government legally required local majority financial control of joint domestic-foreign industrial undertakings.

The government has played an active role in trying to assure that agriculture and industry should have the basic physical and administrative economic infrastructure they required. The basis of the effort in the pre-1967 period was a growing emphasis on planning in order to establish the priorities for utilization of the economy's limited available financial resources. This over a period of more than a decade meant improvement in transport (including the port of Al Aqaba), power, communication, and irrigation facilities. It included industrial plants too large to be undertaken by the private sector alone and research, extension, and credit facilities, as well as the upgrading of training services for both the agricultural and the industrial sectors. In the administrative realm, the effort involved attempts to establish an attractive investment climate and to provide a legislative and administrative framework that would benefit the production and marketing of the economy's output. That much of this effort has not been more effective can be attributed to the difficulties that have battered the economy in recent years and the persistent shortage of administrative expertise and skilled labor where they were most needed (see ch. 6).

Although there are apparently no dependable price indexes, prices are understood to have held fairly steady before the 1967 war. Since then, according to a cost-of-living index instituted in 1967 for Amman, prices had increased from 100 in 1967 to a twelve-month average of about 130 in 1972.

As the government in 1973 launched its three-year development program, it faced an array of serious and potentially long-term problems. Perhaps the most serious was the very high rate of population growth (3.3 percent per year); this growth rate served not only to create or aggravate all sorts of resource and financial shortages but also to do so on a compound basis that tended to render them increasingly costly and frustrating with the passage of time. The obverse of the population growth was the shortage of basic resources—arable land, rainfall and water for irrigation, petroleum, and metals. In nearly the same category were included the precarious state of literacy and the shortage of technical and administrative expertise and skilled manpower.

Somewhat less urgent probably were the greatly increased level of military costs brought on by the 1967 war, the various expenses created by the Palestinian refugees, and the high level of unemployment (an estimated 15 percent or more) in 1970 (see ch. 3). Also troublesome was the shortage of efficient and dependable export outlets to overseas markets, as well as the small size of the market and the marketing difficulties within the country. Exacerbating all the economic problems was the pervasive political instability that currently embraced the whole of the Arab world and the year-to-year unpredictability of the level of foreign budget support, without which in the short run the economy could scarcely survive, much less develop efficiently, and which was becoming increasingly costly (see Public Finance, this ch.).

NATIONAL INCOME

Data dealing with the GDP refer to the whole of prewar Jordan, including both the West Bank and the East Bank. It is understood that these data as they were annually updated by the government after 1966 were not arrived at by summing separately calculated partial data for the two regions. Rather, the 1966 data for the whole country have apparently since then been updated by applying to the 1966 data for both banks the annual sectoral changes observed in the East Bank alone, adjusted for such clearly identifiable and easily calculable differences between the two banks as were observed. It is assumed that annual GDP and GNP estimates for the East Bank represent some 60 percent of the officially presented global data. Because this assumption entails a potentially sizable margin of error and because of the unsophisticated methods used in the official collecting and processing of the data, the national income data should be viewed as possible orders of magnitude rather than as precise measures of the economic dimensions under discussion. With some qualifications, the same observation may probably be made concerning other economic data except perhaps those collected and issued by the Central Bank of Jordan.

Between the years 1961 and 1971 the GDP (at factor cost) increased from around JD111 million (for value of the Jordanian dinar—see Glossary) to a preliminary estimate of about JD202 million, or at an average annual rate of about 6.2 percent compounded (see table 4). The growth over the period was not regular, however, even allowing for the effect of rainfall fluctuations on agricultural output. The period was divided by the impact of the 1967 war. During the prewar years the GDP had grown at an average rate of about 8 percent a year, whereas in the postwar years 1967 to 1971 the average rate of growth apparently declined to around 5 percent a year. The growth rate in 1972 was about 7.1 percent. With the organization of the country's economic efforts embodied in the economic development program of 1973 to 1975, there is reason to suppose that, if political stability can be maintained in the Middle East, the rate of economic growth will increase somewhat.

The GNP, which differs from the GDP by the amount of the net income from abroad (profits, interest, dividends, and migrant worker remittances), was estimated in 1972 at around JD230 million (factor cost). Per capita GNP in the East Bank in 1971 amounted to around JD75, equivalent to about US$210 at the prevailing exchange rate. This compared with estimates equivalent to about US$220 in 1961, US$230 in 1966, and US$240 in 1972. In all cases it should be observed that the per capita income is an average that does not indicate the very sizable range of differences in individual incomes that underlie it.

The sum of domestic consumption (private and public) and gross investment (private and public) exceeded the GNP during the 1966–71 period by annual amounts ranging from JD25 million to JD62 million. Inasmuch as this in effect was borrowing against future domestic resources, it could have represented a substantial lien against consumption and (or) development capacity in the future. Fortunately for Jordan, much of the deficit was financed either by foreign grants or by soft (concessional-term) loans.

DEVELOPMENT PLANNING

Development planning dates back to the establishment of the Jordan Development Board in 1952. In 1955 the International Bank for Reconstruction and Development (IBRD, also known as the World Bank) mounted a major survey mission that presented an extensive and intensive analysis of the economy and drafted proposals for a ten-year development program. In 1961 the Jordan Development Board published a five-year plan (1963–67) for economic development. This program called for outlays over the period of JD127 million, including JD59 million from abroad. The sectors having the top priorities under this plan were agriculture, mining, communications, and industry.

In 1966 that program was replaced by a new one that was intended to carry the planning period forward to 1970 and to reshape its emphasis. The new program proposed total outlays of JD275 million. It was expected that around JD130 million would be provided by the private sector and most of the balance by grants and loans from abroad. Major goals of the new program were reduction of the trade balance deficit (and thus dependence on foreign budget support), increase in per capita income, and reduction in the level of unemployment. The program

Table 4. Industrial Origin of Gross Domestic Product in Jordan (East Bank and West Bank) at Current Prices, 1966–71
(in millions of Jordanian dinars)[1]

	1966	1967	1968	1969	1970	1971[2]	Percent of 1971 GDP[3]	Percent of 1970 Working Force
Industrial Origin of Gross Domestic Product at Factor Cost								
Agriculture, forestry, and livestock ...	27.65	38.74	27.53	36.34	28.66	37.81	19	33
(Crops and forestry)	(15.98)	(29.15)	(13.04)	(23.81)	(18.13)	(23.47)	(12)	...
(Livestock)	(11.67)	(9.59)	(14.49)	(12.53)	(10.53)	(14.34)	(7)	...
Manufacturing and mining	17.27	17.50	20.05	23.12	19.77	20.56	10	7
Construction	9.28	8.69	9.83	10.89	7.79	7.50	4	2
Electricity and water supply	1.97	1.78	2.27	2.09	2.35	2.73	1	0
Transportation	14.42	14.84	14.55	16.01	15.91	16.20	8	3
Wholesale and retail trade	28.92	39.08	29.07	38.36	38.00	39.00	19	7
Banking and finance	2.77	3.40	2.97	4.20	4.19	3.37	2	1
Ownership of dwellings	11.20	11.90	12.33	12.78	13.61	14.41	7	0
Public administration and defense	22.03	26.01	33.25	36.28	37.94	39.00	19	23

Community, social, and personal services	14.10	15.17	16.64	18.27	21.34	22.00	11 / 100 · 10 / 100[4]
Total GDP[3] at factor cost	149.61	177.11	168.49	198.34	189.56	202.58	
Indirect taxes	20.89	17.60	18.42	21.35[5]	20.30	20.84	
Total GDP[3] at market prices	170.50	194.71	186.91	219.69	209.86	223.42	
Net factor income from abroad	15.15	11.24	10.37	14.03	12.64	13.17	
Total Gross National Product (at market prices)	185.65	205.95	197.28	233.72	222.50	236.59	
Minus depreciation allowances	-7.21	-6.76	-8.19	-8.73	-8.35	-8.50	
Minus indirect taxes	-20.89	-17.60	-18.42	-21.35	-20.30	-20.84	

[1] For value of the Jordanian dinar—see Glossary.
[2] Preliminary.
[3] Gross domestic product.
[4] Includes seeking work category of 14 percent (see ch. 3).
[5] Revised.

Source: Adapted from *Statistical Yearbook, 1971*, XXII, Amman, 1972, p. 179; and Jordan, Central Bank of Jordan, *Monthly Statistical Bulletin*, IX, No. 2, Amman, February 1973, table 31.

Table 5. *Projected Outlays on Jordan's Three Year Program by Sector, 1973–75*
(in millions of Jordanian dinars)*

Program	1973	1974	1975	Total	Percent of Total
Economic Development:					
Agriculture	5.296	4.415	3.309	13.020	7.3
Irrigation	7.009	5.385	2.242	14.636	8.2
Mining and industry	5.200	8.040	12.880	26.120	14.5
Tourism and antiquities	2.365	2.595	2.210	7.170	4.0
Electricity	2.050	3.448	4.283	9.781	5.5
Transportation	12.926	12.001	10.885	35.812	20.0
Communications	3.370	2.059	1.283	6.712	3.8
Trade	0.325	0.225	0.225	0.775	0.4
Total	38.541	38.168	37.317	114.026	63.7
Social Development:					
Education	3.004	3.679	4.231	10.914	6.2
Public health	0.400	0.470	0.610	1.480	0.8
Social welfare and labor	0.312	0.511	0.632	1.455	0.8
Housing and government buildings	11.160	11.814	11.916	34.890	19.5
Municipal and village affairs	4.220	4.973	5.565	14.758	8.2
Awqaf (endowments)	0.356	0.434	0.424	1.214	0.7
Statistics	0.020	0.231	0.012	0.263	0.1
Total	19.472	22.112	23.390	64.974	36.3
GRAND TOTAL	58.013	60.280	60.707	179.000	100.0

*For value of the Jordanian dinar—see Glossary.

Source: Adapted from Jordan, Ministry of National Economy, *Investment Conditions and Opportunities in Jordan,* Amman, 1972, p. 77.

aimed to increase the GNP from JD138 million in 1963 to JD191 million in 1970 (at constant, or substantially constant, prices). In the framework of the plan, work was started on the large Khalid irrigation and hydroelectric dam on the Yarmuk River and the smaller Az Zarqa River project and on the grid linking the existing distribution networks in the East and West banks.

The program was predicated on political stability, and practically within a year of its passage the 1967 war rendered it inoperative. In the aftermath of the war long-range or medium-range planning had to give way to ad hoc decisionmaking responding to the needs of the moment and the immediate future.

In 1971, however, with the government's reestablishment of its authority throughout the East Bank, interest in forward planning was renewed, for the time being for the East Bank alone. New planning legislation was passed that took account of the changed economic realities; and the National Planning Council, under the tutelage of the prime minister, replaced the Jordan Development Board. The new legislation gave the National Planning Council a wide range of responsibility, in collaboration with the Ministry of Finance and the Central Bank, for all aspects of social and economic planning. This included the right to contract loans in its own name both at home and abroad. It thus became one of the government's major development agencies. The new planning legislation also created the policy-level Council of Economic Security, which under the chairmanship of the prime minister had as its function the supervision and review of all matters affecting the economic, financial, and monetary situation of the country.

In 1972 the National Planning Council prepared the 1973–75 economic development plan that went into effect in January 1973. Its objectives, which were limited to the East Bank, were to increase employment and manpower training; to increase output while maintaining price stability; to provide optimum distribution of public services among the country's several regions and social groups; and to reduce the trade deficit and the need for foreign budgetary and balance-of-payments support.

The program proposed a total outlay of JD179 million over the period. About 64 percent of the total outlay would be devoted to economic, and about 36 percent of the total to social, development (see table 5). The public sector was expected to contribute JD100 million, or 56 percent of the total outlay, and the private sector JD79 million, or 44 percent of the total. The public sector contribution would be financed from the central government's budget (10 percent), from domestic government borrowing (48 percent), and from foreign grants and loans (42 percent). The private sector was expected to finance its contribution out of private saving and by foreign direct investment and loans. The top priorities of the program by economic sector were transportation; housing and government buildings; agriculture (including irrigation); mining and industry; and municipal and village affairs. The program was expected to raise the level of the GDP (at factor cost) at an average annual rate of 8 percent (compounded) in constant prices over the three-year period, or at about the average rate of increase in the pre-1967 period.

PUBLIC FINANCE

The public sector in Jordan comprises the central government, the National Planning Council, the Jordan River Corporation, and the local government units; the National Planning Council and the Jordan River Corporation serve as the government's major development agencies. Although the local units have some small financial resources of their own (how much is exceedingly difficult to determine) and although the National Planning Council is empowered to borrow both at home and abroad, the fact seems to be that as of late 1973 the central government had provided the bulk of the financing for the public sector.

The central features of the government's public finance history have been the large measure of foreign financing for its current budget that the government has enjoyed and the fact that up to the outbreak of the 1967 war very considerable progress had been made in reducing the extent of such aid. That effort, however, like everything else, was seriously disrupted by the war and its aftermath. On the one hand, expenditures increased rapidly as a function of the increased military needs and the influx of Palestinians. On the other hand, revenues declined as a result of the loss of the West Bank as part of the tax base and because of the persistence of hostilities and civil disturbance. Between 1966 and 1967 both receipts and expenditures of the public sector jumped to new levels and thereafter, despite sizable year-to-year fluctuations, maintained an upward trend (see table 6).

Receipts

Receipts are divided between domestic revenues on the one hand and foreign grants (for budget support) and loans (for specific development projects) on the other. In the immediate postwar years the level of foreign grants was raised substantially. Thereafter, Libya suspended and Kuwait froze their respective contributions to the government's budget support. In partial compensation the government renewed its efforts to increase domestic revenues, and the United States picked up a good part of the reduction in the support that had been provided by the Arab countries. These efforts were accompanied by determination on the part of the government to develop its export- and import-substituting industries, the port of Al Aqaba, and the tourist business in order to reverse the deterioration in the balance of payments.

Domestic revenues, although they declined in relation to total receipts over the 1966–72 period as a whole, showed a healthy recovery

Table 6. *Receipts and Expenditures of the Central Government of Jordan, 1967-73*[1]
(in millions of Jordanian dinars)[2]

	1967	1968	1969	1970	1971[3]	1972[3]	1973[4]
Receipts:							
Domestic	25.50	26.26	32.52	30.26	36.11	38.49	44.20
Foreign grants[5]	40.41	40.11	38.38	35.42	35.10	41.90	87.56
Foreign development loans	4.29	5.44	4.84	2.28	3.74	9.64	27.43
Other foreign	0.22	0.11	0.64	0.42	3.62	1.11	0.0
TOTAL	70.42	71.92	76.38	68.38	78.57	91.14	159.19
Expenditures:							
Recurring:							
Defense and public security	28.06	38.42	45.98	38.13	38.98	44.82	42.40
Administration	5.85	7.41	7.22	7.47	8.66	10.53	n.a.
Social services	7.50	8.07	8.72	9.81	9.66	10.42	n.a.
Economic services	3.25	3.29	3.31	3.62	3.41	4.70	n.a.
Total recurring	44.66	57.19	65.23	59.03	60.71	70.47	96.34[6]
Development[7]	23.50	23.33	23.18	21.68	20.83	29.16	62.85
TOTAL	68.16	80.52	88.41	80.71	81.54	99.63	159.19
Surplus or deficit (−)	2.26	−8.60	−12.03	−12.33	−2.97	−8.49	0.0

n.a.—not available.
[1] Refers to the East Bank only.
[2] For value of the Jordanian dinar—see Glossary.
[3] Preliminary.
[4] Budget estimate.
[5] Includes technical assistance.
[6] Includes JD15.53 million to cover costs of development projects in progress.
[7] Includes outlays of the National Planning Council and the Jordan River Corporation.

Source: Adapted from Jordan, Central Bank of Jordan, *Monthly Statistical Bulletin*, Amman, December 1972 and February 1973, table 26; and Centre d'Etudes et de Documentation Economiques, Financières et Sociales, *L'Economie des Payes Arabes*, Beirut, February 1973, pp. 20–23.

after the sudden drop in 1967 that resulted from the loss of the West Bank. The growth derived from increases in tax rates, in the tax base, and in economic activity in 1971 and 1972 and from improved collection procedures. In 1972 customs duties were the largest domestic revenue source (though declining), followed by excise taxes (rising), interest and profits from government participation in the economy (mainly the Central Bank), and taxes on income. Income taxes were both personal and corporate. The personal tax was progressive. Corporate income was taxed, as such, at a moderate flat rate; it was not also taxed as a part of personal income. Income from agriculture and stock-raising, except for that from irrigated land, was not subject to taxation.

Expenditures

Expenditures are divided between recurring (current) operating expenditures and expenditures for development. In no year have the government's own domestic revenues been sufficient to cover its current expenditures. Foreign assistance was required, therefore, not only for the whole of the development budget but for a sizable proportion of current expenditures as well. Among the current budgeted expenditures, the largest item throughout the 1966-72 period was for defense and public security, reaching 70 percent of total current expenditures in 1969 and declining thereafter to an estimated 63 percent in 1972.

The government's development expenditures underwent an abrupt increase from 1966 to 1967 that reflected the multiple emergency problems created for the government by the Israeli occupation of the West Bank and the massive injection of foreign assistance with which the wealthy Arab countries responded. After remaining virtually unchanged from 1967 to 1969, development expenditures declined somewhat in 1970 and 1971 with the difficult financial and political conditions that prevailed in those years. In 1972 they apparently picked up when the level of foreign assistance increased and, other things being equal, they may probably be expected to increase somewhat further as the 1973-75 development program unfolds.

The projected budget for 1973 calls for special mention because of the large increase it shows in both revenues and expenditures compared with earlier years. This is mainly because the foreign grants item on the receipts side includes some JD47 million corresponding to Kuwait's foreign grants that had been frozen since 1970. If this item were excluded or reduced, the budget would be more in line with the changes shown in preceding years and would show some reduction in both the government's current and its development expenditures.

In 1973 a municipal development program was apparently being undertaken to stimulate local investment and to reduce the rising rate of unemployment in the local units and the consequent migration to the cities. The program emphasized the construction of local roads; municipal street, water, and sewerage systems; and housing, schools, and government buildings. The estimated cost of the program amounted to around JD14 million, and its timing was designed to coincide with the larger, countrywide three-year development program.

Public Debt

The rapid increase in public sector expenditures in 1967 and subsequently was not completely offset by the increase in domestic revenues and in grants and loans from abroad. The consequence was a budgetary deficit in all years after 1967, and the public debt, both domestic and foreign, increased substantially.

According to the Central Bank, the disbursed external debt of the central government outstanding at the end of 1972 totaled the equivalent of about US$170 million. In addition, there apparently was a contracted but undisbursed external debt of around the equivalent of US$60 million, making a total contracted external debt of about the equivalent of US$230 million, at the end of 1972. The largest creditors, in order, were the Federal Republic of Germany (West Germany), the United Kingdom, Kuwait, the International Development Association (IDA, an affiliate of the World Bank), and the United States Agency for International Development (AID). The government also had internal indebtedness, most of it in treasury bills, totaling an estimated US$85 million to US$100 million at the end of 1972.

BANKING, MONEY SUPPLY, AND PRICES

The banking system in 1972 comprised the Central Bank, nine commercial banks, and five specialized credit institutions. The money and capital market was limited mainly to government bills and bonds and to discounted trade bills held by the banking system, in addition to modest amounts of the securities of some of the major industrial corporations held outside the banking system and the corporations themselves. Long-term (three-year) government bonds were introduced for the first time in 1971 and 1972 under repurchase agreements by the Central Bank; most of them were taken up by the commercial banks. Outside the banking system a good deal of small-scale credit was extended by the traditional moneylenders (shopkeepers, landlords, and merchants) at extortionate rates of interest. Interest rates paid by the banks ranged up to 6 percent, and the rates they charged were from 4 percent to 9 percent. The central bank discount rate has been 5 percent.

Banking System

The Central Bank of Jordan was established in 1964 and given more precise definition in 1971; it is government owned and pays 80 percent of its profits into the treasury. It issues the currency, administers the exchange reserves, and acts as the government's fiscal agent. In collaboration with the Economic Security Committee it helps chart and implement the government's monetary policies. The Central Bank supervises the commercial banks and acts to control the money supply. At the end of the 1972 it had assets totaling about JD110.5 million.

At the end of 1971 the commercial banks included four Jordanian banks, three Arab banks, and two banks with headquarters in London. All West Bank branches had been closed in 1967, and data on the commercial banking system in the early 1970s referred only to the East Bank. At the end of 1972 the Jordanian banks accounted for almost two-thirds of commercial bank assets. Assets totaled JD95.5 million, including credit to the private sector of about JD40 million and credit to the public sector of JD16 million; private sector deposits totaled some JD61 million. Most of the outstanding loans were for trade and commerce (42 percent), construction (20 percent), and industry (9 percent).

The specialized credit institutions included the Industrial Development Bank, the Agricultural Credit Corporation, the Municipalities and Villages Loan Fund, the Housing Corporation, and the Jordan Cooperative Organization (see ch. 12). The Agricultural Credit Corporation and the Industrial Development Bank extended medium- and long-term credit for agricultural and private sector industrial development. The Municipalities and Villages Loan Fund provided credit to the public sector, mostly for rural water and power projects, and the Housing Corporation provided credit for residential construction in both the private and the public sectors. At the end of 1972 the five specialized institutions taken together had total assets of JD20.6 million, outstanding loans of JD16.2 million, loans from the government of JD1.8 million, and loans from foreign institutions of JD3.7 million. The bulk of their outstanding loans were for agricultural credit, municipal and village loans, and industry.

Currency

The currency unit is the Jordanian dinar, which was created in 1950 to replace the Palestinian pound; it is divided into 1,000 fils. Jordan was a member of the sterling area, and the dinar was established at par with the pound sterling, or at a dollar rate of US$2.80 per JD1. In 1953 Jordan joined the International Monetary Fund (IMF) and agreed with the IMF on a par value of 2.48828 grams of fine gold, equal to US$2.80.

When the British pound was devalued in 1967 the dinar did not follow suit; it stayed with the dollar in the dollar devaluation of 1971. It did not, however, follow the dollar in its second devaluation, on February 12, 1973, and the exchange rate between them thereupon changed from US$2.80 per JD1 to US$3.11 per JD1.

At the end of 1972 the dinar was not convertible, and no minimum reserves of gold and foreign exchange were required to be held against the note issue. Notes were issued in denominations of JD10, JD5, JD1, and JD0.5, and coins in smaller denominations; the latter, however, represented a very small percentage of the currency outstanding.

Money Supply

The money supply in 1966 totaled JD56 million, of which some 54 percent was in currency and 46 percent in demand deposits. By the end of 1972 the money supply had increased by more than 100 percent to JD115 million, an average of about 12.7 percent per year, compared with a preliminarily estimated average annual increase in the GNP of about 5.8 percent over the same period.

In the Jordanian monetary system the factors that contribute to expansion of the money supply are net inflow of foreign exchange (foreign assets), increases in loans by the banking system to the private sector, and increases in loans by the banking system to the public sector. Factors that act to contract the money supply are increases in government deposits, increases in time and savings deposits, increases in capital and reserves, and increases in other balance sheet liabilities less other assets.

The large increase in currency in circulation in 1967 and 1968 reflected the large inflow of foreign exchange (foreign assets) from Saudi Arabia, Kuwait, and Libya, which was converted into a flight from deposits of all kinds into currency as protection against changes in the political situation. It also apparently reflected a sizable movement of currency from the East Bank to the West Bank, where the currency was hoarded, went into circulation, or went into Israeli banks but did not return to the East Bank. During these years the movement of goods and services between the East Bank and West Bank favored the West Bank. In addition, the Jordan government made sizable payments there for relief and government salaries.

In the years 1969 to 1971 the net inflow of foreign exchange was reversed under the impact of decreased Arab budget support and the deteriorating balance of trade. The decline in foreign assets, however, was more than offset by a rapid increase in bank credit to the government to finance its uncovered budgetary deficits.

In 1972 the net inflow of foreign assets showed a sharp upturn, bank credit to the private and semiprivate sectors increased appreciably, and the public sector apparently did not increase its indebtedness to the banking system. Deposits of all sorts, especially demand deposits, increased; for the first time since 1966 currency in circulation decreased; and the proportion of currency in the money supply declined.

Prices

In mid-1973 the only available guides to price changes were cost-of-living indexes for Amman and Az Zarqa using 1967 as 100. Up to 1966 prices were basically stable, but the Amman and Az Zarqa indexes suggest that thereafter there was a substantial rise in prices. The overall Amman index, after declining to 99.7 in 1968, rose to about 115 in 1970, to 120 at the end of 1971, to 133 at the end of 1972, and to about 140 in April 1973. It should be noted, however, that the rapid increases in the later years reflect not only the expansion in the domestic money supply but also increases in the prices of internationally traded commodities and increases in import prices resulting from Jordan's devaluation of the dinar in fiscal 1971/72 and from the floating of various currencies after 1971.

As presented in the Amman index, food prices rose faster in the post-1967 period than other prices, followed by housing and clothing. Prices apparently rose somewhat less rapidly in all categories in Az Zarza than in Amman.

TRADE AND BALANCE OF PAYMENTS

Structure of Trade

By the 1960s the larger towns and cities had experienced substantial growth, and a new urban economy was developing (see ch. 3). Among other things, this introduced new wants to the countryside, influenced the traditional rural and nomadic patterns of trade, and resulted in a general monetization of the economy. Nevertheless, because of the structure, size, and early stage of growth of the economy, per capita incomes were low, and effective demand was limited, precluding for the most part the domestic development of large production units and markets.

The 1967 war dealt a bitter blow to trade, disrupting the usual pattern of commodity exchanges within the country and introducing political and economic uncertainties that distorted the external marketing process. Although the new cease-fire line along the Jordan River was not completely closed to interbank commodity trade, traffic was frequently interrupted. Before the war and the closure of the Suez Canal, roughly half of Jordan's imports went to the West Bank territory after entering the country through Al Aqaba. By the end of 1967, largely because of payments difficulties, imports to the West Bank had virtually ceased. The movement of fresh agricultural produce from the West Bank to the East Bank for local consumption or export was resumed; this and other exports to the East Bank were abetted by the Israeli decision to allow the Jordanian dinar to continue to circulate freely as legal tender in the occupied territory and to accumulate there.

As elsewhere in the Middle East, most farming in Jordan is on a small scale, and the majority of the farmers deal with middlemen in disposing of their produce. Lack of adequate on-farm transportation services and storage facilities results in waste and financial loss, and absence of standardization and grading for products detracts from their sales value. The existence of many middlemen between the producer and the consumer or exporter is the result partly of the farmer's lack of knowledge of alternatives and partly of the small amounts that he produces.

Cereals, the country's most important farm product, often reach the market through peddlers who proceed through the country at harvest-time with a variety of goods needed by the villagers. The peddlers buy whatever cereals the farmers have to sell and in turn sell the produce to wholesalers. Large producers and landlords often sell directly to the flour mills.

Vegetables, grapes, olives, melons, and watermelons, because they frequently earn foreign exchange, tend to be marketed with somewhat more sophistication and assistance from the public sector than the grains. Livestock is sold locally, at weekly markets, or at local and regional fairs. Phosphates and cement are marketed with a good deal of sophistication and official assistance and supervision. Price supports (at all levels of marketing) are not standard practice, but they are resorted to if conditions of weather or barriers to markets appear to the government to call for them.

In the towns and cities the special feature of the trading structure is the *suq* (bazaar). Practically all buying is carried out on the basis of bargaining; frequently, more time is spent in bargaining than the margin of advantage to be gained is worth. This, however, is the accepted way of doing business, and it brings more than purely economic satisfaction to the parties involved. A good bargainer may even gain social prestige, and a refusal to bargain may be taken as an insult. In some of the Western-style retail establishments in Amman and other large towns, fixed prices are posted. They are usually aimed at the tourist trade and are moderately high by local standards.

Wholesalers tend, if possible, to be importers as well. If so, they ordinarily require substantial capital, ordinarily paying 25 percent upon order to open an import letter of credit and the remainder upon arrival of goods. Importers also usually try to protect themselves against competition by obtaining exclusive agency contracts for particular lines of goods. As a result of large capital requirements and exclusive agency contracts, the wholesaling of imports is concentrated in a few large establishments whose profits tend to be high.

Most retail stores in the cities are small specialized establishments selling one or only a few products. Outside of Amman, where a few large department stores and modern food markets have been built, the specialty store maintains its traditional importance and in most places is the only kind of store in existence. In some of the smaller towns and villages there may be only a few shops carrying a limited range of goods that are sold or bartered for local produce.

Aside from wholesalers and retailers, the trade sector includes commission agents, who represent foreign producers, selling to both wholesalers and retailers. These agents are either Jordanians engaged part time in this work or non-Jordanians who have a territorial franchise that includes Jordan. Chambers of commerce, with which most commercial establishments of any size are affiliated, are active in Amman and the other large cities and towns. The chambers of commerce are organized nationally into the Federation of Chambers of Commerce. Their powers, organization, and operational procedures are regulated by law.

In most parts of the commercial structure credit was still a bottleneck in 1973, though probably less so than previously. Increasing numbers of small farmers were turning to the Agricultural Credit Corporation and the agricultural credit cooperatives for growing portions of their credit needs. Nevertheless, much recourse was still had to the traditional, very high cost moneylenders, especially for emergency purposes, with the result that the small farmer tended to become mired in debt. For the large farmer, the domestic and foreign trade wholesaler-retailer, and the industrialist there existed the commercial banks and special credit institutions. The government, advised by the international agencies, was moving to improve the lot of the small farmer as well as that of the small trader, but the logistics of the problem in highly traditional areas, not so long since monetized and plagued by unemployment or underemployment, were not easily to be resolved.

Foreign Trade

Because Jordan's known natural resources are so meager as to be inadequate, imports are exceptionally important as a means of eking out the existing inadequacies. By the same token, the development of exports with which to pay for those imports must, unless new resources are discovered, consist largely of services, such as tourism, attractive investment opportunities for foreign capital, and the export of trained personnel. This poses to the government the difficult problems of providing social stability and superior services in the case of tourism and investment and superior qualities of education and training in the case of emigrating personnel. In large measure such provision is not wholly under the control of the government, and the government has not recently been able to assure it in sufficient measure to inspire great confidence. As in most other respects, this condition is largely a result of the 1967 war.

Exports increased from around JD8.8 million in 1966 to JD12.2 million in 1968, declined to about JD8.8 million in 1971 and rose to an estimated JD12.6 million in 1972 (see table 7). In that year nearly 32 percent of exports were accounted for by fruits, nuts, and vegetables; about 28 percent by phosphates; 15 percent by cement; and some 3 percent by wet cell batteries.

Major changes in the direction of Jordan's exports between 1966 and 1972 resulted from repercussions of the closure of the Suez Canal and the country's western and, at times, northern borders, together with

Table 7. *Foreign Trade of Jordan by Economic Function, Selected Years, 1966–72*
(in thousands of Jordanian dinars)[1]

	1966	1967	1969	1970	1971	1972	Percent of 1972
Domestic Exports[2]:							
Consumer goods[3]	4,733	5,877	7,085	6,060	5,450	6,196	49
Raw materials[4]	3,634	3,806	4,562	2,586	2,457	3,947	31
Capital goods[5]	341	258	226	672	873	2,463	20
Other	51	43	43	2	37	0	0
TOTAL	8,759	9,984	11,916	9,320	8,817	12,606	100
Imports:							
Consumer goods	31,333	23,870	33,887	33,025	33,441	46,287	48
Foodstuffs	(18,202)	(14,097)	(18,093)	(18,884)	(21,465)	n.a.	n.a.
Other	(13,131)	(9,773)	(15,794)	(14,141)	(11,976)	n.a.	n.a.
Raw materials	14,696	13,722	14,593	15,144	13,612	18,772	20
Capital goods	15,100	14,774	15,239	13,375	17,614	18,626	20
Miscellaneous	7,082	2,682	4,033	4,338	11,960	11,625	12
TOTAL	68,211	55,048	67,752	65,882	76,627	95,310	100

n.a.—not available.
[1] For value of the Jordanian dinar—see Glossary.
[2] Does not include reexports.
[3] Mainly foodstuffs.
[4] Mainly phosphates.
[5] Mainly wet cell batteries and cement.

Source: Adapted from Jordan, Central Bank of Jordan, *Monthly Statistical Bulletin*, Amman, December 1971, December 1972, and February 1973, table 20.

the increase in cement production. In 1972 the Arab countries as a group took some 73 percent of exports, compared with around 64 percent in 1966 (see table 8). India took around 11 percent in 1972, and Japan about 5 percent.

From around JD68 million in 1966 imports declined to JD55 million in 1967, and thereafter increased to JD95 million in 1972. In 1972 consumer goods accounted for almost half of the total, and foodstuffs for about half of the consumer goods. Raw materials were about 20 percent of the total, machinery and transport equipment around 8 percent, and other forms of equipment about 10 percent. Between 1967 and 1972 there were no shifts among the origins of Jordan's major imports that were not readily explicable by the loss of access to Beirut and the eastern Mediterranean.

Balance of Payments

Between 1966 and 1972 the trade balance was consistently unfavorable (see table 9). Services declined sharply after 1967, as a function mainly of reduced tourist receipts and remittances from abroad (a large but unknown percentage of the remittances went to West Bank residents and hence after 1967 were not an input in the East Bank economy). Goods and services together showed a deteriorating trend between 1966 and 1972. Although foreign budgetary support (unrequited transfers) and capital inflows went a long way to redress that trend, the suspension of Libyan and Kuwait aid in fiscal 1970/71 and the large increase in projected imports in 1972 kept the current account substantially in the red for the 1966-72 period as a whole. The capital account (that is, loans and direct investment as distinguished from grants) remained on balance consistently favorable throughout the period, however.

The outcome was that net foreign assets, which had been growing steadily in the years before the 1967 war, continued to do so in 1967 and 1968 because of the large transfers from abroad in those years. During the next three years, however, gold and exchange holdings declined sharply, but in 1972 they again turned upward.

According to the IMF, net foreign assets, which had stood at JD31 million in 1960, JD56 million in 1965, and JD65 million in 1966, increased to JD105 million in 1968, declined thereafter to JD91 million in 1971, and at the end of July 1973 totaled JD117 million. It is to be expected, however, that the purchasing power of a unit of foreign assets varied somewhat between 1960 and 1973 as a result of changes in international prices and of the net effect on the exchange holdings of the shifts in exchange rates among foreign currencies that took place over the period.

Table 8. Direction of the Foreign Trade of Jordan, Selected Years, 1966–72
(in thousands of Jordanian dinars and percent)[1]

| | 1966 | | 1967 | 1969 | 1970 | 1971[2] | 1972[2] | |
	Value	Percent	Value	Value	Value	Value	Value	Percent
Domestic exports, f.o.b.[3]:								
Arab countries	5,647	64	6,429	8,510	7,088	6,686	9,193	73
European Economic Community	441	5	761	1	1	4	51	0
India	1,337	15	1,429	1,482	253	956	1,405	11
Japan	0	0	31	35	17	173	625	5
United Kingdom	3	0	3	1	2	1	0	0
United States	37	1	13	6	2	2	0	0
Yugoslavia	810	9	530	1,016	788	463	201	2
COMECON[4] countries and PRC[5]	371	4	345	394	419	163	211	2
Other countries	113	1	443	471	750	369	920	7
TOTAL	8,759	100[6]	9,984	11,916	9,320	8,817	12,606	100

Imports, c.i.f.[7]:

Arab countries	13,062	19	10,515	14,382	12,914	16,546	16,376	17
European Economic Community	13,713	20	12,106	12,143	12,722	11,279	17,337	18
India	1,546	2	1,106	1,192	1,635	1,071	1,397	2
Japan	2,860	4	2,034	5,149	3,869	4,191	4,598	5
United Kingdom	8,140	12	6,712	9,677	8,816	6,783	8,645	9
United States	11,952	18	6,769	6,230	7,381	18,133	16,887	18
Yugoslavia	362	1	592	478	984	321	234	0
COMECON[4] countries and PRC[5]	7,629	11	5,885	8,955	8,034	4,636	8,002	8
Other countries	8,947	13	9,329	9,546	9,527	13,667	21,834	23
TOTAL	68,211	100	55,048	67,752	65,882	76,627	95,310	100

[1] For value of the Jordanian dinar—see Glossary.
[2] Preliminary.
[3] Free on board. Does not include reexports.
[4] Council for Mutual Economic Assistance.
[5] People's Republic of China.
[6] Does not total because of rounding.
[7] Cost, insurance, and freight.

Source: Adapted from Jordan, Central Bank of Jordan, *Monthly Statistical Bulletin*, Amman, February 1972, December 1972, and February 1973, table 19.

	1966	1967	1971[2]	1972[2]
CURRENT TRANSACTIONS:				
Merchandise (net):				
Exports, f.o.b.[3]..................	10.4	11.3	11.5	17.0
Imports, c.i.f.[4]	−67.3	−54.2	−76.2	−94.8
Trade balance.................	−56.9	−42.9	−64.7	−77.8
Services:				
Oil transit dues	1.4	1.1	3.4	2.1
Travel (net).....................	6.1	1.5	−4.6	−5.0
Investment income (net)	3.2	3.6	4.8	3.3
Remittances from Jordanians abroad......................	10.6	6.6	5.0	7.4
Government, n.i.e.[5] (net)..........	−0.3	2.7	−1.5	−5.9
Other services (net)[6]..............	0.4	−0.4	−1.7	4.1
Total (net).....................	21.4	15.1	5.4	6.0
Goods and services	−35.5	−27.8	−59.3	−71.8
Unrequited transfers:				
Private (net).....................	2.7	2.4	1.1	2.2
Government (net)	31.4	51.6	35.5	66.0
Total (net).....................	34.1	54.0	36.6	68.2
Current Account	−1.4	26.2	−22.7	−3.6
CAPITAL TRANSACTIONS:				
Private (net).......................	0.0	0.0	−1.3	−0.4
Government (net)[7]	4.9	2.0	8.9	9.0
Total (net)....................	4.9	2.0	7.6	8.6
Sum of current plus capital transactions	3.5	28.2	−15.1	5.0
Net additions to foreign assets[8]	−8.6	−33.2	11.8	−6.7
Net errors and omissions..............	5.1	5.0	3.3	1.7

[1]For value of the Jordanian dinar—see Glossary.
[2]Preliminary estimates.
[3]Free on board. Includes reexports, as well as domestic exports.
[4]Cost, insurance, and freight.
[5]Not included elsewhere.
[6]Includes transportation (net).
[7]Includes special drawing rights of JD0.9 million in 1971 and JD0.9 million in 1972.
[8]Minus sign equals increase.

Source: Adapted from Jordan, Central Bank of Jordan, *Monthly Statistical Bulletin,* Amman, December 1972 and February 1973, table 14.

CHAPTER 12

AGRICULTURE AND INDUSTRY

In 1973 Jordan remained a basically agricultural country. Agriculture (including livestock, forestry, and fishing) contributed somewhat less than 20 percent of the gross domestic product (GDP), depending on year-to-year weather conditions; accounted for around one-third of the working force; and provided a livelihood for upwards of three-quarters of the population. It also provided about two-fifths of the country's exports, as well as the raw materials for a good part of the country's manufacturing and handicraft industries. In spite of the proportion of the country's economic resources devoted to agriculture, the country was dependent on imported foodstuffs to maintain itself.

Industry, if defined to include only mining and manufacturing, contributed some 10 to 11 percent to the GDP in the early 1970s. If power and water were added, the contribution would rise to an estimated 12.5 percent; and if the definition were further expanded to include construction, the estimated contribution would be on the order of 16 to 18 percent. At this level the impact of industry on the economy would closely have approximated that of agriculture in the early 1970s; however, the percentage of the working force absorbed by industry in the early 1970s was estimated at some 9 to 9.5 percent. Industry, including minerals, contributed about 50 percent of total exports in 1971.

Agriculture and industry were concentrated in the northwest corner of the country. Both had had readjustment problems resulting from the Arab-Israeli War of June 1967, and both had suffered seriously as a consequence of the civil strife of 1970 and 1971 (see ch. 2; ch. 9). By early 1973, however, this dislocation in the East Bank (see Glossary) appeared to have been repaired or to be in the process of being repaired. The problems of both sectors had nearly narrowed down to the by-no-means easy problem of making the most of limited resources against the pressures of a rapidly rising population.

AGRICULTURE

Structure

The agricultural sector was in the main a subsistence agriculture, based on a large number of villages that vary appreciably in size and organization. The villages are surrounded by agricultural and (or) pastoral land, depending upon the quality of the land and the local landholding pattern. The farm families live in the villages and journey daily to the plot or plots they either own or work on a tenant basis.

According to an agricultural census in 1965, the great majority of the farms (upwards of 90 percent) were owner operated, but in the early 1970s it seemed likely that there was also an appreciable element of tenancy. Most of the farm units were small, and the greater part of the cultivable area was dry-farmed. In addition to the cultivated area, large areas of range were used by roving herds of sheep and goats, as rainfall permitted.

Perhaps the major fact of life in the agricultural picture at the start of the 1970s was that, given the existing water situation, all available usable land was in use; there was no more land. Production could be increased by increasing the productivity of the available land either through increased irrigation and better use of available water or by the substitution of improved production inputs and methods for the existing ones. The attempts to convert marginal areas of potentially arable land from range use to crop use had not been successful.

In the early 1970s an estimated 8 to 10 percent of the cultivable area was partially or fully irrigated. Under the inspiration and guidance of the international collaborators in Jordan's economic development, irrigation formed a major component of the continuing development program. An important by-product of the irrigation program as it affected the Jordan valley was more equitable distribution of the increasingly usable land in the valley.

Most of the progress that had taken place in the agricultural sector through the early 1970s was mainly related to irrigated crops, especially fruit and other tree crops. Improvement in the livestock and forestry sectors had reportedly been marginal, and in the fisheries sector extremely so. Even the field crop sector had shown comparatively little progress, for a number of reasons. Field crops were mainly rain fed, and rainfall was not only scanty at best but exceedingly unpredictable both in total quantity from one year to the next (statistically, two years in every ten are drought years) and in timing in any given year. Compounding this basic situation was the fact that in the years after independence marginally cultivable areas were taken from pastural uses and incorporated into the cropped areas. To a large extent, these marginal areas did not provide a net gain to the cropping area. In addition, they represented a serious reduction of the best of the pasturelands, and they resulted in a large increase in annual erosion of very limited topsoils (see ch. 3). It is probable that no benefits accrued to the agricultural sector or the country from this misallocation of scarce agricultural resources.

The primitive nature of production practices contributed to the inefficient use of both new and old cropland. An important malpractice in view of the almost universal shortage of water and its seasonal concentration under flood conditions was the generalized persistence in plowing across rather than with the contours of the land as called for to restrain flood season runoff and preserve moisture in the dry season. The generally continued use of the shallow stick-type plow was partly a function of tradition and partly the result of inadequate agricultural credit. Similar observations apply to planting, weeding, and threshing methods. The use of improved seeds and fertilizers, although they have shown some increase, in the early 1970s was still low in comparison with their use in many other underdeveloped countries. These problems may be expected to show improvement as the government's extension services improve.

Tractors pose a potential threat. The use of them increased rapidly in the late 1960s and early 1970s. Given the shallow soils in most farming regions, the rapid rainy season runoff, and the inherited ways of plowing, continued increase in the use of tractors raises dangers of floods and loss of the already minimal topsoil. This situation is perhaps most serious in those marginally cultivable areas where good pastureland has been plowed into poor cropland. These areas and fallow land in the proper cropland areas should apparently be placed under forage crops on either a permanent or a rotational basis.

As Jordan headed into its Three Year Program (1973–75), one problem was prominent in the array of difficulties confronting its agricultural sector. As in many other underdeveloped countries with rapidly growing populations, this problem was how to bring about improvements in agricultural production techniques that would result in an increase in the productivity of the staple food grain areas sufficient to eliminate the debilitating importation of foodstuffs and permit the progressive allocation of marginal wheatlands to more productive purposes.

Role of the Government

The government's relationship to the agricultural sector is advisory, implementary, and in some instances regulatory. Most of the land owned by the government has not been of high quality, except where the extension of irrigation has placed a premium on erstwhile noncultivable land; as a consequence, the government has not in a major fashion been in competition with the private production sector.

Neither, in general, has the government tended to become involved in price and production controls. The major use of such controls has been to assure the availability of wheat seed at reasonable prices for the coming planting season and to fix the price of domestically produced tobacco in conjunction with the country's cigarette industry. Strict production controls, however, are in effect in the Jordan valley in connection with the planting of new citrus crops because of the high demands of these crops for short-supply summer irrigation water.

In 1968 the government established the Agricultural Marketing Organization, in which it had a limited participation, in an effort to dilute the pressure on producers exerted by the commission merchants who controlled the country's agricultural marketing. This effort was apparently not successful, and in 1971 that organization was replaced by the wholly government-owned National Marketing Board. The board was assigned responsibility for the promotion of agricultural production and marketing seemingly with the assistance of support prices and in direct competition with the commission agents' monopoly.

In the early 1970s, however, the government's chief role in relation to agriculture was to provide, with assistance from foreign governments and international agencies, the basic infrastructure for the sector. This included the physical infrastructure, such as irrigation, highway, and storage facilities. It also included the exploration, experimentation, testing, credit, and administrative services needed to help keep the agricultural sector abreast of developments abroad and, after those developments were adjusted as necessary to local conditions, bringing them to the attention of and making them available to the farming community. A major limitation on the potential benefits of these functions has been the inadequately coordinated plethora of overlapping and sometimes competing jurisdictions set up within the governmental administration. This situation has of course been aggravated by the particular conditions created by the 1967 war and its aftermath.

More directly, the government aids the farmer by relieving him of payments of taxes on agricultural income. It affords the farmer duty-free imports of farm inputs, such as fertilizers, herbicides, and agricultural machinery. Irrigation water on the East Ghor Canal, moreover, is sold to farmers below cost, and they are provided with agricultural loans at reasonable rates

Agricultural Credit

In the early 1970s the agricultural sector had three main sources of credit. The most important was the credit traditionally obtained from landlords, shopkeepers, and the private commission merchants who did business in all kinds of crop needs and marketed all kinds of produce. The commission merchants provided larger quantities of short-term credit to farmers than any other source. They provided the farmer necessary inputs on credit and undertook to market his crop for him on commission in the wholesale markets. On both types of transaction they have charged high rates of interest, leaving the farmer little to invest in his farm even if he desired to do so. But the commission agent was available when needed, and until recently the farmer often has had no effective alternative means of marketing the cash crop portion of his production.

In an effort to shield the farmer from the commission merchants and other moneylenders, the government has sponsored a multifaceted cooperative movement. The most effective branch of this movement has been credit and saving cooperative societies, of which there apparently were more than 200 in the early 1970s. All were members of the Jordan Cooperative Organization, part of whose ownership was held by the government. The societies borrowed from the organization at 6 percent and lent to their farmer members at 8 percent. They also accepted savings from their members and made some efforts at providing other than purely credit services. Their loans were for short-term seasonal crop purposes and showed sizable annual increases in outstanding totals after 1969.

The major source of medium-term (five to ten years) farm improvement credit in the early 1970s was the Agricultural Credit Corporation (ACC). With support from the government, the International Development Association (IDA), and other foreign and international agencies, the ACC made loans for such varied purposes as land reclamation, water supply improvement, orchard development, farm mechanization, and poultry farming. For such purposes it charged 6 percent. It also made some loans for short-term seasonal purposes, and for these it charged around 8.5 percent. Many loans were secured by a lien on the salary of a relative.

Land Tenure

Land tenure and agrarian reform have apparently presented less of a problem in Jordan than in many other underdeveloped countries. This has been true in part because of the process of official verification and settlement of land titles that was embarked on in the mandated territory in the 1920s and 1930s and that in respect to the East Bank was approaching a conclusion at the end of the 1960s. Under this legislation, land titles had to be certified with a central registry and were not legally transferred until the transfer had been incorporated into the registry.

The types of land tenure in Jordan have resembled those in various Muslim countries that in this respect act according to the precepts of sharia (see Glossary) law. The several types of tenure were systematized by the Ottoman Land Code of 1858 into *mulk, miri, waqf, matruk, niwat,* and *mudawwara.*

Mulk was land held in absolute ownership, including both surface and subsoil rights. In Jordan *mulk* tenure included all areas inside municipal or urban limits. Scarcely any agricultural land fell in this category, but the category included housing sites in the villages. Disposal of *mulk* land was governed by sharia law (see ch. 8).

Miri was land to which a hereditary right of possession and usufruct was granted by the state, although ownership continued to reside in the state. Technically the land was under lease by the state for purposes of cultivation; it was transferable for such purposes, but it carried no subsoil rights which, along with the land's ownership, apparently remained in the possession of the state. Unlike *mulk* land, disposal of *miri* land was governed by the civil code.

Waqf was land of which the use and usufruct had irrevocably, perpetually, and inalienably been transferred to some religious or charitable organization. On its passage to the organization, however, the land might temporarily be used by members of the donor's family or by other specified individuals.

Matruk (literally, left, abandoned) land was separated from *miri* land and left for the general use of the public, mainly for roads and highways, threshing floors, common pasture, woodlots, and other similar purposes. Such lands were restricted to the purposes for which they were designated.

Niwat (literally, remote) land lay more than one-half hour by foot or 1½ miles from the nearest village or town. About 60 percent of land in Jordan was *niwat*, but there was none in the Jordan valley.

Mudawwara (literally, rotated, circulated) lands were those that had belonged to Sultan Abdul Hamid II at the time of the seizure of power by the Young Turks in 1908 and were thereupon taken over as state lands (see ch. 2). They had for the most part formerly been *miri* lands but had been transferred by their holders to the crown for protection from beduin attacks, the holders becoming tenants of the crown.

Before the land registration legislation of the 1920s and 1930s, two systems of working land in the villages prevailed. Under the *mushaa* system the land in the village was held and worked in common, the holdings of the individual villagers being represented by shares and the part of the land that an individual worked changing about every two or more years. Under the *mafruz* system of landholding, which was practiced on hilly areas and areas planted to vines, olives, and trees, the villagers partitioned the land permanently among themselves, subject to sales and changes resulting from boundary disputes.

After the land settlement legislation, individual land titles in the villages were progressively established, affording more security in this respect than is the case in many underdeveloped countries. In the Jordan valley a noticeable feature of land tenure has been the prevalence of joint ownership. Inasmuch as an effect of joint ownership was to reduce the incentive to invest in improvements to the land and its handling, legislation to break up such holdings has been in effect since the mid-1950s.

Water rights have been registered and assigned with the same care as landrights. Because there was a long history of more irrigable land than water available to irrigate it, the allocation of such water as was available had tended to be sanctioned by custom. Although efforts have been made to match the water to the land by legislation, in practice the two often continued to be separate, and some landholders had

206

more water than they needed. In that case they were permitted to sell the surplus.

In 1965 the government's agricultural census, which included both the East Bank and the West Bank (see Glossary), estimated the number of landholdings in the country at approximately 93,500 and their aggregate acreage at some 1.24 million acres. As presented by the census, about 36.4 percent of the total holdings enumerated contained less than 2.5 acres each (average 1.25 acres) and aggregated some 3.4 percent of the total area. An additional 35 percent of total holdings, each containing 12.5 acres or less, accounted for 16.4 percent of the cultivable area. Thus 71 percent of the total number of holdings represented less than 20 percent of the cultivable area. The next 24 percent of total holdings (12.5 to fifty acres each) accounted for almost 40 percent of total cultivable acreage. At the upper end of the size scale, the top 5 percent of total holdings (fifty acres each and above) contained slightly more than 40 percent of total acreage. About half of this acreage, or 20 percent of the total acreage, was accounted for by the top 1 percent of all holdings.

Land Use

Estimates of the amount of land in all of Jordan that is usable for agricultural purposes vary considerably, and with the data available it is not practicable to reconcile these differences. It may probably be presumed that in large part they reflect differing estimates of the amount of cropland lying fallow in any given year and the amount of marginal land included as permanent pasture. And of course the differences in the estimates depend on whether the West Bank is included. In one important respect the estimates are in full agreement: more than 80 percent of the country's area at the start of 1973 was not suitable for cultivation.

It seems likely that in the early 1970s there were in the East Bank and the West Bank together some 3 million acres of agriculturally usable land that was either already accessible or potentially accessible to adequate water. This aggregate area did not include land under forest or land used for seasonal pasturage.

Some 60 percent of the total agriculturally usable area was estimated to lie in the East Bank. Of this area an estimated 60 to 70 percent (roughly 1 million acres) was under crops (including tree crops); the remaining 30 to 40 percent was being held fallow, was not efficiently usable without irrigation, or consisted of nonproductive marginal cropping areas that should be allowed to go back to pasture. In addition to the agriculturally usable land in the East Bank, there were an estimated 150,000 to 250,000 acres under forest and a very sizable but indeterminate area that was used as winter (rainy season) range by nomadic or seminomadic herds of sheep, goats, and camels.

Irrigation

In the early 1970s water remained the limiting factor in the development of agriculture in Jordan. By the same token, the expansion of irrigation facilities to enable extension of the usable area, as well as increased intensiveness of cultivation, was generally considered to be the country's major immediate agricultural problem.

Estimates of the total irrigated area at the start of the 1970s amounted to 60,000 to 75,000 acres of a total estimated area under cultivation, including tree crops, of around 1 million acres in the East Bank. Various estimates have suggested that a total of 150,000 to 160,000 acres in the East Bank is irrigable, including much of the cultivable portion of the Jordan valley, its side wadis, and some of the southern wadis (see ch. 3). The total irrigable area of the Jordan valley was estimated at around 120,000 acres. An estimated 75,000 acres of that area lay in the East Bank, of which some 40,000 to 45,000 acres were irrigated.

With the advice and assistance of the United Kingdom, the United States, and the specialized agencies of the United Nations (UN), especially the United Nations Relief and Works Agency for Palestine Refugees in the Near East (UNRWA), the United Nations Development Program (UNDP), the Food and Agriculture Organization (FAO), and the International Bank for Reconstruction and Development (IBRD, also known as the World Bank), the government, practically since its inception, has placed particular emphasis on a carefully designed large-scale project for the expansion and improvement of irrigation facilities for the Jordan valley and its side wadis to bring irrigation to an estimated 135,000 acres. Impetus was given to this development by the program of the Israelis to utilize the waters of Lake Tiberias (Sea of Galilee) to meet their own irrigation needs.

The first stage of this project was the East Ghor Canal, which was begun in 1958 and completed in 1969. Starting from an underground diversion of the Yarmuk River, the canal paralleled the Jordan River for some forty-eight miles. It serviced upwards of 4,000 farms with an aggregate area of almost 34,000 acres.

The second and major stage of the project, which had the general name of Yarmuk Project, was to include construction of the Khalid ibn al Walid Dam on the Yarmuk River and the Maqarin Dam on the Az Zarqa River; a doubling of the capacity of the East Ghor Canal; a new thirty-seven-mile canal paralleling the existing one; and a system of canals in the river valley floodplain. In addition, the project called for extension of the East Ghor Canal, together with its associated lateral irrigation canals; for land improvements and flood protection; and for pumping stations to lift water to areas above the level of the canals. As a consequence of the Israeli occupation of the Golan Heights in 1967, construction on the Khalid ibn al Walid Dam was suspended, but work on the Maqarin Dam was proceeding at mid-1973.

In the meantime, water impoundment dams were built on a number of side wadis north of the Dead Sea to provide flood control and runoff catchment; to help reclaim erosion areas; and to supply additional water to stabilize dry-weather flow in both the irrigation and drainage systems. South of the Dead Sea a dam on the Wadi al Hasa provided flood control and water impoundment, and a dam on the Wadi al Mawjib enabled diversion of its waters in flood season into the Wadi al Hasa impoundment area to augment the capacity of that system. These facilities were expected to afford irrigation to 15,000 to 20,000 acres.

As the Jordan valley irrigation system progressed, it was planned that many of the existing landholdings there should be reduced to smaller but still economic sizes not to exceed fifty acres nor to be less than eight acres. Land acquisitions by the government were to be payable over ten years; and many land sales to tenants or small farmers were made on credit.

Simultaneously, groundwater studies under UN auspices had indicated the existence of extensive aquifers in the upland areas that could be tapped for groundwater irrigation purposes. Although these aquifers would have to be used with great care, especially for reasons of salinity, they provided a means of bringing limited areas of permanent cultivation to the outlying desert and of furthering the settlement of nomadic and seminomadic groups.

In mid-1973 the government was planning to expand the irrigated area of the Jordan valley by about 20,000 acres. The proposed project would also establish thirty-eight villages and resettle approximately 137,000 people. The cost of the project was estimated at JD32 million (for value of the Jordanian dinar—see Glossary).

Production

In 1971 around 980,000 acres were estimated by the government to be under cultivation in the East Bank. About 824,000 acres (84 percent) were under field crops, 66,000 acres (7 percent) under vegetables, and 90,000 acres (9 percent) in fruit and olive trees. The most important crops in terms of acreage planted were wheat (603,000 acres), barley (130,000 acres), and lentils (51,000 acres). Wheat, the basic staple food in the rural areas, accounted for more than 73 percent of total area under field crops, mainly in the uplands, under dry farming conditions. Wheat output, never very good compared with that obtained in other wheat-producing countries of the area, has varied enormously from year to year, depending primarily on the quantity and timing of the rainfall (see table 10). During the 1961–65 period wheat yields averaged about ten bushels per acre. The yield declined to around 3.3 bushels per acre in 1966, rose to about 14.5 bushels per acre in 1969, fell to about 3.5 in 1970, and was estimated at around thirteen bushels per acre in 1971. It is to be presumed that yields will improve as better seeds are

Table 10. Agricultural Production in Jordan, Selected Years, 1961-72[1]

(in thousands of metric tons)

	Average 1961-65	1966	1967	1968	1969[1]	1970[1]	1971[1/2]	1972[2]
Field Crops:								
Wheat.........	179.7	101.2	239.7	116.2	159.3	55.5	168.2	190
Barley.........	62.6	22.8	77.7	24.1	42.5	5.2	26.2	30
Tobacco	1.2	1.6	2.1	2.1	2.0	1.2	1.1	n.a.
Others.........	40.5	25.4	56.1	19.8	31.3	11.4	31.9	n.a.
Total........	284.0	151.0	375.6	162.2	235.1	73.3	227.4	n.a.
Vegetables:								
Tomatoes......	202.9	179.0	259.7	152.9	150.1	137.4	147.6	n.a.
Others.........	261.0	232.2	282.2	85.6	69.1	70.2	92.9	n.a.
Total........	463.9	411.2	541.9	238.5	219.2	207.6	240.5	n.a.
Fruits:								
Olives.........	72.1	32.7	64.0	36.3	23.9	3.0	18.5	30
Grapes........	74.4	61.9	71.6	19.3	14.2	6.4	18.6	n.a.
Citrus.........	32.1	48.9	61.4	37.3	24.3	48.9	24.0	n.a.
Watermelons...	146.6	47.7	118.4	82.2	53.2	22.8	28.1	n.a.
Others.........	53.4	54.3	64.8	20.1	27.7	22.5	14.5	n.a.
Total........	378.6	245.5	380.2	195.2	143.3	103.6	103.7	n.a.

n.a.—not available.
[1]Pertains to the East Bank only.
[2]Preliminary.

Source: Adapted from Jordan, Central Bank of Jordan, *Eighth Annual Report, 1971*, Amman, 1972, p. 7; and U.S. Department of Agriculture, *Indices of Agricultural Production in Africa and the Near East, 1962-71* (ERS Foreign 265.), Washington, 1972, p. 46.

introduced, together with more and better fertilizers, forage crops, and cultivating methods designed to avoid erosion, to preserve soil moisture, and progressively to eliminate most of the pasturelands that have been brought under wheat.

Preliminary estimates of wheat production in the East Bank in 1972 totaled around 190,000 tons, and the 1972 barley and olive crops also promised substantial increases over the corresponding output in 1971. The forecast for agriculture in 1973, however, was unfavorable, as a result of an extremely severe frost in the Jordan valley.

The most important of the vegetables cultivated in the early 1970s were tomatoes (about one-third of the area in vegetables), melons and watermelons, and eggplants. The area under tomatoes and other vegetables has expanded rapidly as the area under irrigation has expanded. Jordan has a lead time of a number of weeks for early vegetables and fruits in relation to its neighbors. But as its competitors catch up with new varieties and methods, better inputs, including new plant types and stocks, will have to be incorporated in the cultivation process in order to maintain the built-in advantages afforded by the Jordan valley.

Efforts in this direction, as well as a tendency to increase the production of high-value fruit and other tree crops, were in large measure casulaties of the international and civil strife of 1967, 1970, and 1971, which tended to force the farmers out of the Jordan valley and minimized the incentives to medium- and long-term investment there. By 1972 these deterrents appeared to have abated, and a major element in the agricultural sector of the Three Year Program will be the reactivation and intensification of the use of new plants, seeds, and other improved inputs.

Animal Husbandry

Animal husbandry approaches one-third of the value of output of the agricultural sector in years when climatic conditions are propitious. Livestock serves multiple purposes, such as sources of clothing, meat, dairy products, draft services, natural fertilizer, and raw materials for handicrafts. Most farms have a few animals on a subsistence, and possibly also on a petty cash, basis. Mainly, however, the livestock sector on the East Bank is a nomadic or seminomadic way of life, as the beduins move their flocks of sheep and goats over the country's rangeland in their traditional and largely uncontrolled seasonal search for forage. In this pursuit they depend on the natural growth in the spring, on fodder and cereal by-products in the summer, and on a combination of both in the fall and winter. The size of the flocks tends to be a barometer of nature's bounty from year to year, and numbers, rather than quality and condition of the animals, tend to be the measure of livestock wealth.

As in other nomadic areas there is a growing effort on the part of the government to establish permanent settlements for the nomadic herdsmen. One such settlement is located in the Qaal Jafr depression northeast of Maan, where important experiments are being carried out with pumped groundwater for the concomitant drainage problems to avert excessive salinity and for desirable strains of livestock breeds and forage culture. At the same time efforts will be made in irrigated areas and areas watered by wells to improve both the breeding and the feeding of meat and dairy animals. The Three Year Program proposes to expend upward of JD3 million for these purposes, including poultry and eggs, over the plan period.

The livestock population in the East Bank in 1967, officially enumerated, approximated 788,000 sheep, 377,000 goats, 40,700 cattle, and 10,700 camels. By 1971 the sheep, goat, and cattle numbers had declined to 690,600, 361,300, and 34,300, respectively, while camels appeared to have increased to an unexpected 17,300. FAO estimated poultry numbers at 2 million chickens in the 1970–71 period compared with 2.6 million in the 1966–67 period; turkeys were estimated at 22,000 in 1970.

Forests and Forest Products

Protective reproduction of the forest resources was for practical purposes an abandoned economic preoccupation in Jordan. Cutting over the woodlands for fuel and lumber, unrequited by any persistent replacement policy and aggravated by the permanent destruction caused by large herds of goats, by the 1960s had destroyed practically all of the country's forest cover. This was somewhat less true in the East Bank than in the West Bank.

In the early 1970s it was estimated that around 300,000 acres in the East Bank should be set aside for reforestation in order to reduce the erosion caused by flood runoffs, to preserve the available soil moisture, and to reestablish the capacity of the annual rainfall to maintain an adequate water level in the subsurface aquifers. About JD1.5 million were earmarked for this purpose in the Three Year Program.

Official estimates of seedlings planted (including replantings) in the East Bank from 1967 through 1971 totaled approximately 9 million. Firewood harvested in 1971, as estimated (probably on the low side) by the same official sources, amounted to 5,000 tons; charcoal totaled 4,600 tons, and wood (presumably for lumber), 3,640 cubic meters.

Fisheries

Fishing is not yet a developed activity. According to the official statistics, the East Bank catch in the Gulf of Aqaba and in the Jordan and Yarmuk rivers in 1971 amounted to about 150 tons.

INDUSTRY

Before 1950 there was practically no manufacturing industry in the East Bank except for artisans and producers of handicrafts. By the start of the 1970s there were more than 6,000 mining and manufacturing enterprises located in the East Bank, and although most of them continued to be in the artisan category, there were a number that were not. It was estimated that 90 percent or more of the industries employed fewer than five workers each and in the aggregate accounted for somewhat more than half of the total industrial employment. By contrast, the fifteen or so firms employing more than 100 workers per firm accounted for almost 25 percent of total employment engaged in industry. Most of the larger firms were located in the Irbid-Amman-Az Zarqa areas. Practically all the economically critical and strategic industries belonging to pre-1967 Jordan were located there and consequently did not have to be replaced as a result of the Israeli occupation of the West Bank.

The commercial intercourse that prevailed between the East and West banks in the pre-1967 period was resumed by the prompt reopening of the Jordan River bridges after the war. But it was at best only a partial restoration and one that was bound to be increasingly attenuated with the passage of time under the prevailing circumstances.

First, the reopening of the bridges was attended by the institution of tariff duties between the Israeli-occupied Territory (see Glossary) and the East Bank. Second, West Bank laborers were increasingly attracted by the Israelis into Israel proper. Third, the Israelis instituted other incentives to the expansion of commercial intercourse between Israel and the West Bank at the expense of that existing between the two banks in the pre-1967 period.

In the early 1970s the general orientation in favor of private enterprise that characterized the government's relation to the economy as a whole applied to industry. Basically, the government's policy has been one of laissez-faire, especially as it affects the small-scale industry sector. Among the larger production units a good deal of mixed enterprise exists; and in the power, refinery, and communication fields, monopolies—private or public—are customary.

The mixed enterprise and monopoly sector in large part reflects a pragmatic situation resulting from the limited dimension of the market and the limited financial resources of the private sector; it also reflects instances in which the government has intervened to avoid the bankruptcy of privately owned enterprises. At the end of 1971 the government held an equity position in more than twenty-five industrial, marketing, tourism, transport, power, and financing firms that had an aggregate authorized capital of JD34.7 million. The government's participation varied from 3 to 86 percent and averaged about 25 percent overall. This group of firms included all the country's major industrial operations.

Industrial activities that the government would like to see furthered are provided with incentives in the form of feasibility studies, preferential tax and tariff treatment, and financial participation. The government does not appear to entertain a policy bias either against foreign private sector equity participation in industrial activities or against foreign private sector ownership of a given industrial enterprise.

As a control mechanism the government has maintained a licensing requirement for all but the smallest industrial enterprises. In order to get as much benefit as possible from large-scale production techniques, the government has limited the number of production units in any given large-scale industry. After enough units have been established to assure an element of competition, additional capacity has been obtained by enlarging existing units rather than by increasing the number of units. Information available in 1973 suggested that this restriction was to be relaxed.

In 1972 and 1973, legislation covering industrial development financing and industrial development incentives was revised to take account of the revised status of the Israeli-occupied Territory vis-à-vis Jordan and of the need for greater participation in industry by the private sector, both foreign and domestic. In 1972 the Industrial Development

Bank Law of 1965 was updated. Its objectives were defined as encouragement, incentive, and assistance to large- and small-scale industrial projects, employment, industrial estates, and the stock market. Its resources were rendered somewhat more flexible than previously, and its resources were defined to give the bank a preferred claim on the real and intangible property of its borrowers, including real estate.

In 1972 the Encouragement of Investment Law of 1967 was also updated to provide greater incentives to the private sector to invest in approved economic projects. These were projects with priority status in the sectors of industry, tourism, housing, and land reclamation that were expected to be incorporated in the Three Year Program. The projects were designed to provide an added annual gross value of not less than 20 percent of cost and to contribute to the balance of payments by way of export expansion, import substitution, or the attraction of Arab or foreign investment. Projects meeting the various criteria included in the law would be wholly or partially exempted from customs duties and other charges on imports. Income from such projects would be exempted from income and welfare taxes for specified periods. Transfers of interest, profits, and salaries of foreigners were granted privileged status. Exemptions and privileges accorded by the law were guaranteed protection against contrary provisions that might be included in subsequent legislation.

In 1972 the comprehensive Industrial Development Corporation Law was submitted to the National Assembly for passage in 1973. The objectives of this legislation were to improve and coordinate the government's own performance in industry and to bring a greater degree of coherence to the government's relationship with the industrial sector. The corporation was to achieve these objectives by becoming the government's operational agent in the industrial sphere. It would manage the government's own industrial projects (the management of some parts of which had been farmed out under management contracts); it would become the repository of the government's participation in other industrial projects; and it would locate areas where industrialization should be introduced, modernized, or expanded. In the pursuance of its duties the corporation was empowered to purchase the control of existing private industries, to establish new government-owned or mixed industries, and to sell to the private sector government-owned industries or government participation in privately owned industries. The corporation was also empowered to engage in the marketing of the products of any industrial project the government owned or controlled. It was additionally empowered to employ foreign personnel as might be required.

Mining and Quarrying

Mining and quarrying in the early 1970s apparently contributed some JD5 million to JD6 million to the GDP (at factor cost) and employed somewhat in excess of 3,000 workers. Of these, around 1,200 were employed by the Jordan Phosphate Mine Company.

The Jordan Phosphate Mine Company, which is 64 percent government owned, is the country's largest single industrial employer. It has mines and processing plants at Ar Rusayfah near Amman and at Al Hasa (see ch. 3). Proven reserves apparently total 270 million to 300 million tons, with the possibility that they may turn out to be very much larger.

Traditionally, phosphates were mostly shipped south by railroad, transshipped, trucked to Al Aqaba, and shipped from there via the Suez Canal to markets in Lebanon, Turkey, Yugoslavia, and Eastern Europe. Since the closure of the Suez Canal in 1967, exports to the Mediterranean area from Ar Rusayfah have been sent to Beirut for shipment to Turkey and Yugoslavia, and Al Aqaba has been used for exports to new markets in Pakistan, India, and East Asia. Closure of the borders with Iraq and Syria by those countries in 1971 cut off exports to the Mediterranean markets. Exports declined from a high of 1.2 million tons in 1968 to 640,000 tons in 1971 and 709,000 tons in 1972.

Modernization of the processing plants at the mines, as part of the Three Year Program, was expected to raise the company's capacity to a level of 3 million tons or better. It was hoped that with the reopening of the Syrian border phosphate exports might approach 1.5 million tons in 1973 and even higher levels in 1974 and 1975.

Apart from phosphates, Jordan had little in the way of known and assured mineral resources. Recent discoveries of kaolin have opened possibilities for enlarged production and exports of ceramics. Some likely deposits of copper ore have apparently been found in the Wadi al Arabah region, and the government hopes these will prove to be about 150 million tons of ore with a 1-percent pure copper content or better. There have also been some hopeful signs of manganese and of high-grade iron ore, but by 1973 none of the findings of metallic minerals had reached commercial proportions.

The same was true of petroleum. There was every reason to expect it should be in Jordan, but in late 1973 it had not been discovered. There had been a series of arrangements with various concessionaires that gave them considerable freedom of action. One agreement signed in 1972 with a Canadian concern was expected to extend for twenty-five years and to involve outlays by the company of up to 20 million Canadian dollars. The concession was subsequently revoked, however, and at mid-1973 a new concessionaire was being sought.

Meanwhile the country obtains its petroleum needs from the Trans-Arabian Pipeline Company (Tapline), which crosses Jordan on its way to Sidon, Lebanon. The crude petroleum is refined in the government's refinery near Az Zarqa, the capacity of which was raised from 7,000 barrels a day to 15,000 barrels a day in 1970. Certain aspects of the plant were scheduled for further expansion in 1973, and a new lubricants plant was under consideration.

Manufacturing

It is difficult in Jordan to distinguish between manufacturing, on the one hand, and handicrafts, artisanry, and certain service trades, on the other; one distinction is that handicrafts and artisanry tend to be carried on by small units. In the early 1970s it was estimated that of the nearly 6,000 manufacturing enterprises located in the East Bank, more than 5,000 averaged slightly fewer than two workers per enterprise. The next category, about 500 firms employing five to twenty-four workers each, averaged slightly fewer than nine workers per enterprise. The seventy-five largest firms, employing twenty-five or more workers each, averaged eighty-seven workers per firm and aggregated more than 30 percent of all workers employed in manufacturing and artisanry. Among these were included the phosphate company, a refinery, power plants, and companies producing cement, potash, pharmaceuticals, basic metal products, paper products, and tobacco products.

In aggregate employment terms food processing (presumably including beverages) was the leading branch of the manufacturing sector, and after it came the fabricating of metal products and the fabricating of wearing apparel. These were followed by the manufacture of cement, clay products, furniture and fixtures, and shoes. In terms of value in 1971 food processing (including beverages) was also the leading branch of manufacturing (see table 11).

Despite the difficulties that had intervened between 1967 and 1971, available mining and manufacturing data for that period suggest, on balance, a resumption of the rising production trends that preceded the war (see table 12). The decline in the output of phosphates, iron (reinforcing rods), cigarettes, and wet cell batteries reflects the closure of the Syrian border after the domestic disturbances of 1970 and 1971. The data for 1973 are expected to show an increase in production following the reopening of the border on December 1, 1972.

Under the Three Year Program the government earmarked some JD5.5 million of its funds for the development of five major projects in the manufacturing sector. The largest was a proposed plant to convert rejected low-grade phosphate ores to phosphoric acid; this was viewed as the first stage in the development of an expanded fertilizer project. Because the conversion project would cost JD30 million to JD40 million and would mainly be dependent on foreign financing, it was being reviewed in the context of changing international prices.

The same situation applied to a proposed expansion of the Arab Potash Company, which would obtain its raw materials from the high quality potash extractable from the Dead Sea brine. The expanded project would have a capacity of 1 million tons of high potassium content output for export and would cost JD30 million or more. The over-

Table 11. *Contribution of Mining and Manufacturing to the Gross Domestic Product in Jordan at Factor Cost, 1967-71*
(in millions of Jordanian dinars)*

Industry	1967	1968	1969	1970	1971
Mining and quarrying	2.70	3.14	3.28	2.45	2.70
Food manufacturing...........	2.82	2.70	2.86	2.81	2.85
Beverages	0.30	0.43	0.49	0.40	0.50
Tobacco	0.97	0.89	0.95	0.65	0.92
Textiles	1.10	0.93	0.82	0.80	0.87
Clothing and footwear	1.21	1.50	1.86	1.71	1.75
Wood and cork	0.03	0.06	0.08	0.07	0.07
Furniture and fixtures	1.20	1.11	1.34	1.30	1.41
Paper and paper products	0.14	0.11	0.12	0.11	0.13
Printing and publishing........	0.55	0.66	0.49	0.47	0.55
Leather and leather products ...	0.06	0.25	0.21	0.21	0.22
Rubber and rubber products....	0.05	0.05	0.08	0.07	0.08
Chemicals and chemical products	0.86	1.04	1.18	0.93	1.00
Petroleum refinery	2.05	2.36	2.45	1.80	1.95
Nonmetalic mineral products ...	1.47	2.70	3.16	2.89	2.90
Basic metal products	1.11	1.27	2.37	1.97	2.00
Nonelectrical machinery	0.01	0.01	0.02	0.02	0.02
Electrical machinery	0.16	0.19	0.32	0.20	0.22
Transport equipment	0.28	0.28	0.70	0.65	0.66
Miscellaneous................	0.43	0.37	0.34	0.26	0.20
TOTAL	17.50	20.05	23.12	19.77	21.00

*For value of the Jordanian dinar—see Glossary.

Source: Adapted from Jordan, Ministry of National Economy, *Investment Conditions and Opportunities in Jordan,* Amman, 1972, pp. 95-96.

supply of potash on world markets in the early 1970s made further pursuit of this project questionable under current conditions. On the other hand, the implementation of smaller projects for the production of ceramics, sheet glass, and paperboard was being actively promoted within the limits of available foreign financing.

As of mid-1973 only limited success had been achieved in the processing of domestic raw materials, such as the important tomato crop and local hides and skins. A major problem was the absence of an effective quality control of raw materials. As a result, the tanning and leather industries, for example, continued to rely to a large extent on imported raw materials.

Construction

The construction sector includes railway, highway, airport, and port construction and maintenance; the construction and maintenance of irrigation and power dams and associated distribution systems; and residential, commercial, and governmental (including educational and tourist) construction. To the extent that construction involves

Table 12. Production of Principal Industries in Jordan, 1967–71

Product	Unit	1967	1968	1969	1970	1971
Phosphate (dry)	thousand tons	917.8	1,161.9	1,087.3	938.9	640.0
Cement	do	289.2	375.6	480.4	377.6	418.9
Petroleum products	do	392.6	392.9	464.1	445.8	556.7
Tanning:						
Sole leather	tons	329.4	399.3	373.7	276.8	397.4
Upper leather	thousand square feet	1,671.0	1,678.0	1,678.0	1,302.0	1,888.0
Detergents	tons	1,300.0	1,300.0	1,312.0	1,709.0	2,592.0
Liquid batteries	thousand units	45.6	59.6	66.9	66.8	40.0
Cigarettes	tons	1,804.0	1,619.0	1,803.0	1,619.0	1,536.0
Spirits and alcoholic beverages	thousand gallons	505.0	578.0	579.0	571.0	633.0
Paper	tons	n.a.	2,063.0	2,741.0	2,692.0	2,109.0
Electricity	million kilowatt-hours	91.1	104.5	122.7	120.0	133.7
Iron	tons	n.a.	14,400.0	26,551.0	24,070.0	9,214.0
Textiles	thousand yards	443.0	486.0	512.0	478.0	748.0
Fodder	tons	19,941.0	12,463.0	21,533.0	25,603.0	34,204.0

n.a.—not available.

Source: Adapted from Jordan, Central Bank of Jordan, *Eighth Annual Report: 1971*, Amman, 1972, p. 12.

major infrastructure works, its timing tends to depend on foreign financing and to fluctuate with the availability of foreign financing for such major projects.

In 1966, the last full year before the 1967 war, construction contributed an estimated JD9.3 million, or 6.2 percent, to the GDP. Since then, and allowing for the special conditions that led to decreases in construction in 1967 and subsequent years, the annual contribution to the GDP has apparently averaged around 5 to 5.5 percent a year.

The Three Year Program calls for construction outlays by the government over the duration of the plan on the order of JD80 million. The largest item, totaling an estimated JD25 million, would be for transport, including road, rail, and air, and for the development of the port of Al Aqaba. The next largest allocation would be for irrigation (around JD14 million to JD15 million), followed closely by municipal and village affairs (around JD13 million), and at a considerable distance by communication, mining and manufacturing, and power (upwards of JD5 million each).

The Three Year Program foresees the private sector coming forward with construction outlays approaching the same magnitude as those of the government. The largest of the anticipated private sector outlays would be for housing (JD31 million), mining and manufacturing (JD20 million), electric power (JD8 million), and tourism (JD5 million).

Although nonmetallic minerals for construction purposes were available in generally satisfactory quantities and qualities, metallic materials and most lumber products had to be imported. A modern plywood factory, to be dependent on imported lumber, has been proposed as part of the development program for Al Aqaba.

Energy

With neither coal deposits nor any known deposits of petroleum, the East Bank's only indigenous sources of energy are two potential hydroelectric projects. The first is a small (five megawatts) site on the Az Zarqa River, to be developed as part of the irrigation project being carried out there. The other, with a hydroelectric potential of about forty-six megawatts, is located on the Yarmuk River, but its development was halted by the 1967 war.

In mid-1973 the main source of electricity production continued to be petroleum piped from the Tapline to the refinery at Az Zarqa and then delivered to other parts of the country by tank trucks. Electricity is generated for both public and private purposes, but its supply has not been planned or organized. Apart from two regional concession areas in the northwest, it is based on small, isolated units. In 1967 the Jordan Electricity Authority (JEA) was established with the expectation that initially it would bring coordination to bear on the existing power situation and that ultimately it would come to exercise autonomous control over power planning and implementation for the whole country.

Total installed capacity at the start of 1973 was about ninety megawatts. In the north public electricity was provided by two companies: the Jordan Electric Power Company (JEPCO) in the Amman-Az Zarqa area with about thirty-six megawatts of available capacity and the Irbid District Electricity Company (IDECO) in the Irbid area with less than five megawatts of capacity. Both companies are private, with monopoly privileges in their respective concession areas. In the south electricity is provided by isolated enterprises, the largest public one being that of the Al Aqaba Port Authority with a peak demand of three megawatts. The Jordan Phosphate Mine Company at Al Hasa provides its own electricity for that complex with a load of around five megawatts. Since 1971 the refinery at Az Zarqa has also provided its own requirements, which have been approximately five megawatts.

In addition to the public power production in the Amman area, there was private capacity aggregating about the same megawatts as JEPCO. The private capacity included the production of the Jordan Cement Company (fourteen megawatts) a few miles out of Amman and that of a number of smaller plants maintained for standby purposes. There were also some 200 pumping stations in the Jordan valley with a total capacity of around 1.5 megawatts.

By the end of 1973 JEPCO expected to add three six-megawatt diesel units to its Amman system, and by the end of 1974 IDECO expected to complete a new diesel station with three 2.8-megawatt units. Power is transmitted in both systems at thirty-three and 6.6 kilovolts and is distributed at 220/380 volts.

In May 1973 the IDA and the Kuwait Fund for Arab Economic Development each extended a long-term loan of US$10.2 million to the Jordanian government to meet the estimated foreign exchange cost of a new steam-electric power project. The project, which will be located at Az Zarqa, will have a capacity of seventy-eight megawatts, including a twelve-megawatt gas turbine; will cost a total of about US$25 million; and is scheduled to be completed in 1977. It will belong to JEA, which will supervise its construction and which is expected simultaneously to expand its existing distribution and transmission network as required by the new facilities.

The project will represent the first step in a shift from diesel to steam-electric generation and a step toward physical and administrative centralization and coordination of the national power supply. This will involve the main productive concentration at Az Zarqa rather than at Amman and in time will involve a power grid including Irbid and the Jordan valley. In the meantime the new project is expected to meet the country's chief power requirements up to 1977 or 1978.

SECTION IV. NATIONAL SECURITY

CHAPTER 13

NATIONAL DEFENSE AND INTERNAL SECURITY

The Jordanian armed forces in mid-1973 were estimated to have reached a total strength of nearly 70,000. The army, with about 65,000 men and five divisions, was by far the principal component. The air force of some 4,000 had doubled in size since 1971; although semiautonomous, it was under the commander in chief of the armed forces, who was also army commander, at General Headquarters in Amman. The naval element consisted of a coastal patrol force of some 250 officers and men at Al Aqaba and was part of the army.

During the Arab-Israeli War of 1967, the Jordanian air force was destroyed by the initial Israeli air attacks of June 5. During the next three days the army as a whole was severely defeated, and Israel occupied the territory west of the Jordan River seized and held by Jordan in the Arab-Israeli War of 1948 (see fig. 1). Personnel and equipment losses in the 1967 war were extensive, and the first concern of King Hussein I and his government after the cease-fire was the rebuilding and reequipping of the armed forces. This was accomplished rapidly through financial grants from oil-rich Arab states and the resumption in 1970 of major United States budgetary and military assistance. By 1973 the size, state of equipment, and capability of the Jordanian forces substantially exceeded those of June 1967. These conditions, however, were dependent upon the continuance of foreign aid.

Hussein is, constitutionally and in fact, the supreme commander of all forces and has always maintained a close personal connection with them. Jordan has sometimes been called a praetorian state: the continuance of the Hashemite monarchy is widely described by analysts as depending upon the continuing loyalty of the combat forces of the army. On many occasions these forces have been called upon to reestablish public order and as of late 1973 had never failed to do so. Their overall missions are internal security and national defense.

The most severe test of the army in its internal security role occurred in the 1970-71 civil war with the Palestinian (see Glossary) guerrillas—a confrontation that had been developing since the 1967 war. The guerrillas had almost succeeded in establishing a "state within a state" in Jordan and had defied the king and his government. In the civil war, over about nine months' time, the guerrillas were eliminated as an organized force within Jordan by the regular army.

To the Transjordanian (see Glossary) veterans of the old Arab Legion and the British era, many of whom were of tribal background, the Palestinian guerrillas had always been repugnant because of their methods and their hostility to the Hashemite throne (see ch. 5). After the civil war the Transjordanian elite reinforced their domination of the key command positions in the armed forces, and their domination continued in 1973. The professional and traditional loyalty of the majority of the armed forces has thus far precluded a revolutionary political-military overthrow of the kind carried out by some other Middle Eastern armies since World War II. Nevertheless, attempts have been made on a number of occasions; Hussein has escaped assassination many times.

In 1973, the national police, called the Public Security Force, numbered about 7,500. The police were subordinate to the Ministry of Interior, but they can be assimilated under the Ministry of Defense in war and operationally controlled by the royally appointed military governor general in periods of martial law. During the fifteen years before 1967, crimes of a nonpolitical nature showed some increase but no distinct trend. The new influx of indigent refugees in 1967 greatly increased the density of urban population, especially in Amman, and was accompanied by a corresponding increase in such crimes as larceny and narcotics offenses.

In 1973, as throughout the earlier history of the country, the principal threat to internal security was not from crime but from political and ideological causes. Partisan political party activity in Jordan was forbidden, and the remnant, clandestine, and closely watched Communist Party was not considered dangerous. Opposition to the Hashemite monarchy and its Transjordanian supporters, however, was by no means dead in a population composed of a majority of Palestinians inclined toward the doctrines and promises of radical Arab nationalism. Future problems of stability and security were believed by analysts likely to occur in this context (see ch. 9; ch. 2).

ARMED FORCES IN THE NATIONAL LIFE

Missions and Roles of the Armed Forces

The constitution, as amended, states that "the duties of the Army shall be restricted to the defense of the realm and its safety" and specifies that recruitment and organization of the army and the rights and duties of its members shall be defined by law. By interpretation the word *army*, and the legitimation attached to it, includes air and naval forces also. A separate but parallel specification, however, is made for police and gendarmerie forces. Provision is made for the declaration of a state of emergency by decision of the Council of Ministers promulgated by royal decree when required to "ensure the defense of the realm." In this situation ordinary laws are suspended, and the Defense Law comes into force. Under martial law, which is proclaimed in the same manner as the state of emergency, the king rules by decree.

The Jordanian armed forces, thus constitutionally established and legitimized, have the usual and primary mission of defending the country against armed attack. In particular, this mission is oriented against Israel, but it is not and has not been exclusively so—as shown by the requirement to defeat a Syrian invasion of September 1970 (see ch. 2). Jordanian forces also have the mission of maintaining internal security when the requirement exceeds police capabilities. This mission, in fact, preceded that of defense against attack from external sources, and the operational engagement of Jordanian army units has more often occurred in this role than against outside enemies.

The Jordanian civil war of September 1970 to July 1971 was, in a sense, an internal security matter in which the regular forces finally defeated and cleared Jordan of Palestinian guerrillas, or fedayeen. The continuance of the existing form of government, however, was at stake in this case, and the degree of external assistance and sponsorship received by the guerrillas gave this conflict characteristics of an external attack as well as an internal insurgency.

King Hussein as Supreme Commander

Constitutionally, the position of the king in relation to the armed forces is extremely clear. Under Article 32 "the king is the Supreme Commander of the Army, Naval and Air Forces." The words *supreme commander* have a similar connotation here to commander in chief as applied to the president of the United States. The Arabic expression translated as commander in chief is applied in Jordan to the commanding general of the Armed Forces General Command, the senior officer of the uniformed services. In further establishment of the royal powers and prerogatives, the constitution states that "the king declares war, concludes peace, and signs treaties."

Throughout, the great majority of officers and troops have remained disciplined and loyal to the king and his government. Prime ministers and cabinets have frequently changed, but Hussein, armed with extensive constitutional powers as king, has remained as the dominant focus of the country's leadership, not only symbolically but operationally. He is closely identified with the functioning of all branches of government but particularly with the armed forces and the development of their capability to perform their missions.

Impact on the National Life

Forces as large and expensive as those of Jordan are highly visible and influential in so small a country. Among the various social, economic, and political institutions affecting the national life, with the exception of the monarchy itself and possibly Islam, none has been more pervasive in its presence and power than the armed forces. This condition began with the formation of the first units early in the national life of the country and developed as the country developed. Soon after becoming king in 1953, Hussein remarked to the British commander of Jordanian forces, Lieutenant General Sir John Bagot Glubb, better known as Glubb Pasha, "Everywhere I go in Jordan I find the Arab Legion doing everything." Years later, after the Arab Legion had become expanded and highly organized, a foreign observer's remark intended as an exaggerated jest nevertheless epitomized the impression often gained by visitors: "Jordan is really an army with a country attached to it."

When the Amirate of Transjordan was formed after World War I, the small scattered police elements left over from Ottoman days were inadequate to maintain order and establish central government control (see ch. 2). The police were expanded, and a miniature army with balanced elements of infantry, cavalry, and artillery was created in 1920 and 1921. In 1923 the police, numbering about 300, and the military force of about 1,000 were combined under Arab Legion Headquarters. The force was originally called the Arab Army (Al Jaysh Al Arabi) as a perpetuation of the force led by the Hashemites in World War I against the Turks, and this title was officially retained in Arabic. In English, however, the name was, and remained until 1956, the Arab Legion. In common parlance it was simply *al jaysh* or, even among the Arabs, the legion.

Initially, public reaction to the forces was indifferent or hostile, and recruiting was difficult. As time passed, however, the new forces developed rapidly in organization, discipline, and training; tribal uprisings and raidings were suppressed, and crime diminished; civic assistance actions were often performed by military and police units; and the Arab Legion became a proud and respected regular, professional force noted not only for firmness and effectiveness but also for discipline and justice in dealing with the civil population.

Recruiting became easy, not the least inducement being the economic advantages of the pay scales in the enlisted grades. These were generous by comparison with the conscript scales of most other Middle Eastern armies. The legion was officered, trained, and paid for by Great Britain, but the troopers were all Arabs. British officers with the legion were mostly, like Glubb, detached from the British service and engaged as contract employees of the Transjordanian government; some, however, were attached, or seconded, from the British service. One of the legion's most effective units and possibly its best known was the camel-mounted Desert Patrol organized by Glubb in 1930 (see ch. 2).

From the start the primary mission of the Arab Legion was the establishment of the authority of the central government and the maintenance of internal security. Under the early agreements between Transjordan and Great Britain, defense of the borders against external attack was a British responsibility. To this end, a British Royal Air Force (RAF) squadron with an armored car unit attached was stationed in Jordan and drove out a Wahabi tribal invasion from Saudi Arabia in 1924. In 1926 Great Britain organized the Transjordan Frontier Force (TJFF) for the border defense role. This British-officered force of about 1,000 men, recruited throughout the Middle East, was part of the British Imperial Forces. The TJFF had supplementary police duties in Palestine as well as the border defense mission in Transjordan and was under the command of the British high commissioner for Palestine, rather than Amir Abdullah (later, King Abdullah Ibn al Hussein) of Transjordan. It was not part of the Arab Legion, although a confusion to this effect may be found in some references. After Transjordan became an independent kingdom, many TJFF personnel were gradually absorbed into the Arab Legion, and the TJFF itself was disestablished.

By 1938 the Arab Legion (including police) numbered no more than 1,200 men, and by 1942 only about 1,400. The Arab Legion had been expanded to 8,000 by the end of World War II but quickly declined in the postwar economy measures to 6,000 by the time the British gave up the mandate for Palestine on May 14, 1948. Of this number, about 4,500 were combat troops available for employment in Palestine, and these were promptly committed in the Arab-Israeli War of 1948 that then ensued. As another consequence of the British withdrawal, it became necessary for the Arab Legion for the first time to provide its own technical service support, these services having previously been provided by the British. Reserves of personnel, ammunition, and supplies were also lacking for, as Glubb has written, "In its twenty-eight years of life, it had never been contemplated that the Arab Legion would fight an independent war."

During the 1948 war the Arab Legion was quickly expanded to 10,000. Afterward, faced with the task of guarding the border with Israel, the strong possibility of renewed hostilities, and the general requirements of an independent nation, a major expansion was undertaken—still underwritten by British assistance and subsidies. The Jordanian forces, in substantial numbers and complexity of organization, are thus a post-World War II development.

By 1956 the legion's numbers were some 25,000. After Hussein's dismissal of Glubb on March 1, 1956, the name Arab Legion was changed to the Jordan Arab Army; the national police, numbering about 6,000, were then separated and placed under a director of public security subordinate to the minister of interior. As the population increased and the economy grew, assisted from 1957 onward by extensive United States and lesser British aid, the total forces grew in numbers and complexity (see table 13).

In a small country without major resources, where the original population of less than 500,000 was twice within twenty years suddenly expanded by hundreds of thousands of destitute refugees, the high national expenditures for the armed forces have always been a matter of concern to and periodic criticism by some civilian political leaders, heads of other ministries, and foreign aid donors. The pay of the troops, however, the employment that the military service provides, and the contracts and support services generated by the force establishment are a substantial factor in the economy.

Table 13. *Jordanian Military Force Levels and Expenditures, 1967–72*

Year	Approximate Force Strengths[1]				Military Expenditures[1]	
	Army	Navy	Air Force	Total	Amount[2]	Percent of GNP[3]
1967	48,000	250	1,750	50,000[4]	69.6	12.1
1968	53,000	250	1,750	55,000	98.5	17.8
1969	53,000	250	2,000	55,250	109.0	16.7
1970	58,000	250	2,000	60,250	92.6	14.9
1971	58,000	250	2,000	60,250	95.6	14.4
1972	65,000	250	4,000	69,250	112.0	13.8

[1] All data are estimated approximations; those for 1972 are the most tentative.
[2] In millions of current US$.
[3] Gross national product. Differing GNP data may be found, based upon different methods of calculation. The purpose here is to show the trend, based on one source.
[4] Immediately after the June 1967 war, effective strength was probably not more than 32,000 but was quickly restored.

Source: Adapted from Jordan, *Monthly Statistical Bulletin*, Amman, IX, No. 2, February 1973, tables 29 and 31; *Statistical Yearbook, 1971*, XXII, Amman, 1972, p. 185; and *The Military Balance: 1972–1973*, London, 1972, p. 32.

Public services by the forces have included such major items as bridge and road construction and disaster relief, organized campaigns against locust infestation, and innumerable lesser actions, such as well and cistern repair and desert rescue. The army has conducted literacy training for many recruits and has provided a four-year home and vocational school for selected boys who, with family consent, volunteer at age thirteen on condition of serving at least one enlistment after completion of the school. Technical skills learned in the military service have to some extent reverted to and benefited the society at large although, with a force largely composed of long-term professionals, this factor may be overrated, as J. C. Hurewitz has pointed out.

The ability and willingness of the Jordanian regular forces to maintain or restore public order whenever called upon to do so has been the mainstay of the Hashemite monarchy to such an extent that some experienced observers have estimated the overthrow of the government to be impossible without massive external intervention or subversion of a majority of the combat units of the Jordanian forces. Such subversion had not occurred by late 1973, although a number of subversive plots attempting to involve the army or air force had been unsuccessfully attempted.

After the war of 1948 the population of Jordan became predominantly Palestinian, a condition further augmented after the war of 1967. Between Transjordanians and Palestinians there were and continued to be in 1973 certain differences in cultural and political outlook (see ch. 5; ch. 9). Among Transjordanians themselves, those from the central and southern regions below Amman often were differentiated from those of the area north of Amman, who were oriented more to the town and village life of southern Syria and sometimes made common cause with the Palestinians.

In 1969 and early 1970 concessions to the Palestinian guerrillas at the height of their power resulted in the retirement, transfer, or downgrading of a number of Transjordanian officers who opposed the Palestinians' methods and politics. This attempt to reorient the senior military command ended when the guerrillas went down to defeat in the 1970–71 Jordanian civil war. The military forces, although they contain many men of Palestinian or northern Jordanian origin, did not split along East Bank-West Bank lines; and in 1973 most of the important command and senior staff positions continued to be held by those of Transjordanian and beduin background.

Manpower, Recruitment, and Mobilization

Because of changes and dislocations incident to the 1967 war with Israel and the subsequent 1970–71 civil war, the population has experienced much turbulence, and reliable statistics were not available. The population of the East Bank in 1973 was estimated by experienced analysts at about 1.84 million. This was a predominantly young population, an estimated 65 percent being below the age of twenty-four years. Of these, about 54 percent were males. The relatively large size of the Jordanian military establishment compared to this population made the armed forces a major vocational group in the national society, second only to agriculture. The good pay scales of the military services and an overall national unemployment rate of at least 8 percent (and probably considerably more) indicated that availability of manpower was not likely to become a problem in the mid-1970s (see ch. 3).

After an Israeli raid on a border village in 1966, the government promulgated an emergency conscription act under which physically fit males from eighteen to forty years of age would be drafted for training and service with regular units for periods of up to two years. The same law provided the loophole of a fixed fee payment in lieu of service, as well as other exemption provisions. This act was not intended to create a conscript army and, in fact, did not do so. Military units kept their original character; recruiting continued to be more than adequate; and in 1971 conscription ceased, and the law became inoperative. The forces again became fully voluntary and continued to be so in late 1973.

No organized reserve structure is maintained. Discharged veterans, if physically fit, continue to be subject to recall up to age forty and would be mobilized through the principal bases at Amman, Az Zarqa, and Al Mafraq. Main reliance, however, continued to be placed upon existing forces, both because of the rapidity of action and short distances involved in the likely forms of engagement and because of the ease of recruiting full-time regulars up to the limit of budget capabilities. In case of extended periods of engagement, a mobilization process would be implemented to expand support services and provide combat replacements.

The manpower available for military service compares favorably in health and literacy with that of the developing countries of the region. An adult literacy rate of 55 percent has been claimed by government sources; other analysts have given 45 percent—still a comparatively favorable figure. Standards of recruitment developed in the old Arab Legion continued to be maintained, including screening to exclude subversive activists and those of doubtful loyalty. The all-volunteer system made selection, on whatever bases, easier and more adaptable for government purposes than if the conscript system had been employed (see ch. 6).

The Jordanian soldier is typically tough and capable of endurance, especially under circumstances with which he is familiar. Transjordanians of beduin origin or tribal background have a particular affinity for and pride in military service. A shortage of well-qualified technicians continued to be the main personnel procurement problem, but it had become progressively less severe since the mid-1950s. Palestinians tended to be more numerous in the air force and in the technical services of the army, whereas Transjordanian Muslims predominated in the combat arms of infantry and armor.

Military Expenditures and Foreign Aid

The disasters of the 1967 war included, in addition to casualties and prisoner losses, other personnel losses caused by the confusion and disorganization of the short but intense period of combat. Equipment losses of major items, such as tanks, artillery, armored personnel carriers, and wheeled vehicles, were extensive. An intensive program of reorganization and reequipping was promptly begun, made possible by the grants from the Khartoum Agreement donors, several of the Arab shaykhdoms of the Persian Gulf, and the resumption of United States military aid and budget support (see ch. 2).

Military expenditures between 1967 and 1973 varied from about 45 percent to about 50 percent of total annual government outlays, although in 1968 military expenditures may have been as high as 56 percent. Of these amounts, personnel and personnel-related costs formed the largest single, recurring item, accounting for nearly 50 percent of military expenditures.

In relation to the country's size, resources, and state of development at any given time since the state was formed, the maintenance of armed forces as large as those of Jordan was possible only with extensive foreign aid. The record of foreign military aid may be described as having occurred in three periods: British, United States, and the post-1967 period of Arab and United States aid. This broad categorization of principal donors refers to military aid only; other forms of economic aid come from a wide range of Western and Arab sources (see ch. 11).

After the establishment of diplomatic relations between Jordan and the Soviet Union in 1963, offers of military aid were made by the Soviet Union on a number of occasions. Such offers, as of mid-1973, were never accepted by Jordan, although the government seriously considered accepting them at several intervals during the politically troubled years 1967 through 1970.

British aid and assistance were by direct, controlled subsidies in conformity with a special treaty relationship to Great Britain not terminated until March 1957 (see ch. 2). During the last years of the British subsidy, the annual payment for the Arab Legion was the equivalent of about US$33.6 million. This system had the advantage, for Jordanian planning and purchasing officers, of predictability because it involved a known and recurring commitment on the part of Great Britain. This subsidy, however, was carefully budgeted in advance of each fiscal year, and Jordanian civil and military officials had little or no control over disbursements and allocations thereafter.

After 1957 a British presence was retained; at Hussein's invitation, a reinforced British brigade and an RAF squadron contributed significantly to the preservation of political stability and internal security during mid-1958 and must be counted as military aid in the most direct form. British aid, no longer under a treaty arrangement, in time became relatively minor, taking the form of development loans and some continuing military sales.

From 1957 to 1967 the United States became the principal source not only of military aid but of economic aid and direct budgetary support. The first United States grant, in 1957, was of an emergency nature after the termination of the British subsidy and the failure of the short-lived Arab Solidarity Agreement. This grant brought into Jordan for the first time, although in modest numbers, major items of United States equipment, including tanks, artillery, and recoilless rifles. Jordan was also taken under the United States Military Assistance Program (MAP) for certain training assistance and spare parts supply.

From 1958 onward the United States provided direct budgetary assistance to Jordan, over and above the MAP and economic and developmental assistance, of about US$40 million annually. The financial grants, like the MAP grants, differed from the old arrangement with the British in two important ways. They were not made under long-term treaty commitments and hence were not firmly assured, but their disposition was almost entirely in Jordanian hands—there were few conditions, or strings, attached. The budget subsidy was not designated for military or any other specific purpose. It was noted, however, that in the years 1959 to 1963 the sum of the United States budget subsidy and MAP grants virtually equaled the annual Jordanian military budget. The United States budget subsidy was progressively reduced after 1963 and terminated in 1967, although a small residual was paid in 1968.

Jordan made a large-scale purchase of ground force equipment from the United States in 1965 and of air force equipment (F-104 aircraft and support gear) in early 1967. The economic situation of Jordan had by then improved considerably and, in addition, some funds for military purposes had become available through the United Arab Command formed in January 1964 (see ch. 2). The disasters of the war temporarily wiped out the economy and military logistics. Massive assistance was, however, soon forthcoming from the oil-rich Arab states at the Khartoum Conference of September 1967. Saudi Arabia, Kuwait, and Libya undertook to provide annual subsidies, paid quarterly, to both Jordan and the United Arab Republic (UAR). These schedules were adhered to, and Saudi Arabia and some of the shaykhdoms made additional grants. It was intended that these money grants be used to restore the Jordanian defense establishment and economy. During the years 1968, 1969, and 1970 Jordan received from Arab sources the equivalent of US$105.3 million, US$105.15 million, and US$92.6 million, respectively.

Libya and Kuwait, disapproving of Jordan's handling of the Palestinian guerrilla problem, cut off their subsidies in late 1970 and by mid-1973 had not resumed them. Cash grants from Arab sources in 1971, therefore, fell to US$49 million, representing mainly the Saudi Arabian subsidy. The United States then reentered with budgetary and MAP aid (economic development aid was never terminated). During calendar years 1971 and 1972 United States direct budgetary aid in effect made up the difference caused by the Libyan and Kuwaiti termination.

MAP shipments were resumed to Jordan in 1968 but under residual commitments or new purchases. A new program of military aid under MAP was laid out by the United States in 1971 on a three-year planning basis totaling about US$120 million. The last stage of this plan, somewhat modified in form, was scheduled for completion in United States fiscal year 1974. During the same year direct budget support was scheduled for continuance, at a somewhat higher level than in the two preceding years.

In addition to military aid and direct budget support, Jordan continued to be in receipt of technical assistance and development loans from a variety of sources, particularly the United States Agency for International Development (AID), Saudi Arabia, the Federal Republic of Germany (West Germany), and Great Britain. As these measures gradually benefit the economy and stability of the country, it is expected that they will also produce indirect benefits for the armed forces, for example, in the country's infrastructure and in the health and literacy of manpower.

ADMINISTRATION AND ORGANIZATION

The Ministry of Defense

The primary functions of the Ministry of Defense are administrative and logistical. The military budget is assembled from army and air force recommendations, usually made through a careful process of priority selections and compromises among items that are necessary and those that are desirable, within guidelines furnished by the king or prime minister as to resources likely to be available. Principal line items of the budget and the amounts allocated to them are often referred to individually as *votes*, a British usage to which Jordanian finance officers became accustomed by their training under British budget and accounting procedures.

After the military budget is completed, the ministry defends it as necessary within the cabinet and parliament. After it is approved, the ministry maintains an overall review of expenditures and administrative supervision of accounts. It also performs certain functions in contracting for construction, allocating real estate, and procuring indigenous supplies, such as rations, clothing, and building materials.

The ministry does not participate in the operational control and direction of the armed forces. Although in theory the commander in chief of the armed services answers to the minister of defense, in practice the minister has not usually issued operational or policy directives to the commanding general unless these have the sanction of the prime minister or, more important, the king.

At various times since 1948 the prime minister has chosen to hold the defense portfolio himself. Usually this has been a characteristic of strong prime ministers who, for reasons of the time, have desired to strengthen and simplify their relationship with the armed forces command. In mid-1973 Prime Minister Zaid Rifai was following this course.

The Commander in Chief and General Staff

General Headquarters of the Jordanian armed forces are located at Amman. This installation is sometimes referred to in the press as the Armed Forces General Command; however, the simpler designation of General Headquarters is an accurate translation of Qiadat al Am, the usual usage employed. The older expression Qiadat al Jaysh (Army Headquarters) is often heard, or simply Qiadat.

The commander in chief in 1973 continued to be Field Marshal Habis al Majali, cousin of the pro-Western Prime Minister Hazza al Majali who was assassinated in August 1960 (see ch. 2). Majali, the only Jordanian officer below the king ever to hold the rank of field marshal, was promoted to this grade in the mid-1960s. Except for an interval in the years 1967 to 1970, he has been commander in chief since May 1957. Majali was recalled to duty by Hussein in mid-September 1970 to direct the war then launched against the Palestinian guerrillas and to act again, as he had often done in the past, as military governor general under martial law. Majali's seniority, experience, and overall prestige have all been factors contributing to his virtual autonomy from the Ministry of Defense.

In late 1973 the chief of staff was Major General Sharif Zaid bin Shakir, who was appointed on March 4, 1972. He was distinguished for his performance as an armor commander in the 1967 war, against the Syrians in 1970, and against the guerrillas in 1970 and 1971. As chief of staff Shakir plays a key role in the daily conduct of all affairs at General Headquarters.

The Jordanian General Staff itself continued to be organized basically in the British form persisting from Arab Legion days, with some later modifications from Jordanian experience and United States influence. The principal staff officers after the chief of staff were the director of operations and the director of military intelligence, supported by a number of what in United States parlance would be called special staff sections, such as the adjutant general, quartermaster general, surgeon general, finance officer, signals officer, and others. In 1973 the new Directorate of General Intelligence was established under Major General Muhammad Rasul al Kilani. Although the director was presumed to be answerable to the commander in chief, the relationship of the directorate to the rest of the staff was not clearly known. The principal routine duties of the General Staff involve the administration and operations of the Jordan Arab Army. The commander of the semiautonomous Royal Jordanian Air Force is subordinate to the commander in chief and the chief of staff, derives some logistic support from the army, and carries out a degree of policy coordination with the principal officers of the General Headquarters staff. For regular operations and administration, however, the air force has its own staff.

The Army and Navy

The major formations organized within the overall army strength of about 65,000 consisted of five divisions: two armored, one mechanized, and two infantry. The combat force is thus distinctly armor heavy. These divisions are smaller than those of the United States Army, however, since they do not include as much organic logistic and administrative support. Higher echelon logistic functions are performed by central base facilities and separate units serving more than one division. The ratio of combat to support strength is therefore highly favorable.

The command channel from division headquarters is directly upward to General Headquarters and downward through the pyramid of subordinate divisional units. From top to bottom, the governing organizational form is triangular: the division normally has three brigades, each brigade has three battalions, and so on. In adopting the triangular principle, the Jordanians shifted to basic United States practice. Within specific units, however, traces of British usage remain. British forms of organization in particular endure strongly in administrative, maintenance, and other technical units.

In addition to divisional units, separate combat elements included a special forces brigade and at least twenty battalions of field artillery and air defense artillery from which fire support attachments or allocations are made to the divisions. The main base areas for the army are the complexes at Amman and Az Zarqa, and there are lesser installations in the area of Irbid-Al Mafraq and at Maan, Al Aqaba, and elsewhere.

Principal items of armored equipment are procured from the United States and the United Kingdom and include medium and heavy tanks, armored cars, Saracen armored personnel carriers, numerous self-propelled antiaircraft guns, and self-propelled howitzers. Artillery equipment includes 8-inch howitzers and 155-mm guns, numerous 155-mm and 105-mm howitzers, and a reserve of older British twenty-five-pounders. Infantry weapons were increasingly of United States types; for example, the M-16 rifle was being assimilated in 1973. Some protection against low-flying aircraft was provided in tactical units and for static point defense by the dual automatic 40-mm guns on M-42 mounts, but main reliance for air defense was placed upon the Royal Jordanian Air Force.

Equipment and weapons of British origin were not limited to obsolescent items left over from the late Glubb era. Quartermaster items of individual clothing and personal gear, for example, continued to be mainly of British origin or style. As a rough generalization, however, it was estimated that in 1973 the Jordanian army was equipped and organized about 70 percent along United States lines, the balance being British.

Junior officer procurement for the army and air force is provided by the Jordanian Military Academy located at Ar Rusayfah, near Az Zarqa. Applicants, carefully screened for loyalty, are expected to be secondary school graduates. The course is usually of two years' duration (although classes may be graduated early) and follows a program closer to that of the British Royal Military Academy than to that of the United States. Upon graduation, cadets are commissioned as second lieutenants. Direct commissioning from the enlisted ranks is also possible and not infrequently occurs.

Advanced officer training is provided by the Jordanian Staff College located southwest of Amman and by allocations at the United States Army Command and General Staff College at Fort Leavenworth, the British Army Staff College at Camberley, and lower level branch schools in both the United States and Great Britain. The course at the Jordanian Staff College is about one year in duration and is modeled closely after Camberley, although the influence of Fort Leavenworth had increased markedly by 1973.

The naval element of the Jordanian armed forces is a force of about 250 men, based at Al Aqaba. It has about ten small craft used for coast guard, customs, and harbor security functions. This small, stabilized force is, in fact, part of the army but is tabulated separately to account for the function.

The Air Force

During 1971 and 1972 the small Royal Jordanian Air Force underwent an expansion in strength of 100 percent—from about 2,000 to about 4,000—in order to handle new acquisitions. Increasingly, because of its growing capability and power potential since being rebuilt after the destruction of 1967, the air force was becoming an important factor in military calculations and Jordanian policy. Its missions are air defense, tactical bombardment, close support of ground units, and transport. Some degree of capability exists under each of these headings, but none was yet sufficiently developed to make full use of equipment on hand or on order. The air force commander in 1973 was Brigadier Abud Salim Hasan.

Air force headquarters are near Amman, at an area locally called Marka, where the main airstrip and some facilities are jointly used with the civil international airport. The second major, all-weather, all-capacity airfield is at Al Mafraq and is exclusively an air force installation. Other airfields of lesser size are at Maan, Al Aqaba, and elsewhere, including a number of emergency strips in the desert. The modern air force formations included one fighter-interceptor squadron, two fighter-bomber ground attack squadrons, one transport squadron, and one helicopter squadron. In addition, a number of older miscellaneous aircraft were on hand for training and as reserves. In 1973 a number of F-5E fighters were to be supplied by the United States, and observers anticipated that these high-performance, short-range aircraft would be formed into another interceptor squadron with a primary air defense role.

Air force personnel are carefully selected and contain a larger percentage of Palestinians than the armor and infantry units of the army. The air force has no separate academy but secures its new officers by transfer from the army or by direct commissioning. Pilot training is accomplished in the United States and Great Britain by arrangement with those countries, who also make available technical training for nonrated officer and noncommissioned officer positions.

Uniforms, Ranks, and Insignia

Army uniforms are of brown wool and, for both officers and enlisted men in field and garrison duty, are similar to those of the British army. Lighter weight khaki uniforms of desert tan are worn in summer. Senior officers and all who have graduated from the staff college wear red lapel patches and red hatbands. In the field, branch and service are indicated by the color of the beret: brown for infantry, black for armor, blue for artillery, and maroon for engineers. Except in combat or field exercises, both officers and enlisted men frequently wear the red-and-white-checkered Arab headcloth called the *kafiya*, held in place by a two-looped black cord called the *aigal*. The headcloth is also frequently called a *shmaag*.

Air force uniforms are of "RAF blue" and, in fact, are about the same as those of the RAF. The *kafiya* is almost never worn by air force personnel.

The rank structure of the Jordanian army is like that of the United States and British armies, although there are fewer enlisted grades. Insignia of rank are worn on shoulder straps by officers; chevrons are worn, with the point down, by enlisted men on upper right and left sleeves. On each shoulder, at the outer limit of the strap, all wear a gold-colored metallic arc spelling out in Arabic "The Arab Army." Many units have authorized shoulder patches, or flashes, but these are not worn during periods of combat or internal stress.

The system of officer insignia is based on combinations of seven-pointed stars (sometimes called pips), crowns, crossed sabers, and wreaths (see table 14). Although there are minor differences in design of these insignia, the system itself is the same as that of the British army. In the army the basic color of the metal of insignia and buttons is gold; in the air force, silver. Air force ranks and insignia are the same as those of the army; rated personnel wear wings and other rating badges somewhat similar in design to those of the British RAF.

Pay and Allowances and Awards

The pay and allowances of the Jordanian services, particularly in enlisted ranks, have always been among the highest in the Middle East and North Africa. Longevity pay and servant allowances (for lieutenant colonels and higher officers) are paid to officers, and cost-of-living allowances and family allowances are provided for enlisted

Table 14. Jordanian Military Ranks and Insignia, 1973

Rank	Arabic Designation	Insignia
Supreme Commander .	Al Malik (the king)....	Crossed sabers within a wreath and one crown
Field Marshal........	Mushir.............	Crossed sabers within a wreath
General	Fariq Awal	Crossed sabers, one star, and one crown
Lieutenant General ...	Fariq...............	Crossed sabers and one crown
Major General.......	Amir Liwa..........	Crossed sabers and one star
Brigadier*..........	Zaim*..............	Crown and three stars
Colonel.............	Aqid	Crown and two stars
Lieutenant Colonel....	Muqaddam	Crown and one star
Major	Raid	Crown
Captain	Rais................	Three stars
First Lieutenant......	Mulazim Awal	Two stars
Second Lieutenant....	Mulazim Thani.......	One star
Cadet	Murashah	White bar
Warrant Officer......	Wakil..............	Crown enveloped by wreath
Staff Sergeant	Naqib..............	Crown and three chevrons
Sergeant............	Naib...............	Three chevrons
Corporal............	Arif................	Two chevrons
Private First Class....	Jundi Awal	One chevron
Private.............	Jundi..............	...

*This rank is translated as brigadier, not brigadier general, but may be regarded as either depending upon whether British or United States customs, respectively, are being followed.

men to augment the base pay. Other types of allowances are also paid for special qualifications, for example, to men with flight ratings, doctors, and registered engineers.

The constitution gives the king power to confer decorations, honors, and awards, and a regularized system of decorations has long been in effect. Ribbons representing awarded medals and campaign services are worn over the left breast pocket of army, air force, and police uniforms in the same manner as in the United States armed services.

On September 18, 1972, a new medal, the Hashemite Order of Grace (Al Nahda Al Hashemi Al Naamat) was established by royal decree as the highest award for valor in "acts of heroism" by members of the military and police forces. Older awards, in descending order of precedence, are: the Order of Military Gallantry (Al Nahda Agdam), the Order of the Renaissance (Al Nahda Al Baath), and the Star of Jordan (Al Kawkab al Urdani). Service medals for World War II, Palestine, and subsequent campaigns and for twenty years' honorable service are also awarded.

Military Justice

The constitution provides for the establishment of military justice, and the Military Criminal Law promulgated on August 16, 1952, is applicable to all personnel subject to military authority. The commander in chief of the armed forces or his designate has authority to bring individuals subject to this law to trial by court-martial for violations of it. Sentences by the military tribunal are not effective unless signed by the commander in chief or chief of staff.

An individual found guilty under the Military Criminal Law may be sentenced to execution, life imprisonment, five years' confinement, dishonorable discharge, withholding of pay for three months, three months' imprisonment, loss of rank, loss of promotion, or reprimand. The king must approve all executions and is the source of all pardons.

When martial law or the defense law of emergencies is in effect, its provisions are enforced by the military governor general designated by the king. Members of the military services, however, remain subject to the normal provisions of the military justice system and to any special laws that may be passed for these contingencies.

THE PUBLIC SECURITY FORCE

The Public Security Force constitutes the national police of Jordan and is charged with the standard police functions of law enforcement and security. The police are directed and administered by the Ministry of Interior but are directly responsible to the military governor general during martial law periods. In time of war the police are taken under the Ministry of Defense and armed forces command.

In 1973 the Public Security Force totaled about 7,500 men, an increase of only about 1,500 since 1960. The force is commanded by the director general of public security, usually a major general detached from the army, who reports to the minister of interior. Headquarters, supply bases, and the police academy for officer cadets and policemen are at Amman. The countrywide system is divided into districts corresponding to the administrative divisions of the country. In each of these a chief of police is in command, and central forces, subdistricts, and smaller posts are allotted according to the size and population of the district.

Broadly, the police and their areas of attention may be classed as metropolitan (Amman), rural (small towns and villages), and desert (east of the Hejaz Railway). In Amman the police are fully motorized, have good communications, and are organized for traffic duty, public assistance, and crime prevention and investigation much on the European pattern. In the rural areas some police elements employ horses, and in the desert districts the old system of camel-mounted desert patrols survives—supplemented by improved communications and vehicles.

Police ranks and insignia are the same as those of the army, although the job titles are necessarily different. Pay scales are about the same as those of the army but differ somewhat in the specialized allowances. The basic metal color of police insignia is silver rather than gold. Police uniforms in metropolitan areas are dark blue in winter, light tan in summer. A distinctive sun helmet topped with a short metal spike is sometimes worn by city police. The rural police wear an olive drab uniform lighter in shade than the army brown but otherwise similar. The desert police retain their traditional Arab garb. The police are armed with some light automatic weapons, rifles, revolvers, and nightsticks and have available some special items of crowd and riot control equipment.

In the late 1950s the police did not usually fare as well as the army and air force in fiscal allocations, but in the early 1960s increased allocations and attention were given to the Public Security Force. Normal police functions have usually been effectively performed. Standards of education for entrance are higher than for the army, and a higher proportion of Palestinians is found in the police than in the army. Government policy has usually been to encourage a Palestinian character in the police forces (except in the desert).

The police have on the whole been respected by the population. Municipal police are not the principal means of control of the major riots that have periodically occurred in Jordan because their capability in such cases is quickly exceeded. Combat forces of the army and beduins of the desert police are employed in these extreme circumstances.

INTERNAL SECURITY

Crime, Prosecution, and Penal System

The rate of ordinary, or nonpolitical, crime before the 1967 war was considered low in relation to the total population. With the increase in urban density after that war, the new influx of indigent refugees, and the stresses of the 1970–71 civil war, crime showed some increase in a subdued but restless population that had become two-thirds Palestinian in composition and included many who did not prefer the Hashemite monarchy and rule by the Transjordanian civil and military elite.

Most of the reported crime occurs in Amman and other urban areas. Between 1968 and 1972 there did not appear to be a distinct trend in the amount of reported crime. Narcotics offenses and crimes against property, such as larceny and housebreaking, appeared to be increasing faster than crimes against the individual, such as murder, rape, and aggravated assault. The pervasive presence, almost omnipresence, of the military and police forces throughout the country was maintained principally to keep order and guard against political crimes of subversion and incitation but also had a dampening effect on ordinary crime, and this category in 1973 was still not regarded as high in view of prevailing circumstances.

Statistics of the number of crimes committed and the number of individuals convicted, however, are not highly reliable indicators of the absolute amount of crime. Crimes committed in remote areas are often not investigated or prosecuted because they are settled privately rather than reported to civil authorities. Should they be reported and prosecuted, the prison penalty is often minimized if the families involved agree on a financial settlement.

Procedures and prosecution, like the code of criminal law, resemble the French system. Persons suspected are taken to the nearest police station for interrogation. Usually a warrant is required for arrest; the warrant must be issued by a magistrate and must state specific charges. The police magistrate first informs the accused of the charges and questions him and any available witnesses to determine if there is a prima facie case against the accused, who has a right to counsel at this preliminary investigation. If the magistrate finds evidence of guilt, the case is transmitted for further investigation to the local public prosecutor. This official is attached to every magistrate's court and every court of first instance.

The public prosecutor, upon concluding that public action against the accused is necessary, institutes a trial by issuing an indictment (formal accusation) to the appropriate court. The magistrate courts handle only petty criminal offenses. The courts of first instance try minor criminal cases before one judge and major felonies before three judges; cases may be appealed to the higher courts (see ch. 8). Trials are open except in specified cases. The defendant is presumed innocent until proved guilty and has the right to counsel—to be provided free if he is unable to pay. He also has rights of cross-examination and is protected against self-incrimination. The role of the judge is paramount; there is no jury system.

The prison system is administered by the Prison Section of the Public Security Directorate. As of 1973 there were about twenty-five prisons and jails in use. All except the Amman Central Prison are under the management of the district police commanders and are sometimes referred to as police jails. In addition to the Amman prison, there are other area prisons. The smaller district jails are located in or near the district or subdistrict police headquarters. Generally, convicted offenders with more than a year to serve are transferred to Amman Central Prison, those with three months to one year are sent to area prisons, and those sentenced to three months or less are kept in the district jails. Prison staff personnel are part of the Public Security Force.

Subversion and Political Security

The chief threat to internal security has been from political crimes or acts involving attempts to overthrow or discredit the monarchy and its government. The methods used include the whole spectrum of subversion techniques, including conspiracy, assassination, incitation to riot, organized armed insurgency, general terrorism, and aircraft hijacking (see ch. 2; ch. 9). The main sources of these attempts have been individuals and groups associated with the broad motivations of radical Arab nationalism and its ideologies, the specific Palestinian cause against Israel, and specific hostilities toward the Hashemites and their principal supporters.

The Communist Party of Jordan has always been illegal and, like all political parties in 1973, continued to be outlawed. Its leaders were identified as Fuad Nasir (secretary general) and Fahmi Salifiti, and its total membership was estimated to be fewer than 500. The party attempts from time to time to publish a newspaper called *Al Jamahir*, but the organization is closely watched by security agencies. Otherwise it is ignored by the government and scorned by the Palestinian guerrillas, because it has never taken any decisive action. In late 1971 the party reportedly split between adherents of the Soviet Union and adherents to the People's Republic of China (PRC). It was not considered a great threat.

The most serious danger to the regime occurred in the Palestinian guerrilla insurgency of 1970 and 1971. After this effort was defeated, visible organizations of the Palestine Liberation Organization (PLO) such as Al Fatah were driven out of Jordan, but observers believed that clandestine agents remained and that the Palestinian hostility to the Hashemites had not abated. On August 24, 1973, an Al Fatah spokesman was quoted in the press as demanding the abolition of Hussein's monarchy.

Many assassinations and attempted ones have occurred since 1951 when King Abdullah was killed, including the murders of Prime Minister Hazza al Majali on August 29, 1960, and of Prime Minister Wasfi al Tal on November 28, 1971 (see ch. 9). Hussein by late 1973 had survived at least seven attempted assassinations. All past evidence has shown, however, that assassinations in themselves are politically ineffective and that the government system cannot be internally overthrown without subverting, manipulating, or neutralizing a major part of the combat forces. A number of attempts to subvert the military from within have been made, and after each known or suspected plot a purge of officers—not usually in large numbers—has occurred.

In early November 1972 an acting commander of a Jordanian armored unit was identified as possessing JD20,000 (for value of the Jordanian dinar—see Glossary) from Palestinian guerrilla sources to finance a coup d'etat. Some 300 army and civilian personnel were arrested. The discovery of the plot reportedly caused an air force officer who was involved in it to fly over the royal palace on November 6, 1972, and attempt to kill the king by rocket fire. The pilot failed and was killed in the crash of the aircraft immediately thereafter. Hussein was hospitalized from November 18 through 20, but on November 27, 1972, returned to his duties; in an interview with the Lebanese press he confirmed that an attempt had been made to overthrow his government.

At about the same time the Iraqi press stated that a new organization, the Jordanian Revolutionary People's Party, was being formed to oppose Hussein on behalf of the Jordanian and Palestinian people. Its effectiveness was not at once known, but it was added to the list of clandestine groups against which the security agencies of the military and police forces constantly operate. Another late addition was the Revolutionary Popular Front for the Liberation of Palestine, identified in November 1972 as a breakaway group from the Popular Front for the Liberation of Palestine (PFLP) of George Habbash (see ch. 9).

On February 15, 1973, the Ministry of Interior announced the arrest of an armed Palestinian group attempting to enter the country from Syria with the objectives of assassinating Hussein and overthrowing the government or creating as much disruption as possible. Their leader, Muhammad Daud Auda (also known as Abu Daud), then made a widely publicized confession on television and in the press describing in detail the inner workings and methods of Al Fatah. On September 18, 1973, Abu Daud and a large number of Palestinian fedayeen were granted amnesty by the king and were released from prison (see ch. 9).

The principal threat to internal security, then, was adjudged to be still from political-subversive sources, principally from the Palestinian guerrilla movements. The capability of the security agencies against this threat was seen by observers as extensive, however, and the effectiveness of the subversives had not been impressive.

BIBLIOGRAPHY

Section I. Social

Abdullah, King of Jordan. *Memoirs of King Abdullah of Transjordan.* London: Jonathan Cape, 1950.

Abu-Lughod, Ibrahim (ed.). *The Transformation of Palestine.* Evanston: Northwestern University Press, 1971.

Akhiemer, Yosef. "The Jordanization of Jordan," *Atlas,* XX, No. 6, June 1971, 30-31.

Albright, William F. *Archaeology of Palestine.* (Rev. ed.) Gloucester: Peter Smith, 1972.

―――. "Some Remarks on the Archaeological Chronology of Palestine Before About 1500 B.C." Pages 47-59 in Robert W. Ehrich (ed.), *Chronologies in Old World Archaeology.* Chicago: University of Chicago Press, 1965.

Antonious, Soraya. "The Samaritans," *Middle East Forum* [Beirut], XXXVII, No. 10, December 1961, 30-31.

Antonius, George. *The Arab Awakening: The Story of the Arab National Movement.* New York: Capricorn Books, 1965.

Antoun, Richard T. *Arab Village: A Social Structural Study of a Transjordanian Peasant Community.* Bloomington: Indiana University Press, 1972.

―――. "Conservatism and Change in the Village Community: A Jordanian Case Study," *Human Organization,* XXIV, No. 4, Spring 1965, 4-10.

―――. "On the Modesty of Women in Arab Muslim Villages: A Study in the Accommodation of Traditions," *American Anthropologist,* LXX, No. 4, August 1968, 671-697.

―――. "On the Significance of Names in an Arab Village," *Ethnology,* XXII, No. 7, 1968, 158-170.

―――. "The Social Significance of Ramadan in an Arab Village," *Muslim World,* LVIII, January-April 1968, 36-42, 95-104.

Aruri, Naseer H. *Jordan: A Study in Political Development (1921-1965).* The Hague: Martinus Nijhoff, 1972.

Awad, Mohamed. "Living Conditions of Nomadic, Semi-Nomadic, and Settled Tribal Groups." Pages 135-148 in Abdulla M. Lutfiyya and Charles W. Churchill (eds.), *Readings in Arab Middle Eastern Societies and Cultures.* The Hague: Mouton, 1970.

Azra'i, Musa al. "Improvement of Public Services in Villages and Towns," *al-Ra'i* [Amman], February 16, 1973. [Translated by U.S.

Department of Commerce, Office of Technical Services, Joint Publications Research Service (Washington). JPRS: 58,717, *Translations on Near East*, No. 935, 1973.]

"Badw." Pages 872–892 in H.A.R. Gibb, et al. (eds.), *The Encyclopedia of Islam*, I. London: Luzac, 1960.

Ben-Moshe, Eliezer. "Fall of Jordanian Monarchy Seen," *Zot Ha'aretz* [Jerusalem], June 11, 1971. [Translated by U.S. Department of Commerce, Office of Technical Services, Joint Publications Research Service (Washington). JPRS: 53,638, *Translations on Near East*, No. 629, 1971.]

Berger, Morroe. *The Arab World Today*. New York: Doubleday, 1962.

Bernadotte, Folke. *To Jerusalem*. London: Hodder and Stoughton, 1951.

Bromage, T. N. "Jordan," *Journal of the Royal Central Asian Society* [London], XLIX, 1962, 17–22.

Brown, Neville. "Palestinian Nationalism and the Jordanian State," *World Today* [London], XXVI, No. 9, September 1970, 370–378.

Bukhari, Najati al. *Education in Jordan*. Amman: Jordan, Ministry of Culture and Information, 1972.

Calverly, Edwin E. "The Fundamental Structure of Islam." Pages 62–79 in Benjamin Rivlin and Joseph S. Szyliowicz (eds.), *The Contemporary Middle East: Tradition and Innovation*. New York: Random House, 1965.

Chejne, Anwar G. *The Arabic Language: Its Role in History*. Minneapolis: University of Minnesota Press, 1969.

Chelhod, Joseph. "Problèmes d'ethnologie jordanienne: Nomadisme et sedentarisation," *Objets et Mondes* [Paris], VII, No. 2, Summer 1967, 85–102.

Churchill, Charles W. "An American Sociologist's View of Seven Arab Cities," *Mid-East Economic Papers* [Beirut , 1967, 13–39.

Clarke, J. I., and Fisher, W. B. (eds.). *Populations of the Middle East and North Africa: A Geographical Approach*. London: University of London Press, 1972.

Cleveland, Ray L. "A Classification for the Arabic Dialects of Jordan," *Bulletin of the American Schools of Oriental Research*, No. 171, October 1963, 56–63.

——. "Notes on an Arabic Dialect of Southern Palestine," *Bulletin of the American Schools of Oriental Research*, No. 185, February 1967, 43–57.

Cohen, Abner. *Arab Border Villages in Israel*. Manchester: Manchester University Press, 1965.

Cooley, John K. "Israelis Put Down Roots in Arab Soil," *Christian Science Monitor*, May 30, 1973, Section 2, 7.

Cressey, George B. *Crossroads: Land and Life in Southwest Asia*. (Lippincott Geography Series.) Philadelphia: Lippincott, 1960.

"Cultural Institute to Train Workers in Various Fields," *Al Dustur*,

Amman, November 23, 1972, 5. [Translated by U.S. Department of Commerce, Office of Technical Services, Joint Publications Research Service (Washington). JPRS: 58,379. *Translations on Near East,* No. 910, 1973, 48-51.]

Davis, John H. *The Evasive Peace.* London: John Murray, 1968.

Davison, Roderic H. *Turkey.* Englewood Cliffs: Prentice-Hall, 1968.

Dearden, Ann. *Jordan.* London: Robert Hale, 1958.

Dickson, Harold R. P. *The Arab of the Desert.* London: Allen and Unwin, 1949.

Dodd, Peter, and Barakat, Halim. *River Without Bridges: A Study of the Exodus of the 1967 Palestinian Arab Refugees.* (Monograph Series No. 10.) Beirut: Institute for Palestine Studies, 1969.

Dodge, Bayard. *Muslim Education in Medieval Times.* Washington: Middle East Institute, 1962.

Duncan, Alistair. *The Noble Sanctuary: Portrait of a Holy Place in Arab Jerusalem.* London: Longmans, 1972.

Editor and Publisher International Yearbook, 1973. London: Editor and Publisher, 1973.

Fisher, Sydney N. *The Middle East.* New York: Knopf, 1959.

Fisher, William B. *The Middle East: A Physical, Social and Regional Geography.* London: Methuen, 1971.

Fuller, Anne H. "The Peasant World of Time and Space." Pages 112-118 in Ailon Shiloh (ed.), *Peoples and Cultures of the Middle East.* New York: Random House, 1969.

———. "The World of Kin." Pages 526-534 in A. M. Lutfiyya and Charles W. Churchill (eds.), *Readings in Arab Middle Eastern Cultures and Societies.* The Hague: Mouton, 1970.

Gibb, H. A. R. *Mohammedanism.* New York: Oxford University Press, 1953.

Glubb, Sir John Bagot. *Britain and the Arabs.* London: Hodder and Stoughton, 1958.

———. *A Soldier with the Arabs.* New York: Harper, 1957.

———. *The Story of the Arab Legion.* London: Hodder and Stoughton, 1948.

———. *Syria, Lebanon, Jordan.* New York: Walker, 1967.

Great Britain. Naval Intelligence Division. *Palestine and Transjordan.* (World War II Handbook Series, BR 514.) London: Oxford University Press, 1943.

———. *Western Arabia and the Red Sea.* (World War II Handbook Series, BR 527.) London: Oxford University Press, 1946.

Guillaume, Alfred. *Islam.* Baltimore: Penguin Books, 1968.

Halpern, Ben. *The Idea of the Jewish State.* Cambridge: Harvard University Press, 1961.

Halpern, Manfred. *The Politics of Social Change in the Middle East and North Africa.* Princeton: Princeton University Press, 1965.

Hamady, Sania. *Temperament and Character of the Arabs.* New York:

Twayne, 1960.

Harkaby, Yehoshafat. *Arab Attitudes to Israel.* Jerusalem: Israel Universities Press, 1972.

Harris, George L., et al. *Jordan: Its People, Its Society, Its Culture.* New Haven: Human Relations Area Files, 1958.

Hasson, Khan Shib Syed Hamood. *Arab Marriage Customs.* Aden: Caxton Printing Works, 1934.

Hayes, Robert C. *Labor Law and Practice in the Hashemite Kingdom of Jordan.* (BLS Report No. 322.) Washington: U.S. Department of Labor, Bureau of Labor Statistics, 1967.

Hindle, P. "Aqaba: An Old Port Revived," *Geographical Journal* [London], CXXXII, March 1966, 64–67.

Hitti, Philip K. *History of Syria.* New York: Macmillan, 1951.

———. *History of the Arabs from the Earliest Times to the Present.* (5th ed.) New York: St. Martin's Press, 1953.

———. *Islam, A Way of Life.* Minneapolis: University of Minnesota Press, 1970.

———. *The Near East in History.* New York: Van Nostrand, 1961.

Hoagland, Jim. "Israeli Attitude Toward Arab Land Return Hardens," *Washington Post,* June 5, 1973, A14.

Hollis, Christopher, and Brownrigg, Ronald. *Holy Places: Jewish, Christian, and Muslim Monuments in the Holy Land.* London: Weidenfeld and Nicolson, 1969.

Hollman, Dieter. "Profile of Yasir Arafat Drawn," *Horizont* [East Berlin], April 1973, 14–15. [Translated by U.S. Department of Commerce, Office of Technical Services, Joint Publications Research Service (Washington). JPRS: 58,860, *Translations on Near East,* No. 944, April 26, 1973, 1–6.]

Holt, P. M.; Lambton, Ann K. S.; and Lewis, Bernard (eds.). *The Cambridge History of Islam,* I and II. Cambridge: Cambridge University Press, 1970.

Hourani, Albert. *Arabic Thought in The Liberal Age: 1798-1939.* New York: Oxford University Press, 1967.

Howard, Harry N. "Jordan in Turmoil," *Current History,* LXII, No. 365, January 1972, 14–19, 49.

Hurewitz, J. C. *Diplomacy in the Near and Middle East.* 2 vols. Princeton: Van Nostrand, 1956.

———. *Middle East Politics: The Military Dimension.* New York: Praeger, 1969.

International Bank for Reconstruction and Development. *The Economic Development of Jordan.* Baltimore: Johns Hopkins University Press, 1957.

International Labor Organization. *Labor Force Projections, 1965–1985.* Geneva: International Labor Office, 1971.

Johns, Richard. "The Creeping Settlement," *Financial Times* [London], May 16, 1973, 8.

Jones, L. W. "Rapid Population Growth in Baghdad and Amman," *Middle East Journal*, XXIII, No. 2, Spring 1969, 209-215.

Jordan. *Seven Year Program for Economic Development, 1964-1970.* Amman: Jordan Development Board, n.d.

Jordan. Department of Statistics. *Analysis of the Population Statistics of Jordan*, I. Amman: Department of Statistics Press, 1966.

Jordan. Ministry of Culture and Information. *The Hashemite Kingdom of Jordan.* Amman: Jordanian Press Foundation, 1973.

Karpat, Kemal H. (ed.) *Political and Social Thought in the Contemporary Middle East.* New York: Praeger, 1968.

Katbeh, Ziad. "Hygienische Verhältnisse in Jordanien" (Hygienic Conditions in Jordan). (Doctoral dissertation submitted to the Medical Faculty of the University of Saarland.) Saarbruck, Saarland, West Germany: Institute of Sanitation and Microbiology, University of Saarland, 1965.

Khalidi, Usama. "The UNRWA Diet," *Arab World*, XVI, No. 1, January 1970, 13-15.

Khouri, Fred J. *The Arab-Israeli Dilemma.* Syracuse. Syracuse University Press, 1968.

Kimche, David, and Bawly, Dan. *The Sandstorm.* New York: Stein and Day, 1968.

Klieman, Aaron S. *Foundations of British Policy in the Arab World.* Baltimore: Johns Hopkins University Press, 1970.

"Lack of Work Opportunities Cause of Manpower Migration," *Al-Dustur* [Amman], November 15, 1972. [Translated by U.S. Department of Commerce, Office of Technical Services, Joint Publications Research Service (Washington). JPRS: 58,379, *Translations on Near East*, No. 910, 1972.]

Laqueur, Walter Z. *The Road to Jerusalem: Origins of the Arab-Israeli Conflict, 1967.* New York: Macmillan, 1968.

Laqueur, Walter Z. (ed.) *The Israel-Arab Reader: A Documentary History of the Middle East Conflict.* New York: Bantam Books, 1971.

Lawrence, T. E. *Seven Pillars of Wisdom.* Garden City: Doubleday, 1935.

Lenczowski, George. *The Middle East in World Affairs.* Ithaca: Cornell University Press, 1956.

Lenczowski, George (ed.). *The Political Awakening in the Middle East.* Englewood Cliffs: Prentice-Hall, 1970.

Lengyel, Emil. *The Changing Middle East.* New York: John Day, 1960.

Lerner, Daniel. *The Passing of Traditional Society: Modernizing the Middle East.* Glencoe: Free Press, 1958.

Leslie, Jack. "When the Sky Is Not the Limit: An Imaginary Dialogue," *New Middle East* [London], No. 52-53, January-February 1973, 31-33.

Levy, Robert. *The Social Structure of Islam.* Cambridge: Cambridge

University Press, 1953.

Lewis, Bernard. *The Middle East and the West.* Bloomington: Indiana University Press, 1964.

Lias, Godfrey. *Glubb's Legion.* London: Evans Brothers, 1956.

Little, Selby F. "Fedayeen: Palestinian Commandos," *Military Review,* L, No. 11, November 1970, 49–55.

Little, Tom. "The Nature of the Palestinian Resistance Movement," *Asian Affairs* [London], LVII, (New Series I), Pt. 1, June 1970, 157–169.

Longrigg, Stephen H. *The Modern Middle East.* Chicago: Aldine, 1967.

Louvish, Misha. *The Challenge of Israel.* Jerusalem: Israel Universities Press, 1968.

Lutfiyya, Abdulla M. *Baytin, a Jordanian Village: A Study of Social Institutions and Social Change in a Folk Community.* The Hague: Mouton, 1966.

———. "Islam and Village Culture." Pages 44–60 in Abdulla M. Lutfiyya and Charles W. Churchill (eds.), *Readings in Arab Middle Eastern Societies and Cultures.* The Hague: Mouton, 1970.

MacLeish, Kenneth. "Reunited Jerusalem Faces Its Problems," *National Geographic,* CXXXIV, No. 6, December 1968, 835–871.

Mansfield, Peter. "Jordan." Page 449 in *Britannica Book of the Year: 1970.* Chicago: William Benton, 1970.

———. "Jordan." Pages 429–431 in *Britannica Book of the Year: 1971.* Chicago: William Benton, 1971.

———. "Jordan." Page 399 in *Britannica Book of the Year: 1972.* Chicago: William Benton, 1972.

———. "Jordan." Pages 393–394 in *Britannica Book of the Year: 1973.* Chicago: William Benton, 1973.

———. *Nasser's Egypt.* Baltimore: Penguin Books, 1969.

Mansfield, Peter (ed.). *The Middle East: A Political and Economic Survey.* (4th ed.) New York: Oxford University Press, 1973.

Marden, Louis. "The Other Side of Jordan," *National Geographic,* CXXVI, No. 6, December 1964, 790–825.

Mazur, Michael P. "Economic Development in Jordan." Chapter 5 in Charles A. Cooper and Sidney S. Alexander (eds.), *Economic Development and Population Growth in the Middle East.* New York: American Elsevier, 1972.

Mehdi, M. R. "Palestinian Renaissance: Rebirth of a Culture," *New Middle East* [London], No. 56, May 1973, 31–32.

Mes, Adam. *The Renaissance of Islam.* London: Luzac, 1937.

Middle East and North Africa, 1971–72. (18th ed.) London: Europa Publications, 1971.

Middle East and North Africa, 1972–73. (19th ed.) London: Europa Publications, 1972.

Muller, Siegfried H. *The World's Living Languages: Basic Facts of Their Structure, Kinship, Location and Number of Speakers.* New

York: Frederick Ungar, 1964.

Nakleh, Emile A. "The Anatomy of Violence: Theoretical Reflections on Palestinian Resistance," *Middle East Journal*, XXV, No. 2, Spring 1971, 180–200.

National Geographic Society. *Holy Land Today*. Washington: 1964.

Nolte, Richard H. "The Islamic Dimension." Pages 1–13 in *People, Power, and Political Systems: Prospects in the Middle East, A Summary Record of the 25th Anniversary Conference*. Washington: Middle East Institute, 1971.

————. *The Modern Middle East*. New York: Atherton, 1963.

Nuseibeh, Hazem Z. *The Ideas of Arab Nationalism*. Ithaca: Cornell University Press, 1956.

Nutting, Anthony. *No End of a Lesson*. New York: Potter, 1967.

O'Ballance, Edgar. *The Third Arab-Israeli War*. Hamden: Archon Books, 1972.

Patai, Raphael. "The Dynamics of Westernization in the Middle East," *Middle East Journal*, IX, No. 1, Winter 1955, 1–16.

————. *Golden River to Golden Road: Society, Culture, and Change in the Middle East*. (3d ed.). Philadelphia: University of Pennsylvania Press, 1969.

————. *The Kingdom of Jordan*. Princeton: Princeton University Press, 1958.

————. *On Culture Contact and Its Workings in Modern Palestine*. New York: American Anthropological Association, 1947.

Peake, Frederick G. *The Chief Tribes and Clans of Trans-Jordan*. Amman: n.pub., 1938.

Peake, Frederick G. (Peake Pasha). *A History of Jordan and Its Tribes*. Coral Gables: University of Miami Press, 1958.

Peretz, Don. "Israel's New Arab Dilemma," *Middle East Journal*, XX, No. 1, Winter 1968, 45–57.

Peristiany, John. *Honor and Shame*. Chicago: University of Chicago Press, 1966.

Phillips, Paul Grounds. *The Hashemite Kingdom of Jordan: Prolegomena to a Technical Assistance Program*. (Research Paper No. 3.) Chicago: University of Chicago Press, 1954.

Pitt-Rivers, Julian. *Introduction to Mediterranean Countrymen*. The Hague: Mouton, 1963.

Pleissman, M. *On the Significance of Barka*. Washington: Catholic University of America Press, 1920.

"The Poetry of Fadwa Touqan," *New Middle East* [London], No. 55, April 1973, 11–12.

Qubain, Fahim I. *Education and Science in the Arab World*. Baltimore: John Hopkins University Press, 1966.

Qutub, Ishaq Y. "The Impact of Industrialization on Social Mobility in Jordan," *Development and Change* [The Hague], I, No. 2, 1969, 29–49.

Qutub, Ishaq Y. "The Rise of the Middle Class," *Middle East Forum* [Bierut], XXXVII, No. 10, December 1961, 41-44.

————. "Social Trends in Arab Cities," *Middle East Forum* [Beirut], XL, No. 1, January 1964, 25-28.

"Radio Jordan Structure and Problems," *al'Ra'i* [Amman], March 1, 1973. [Translated by U.S. Department of Commerce, Office of Technical Services, Joint Publications Research Service (Washington). JPRS: 58,957, *Translations on Near East*, No. 951, May 8, 1973.]

Rafael, Gideon. "UN Resolution 242: A Common Denominator," *New Middle East* [London], No. 57, June 1973, 26-32.

Reddaway, John. "What Future for the Palestinians?," *Middle East International* [London], No. 24, June 1973, 9-12.

Reich, Bernard. *Crisis in the Middle East, 1967: Implications for U.S. Policy.* (Report RAC-R-39.) Washington: Research Analysis Corporation, February 1968.

Reisman, Michael. *The Art of the Possible.* Princeton: Princeton University Press, 1970.

Rogers, William. "A Lasting Peace in the Middle East: An American View." (State Department Press Release 371.) Washington: U.S. Department of State, December 9, 1969.

Rosenfeld, Henry. "Processes of Structural Change Within the Arab Village Extended Family," *American Anthropologist*, LX, No. 6, December 1958, 1127-1139.

Rubenstein, Amnon. "The Occupation: A Sort of Social Revolution," *New York Times Magazine*, May 6, 1973, 9ff.

Säve-Söderbergh, T. "The Hyksos Rule in Egypt," *Journal of Egyptian Archaeology* [London], XXXVII, 1951, 53-71.

Seton-Williams, M. V., and Hitchins, Verity Elizabeth. "Jordan." Pages 81-84 in *Encyclopaedia Britannica*, XIII. Chicago: William Benton, 1969.

Sharabi, Hisham. *Palestine Guerrillas: Their Credibility and Effectiveness.* (U.S. Department of State, Office of External Research, Foreign Affairs Research Paper No. 11049.) Washington: FAR, 1970.

Shiloh, Ailon. "The Interaction of the Middle Eastern and Western Systems of Medicine." Pages 372-386 in Ailon Shiloh (ed.), *Peoples and Cultures of the Middle East.* New York: Random House, 1969.

Shorter Encyclopedia of Islam. (Eds., H. A. R. Gibb and J. H. Kramers.) Ithaca: Cornell University Press, 1953.

Shwadran, Benjamin. *Jordan: A State of Tension.* New York: Council for Middle Eastern Affairs, 1959.

Smith, C. G. "Diversion of Jordan Waters," *World Today* [London], XXII, No. 11, November 1966, 491-498.

Snow, Peter. *Hussein: A Biography.* Washington: Robert B. Luce, 1972.

"Social Services and Labor Centers to Be Opened Throughout Kingdom," *Al-Dustur* [Amman], December 1, 1972. [Translated by U.S. Department of Commerce, Office of Technical Services, Joint Publications Research Service (Washington). JPRS: 58,379, *Translations on Near East*, No. 910, 1972.]

Sparrow, Gerald. *Modern Jordan*. London: Allen and Unwin, 1961.

Statistical Yearbook, 1971. New York: United Nations Statistical Office, 1972.

Statistical Yearbook, 1971, XXII. Amman: Jordan, Department of Statistics Press, 1972.

Stevens, Georgiana G. *Jordan River Partition*. Stanford: Hoover Institute on War, Revolution and Peace, 1965.

Swartz, Marc J., et al. *From Contest to Council: Political Anthropology*. Chicago: Aldine, 1966.

Sweet, Louise E. "Camel Raiding of North Arabian Bedouin: A Mechanism of Ecological Adaptation." Pages 264–289 in Louise E. Sweet (ed.), *Peoples and Cultures of the Middle East*, I: Depth and Diversity. Garden City: Natural History Press, 1970.

————. *Tell Toqaon: A Syrian Village*. Ann Arbor: University of Michigan Press, 1970.

"Swords for God: The Story of the Crusades," *Aramco World Magazine*, XXI, No. 3, May-June 1970, 1–40.

Taylor, Alan R., and Tetue, Richard N. (eds.) *Palestine: A Search for Truth*. Washington: Public Affairs Press, 1970.

Thomas, Lowell. *With Lawrence in Arabia*. Garden City: Garden City Publishing, 1924.

Tibawai, A. L. *Arab Education in Mandatory Palestine*. London: Luzac, 1957.

Tritton, A. D. *Materials on Muslim Education in the Middle Ages*. London: Luzac, 1957.

United Nations. *Compendium of Social Statistics, 1967*. New York: UN, 1968.

United Nations Economic and Social Office in Beirut. "Demographic Characteristics of Youth in Arab Countries in the Middle East: Present Situations and Growth Prospects 1970-1990." Pages 71-104 in *Studies on Selected Development Problems in Various Countries in the Middle East, 1970*. New York: UN, 1970.

————. "Nomadic Populations in Selected Countries in the Middle East and Related Issues of Sedentarization and Settlement." Pages 105-118 in *Studies on Selected Development Problems in Various Countries in the Middle East, 1970*, New York: UN, 1970.

————. "Settlement Patterns and Problems and Related Measures and Policies in Various Countries in the Middle East." Pages 31-40 in *Studies on Selected Development Problems in Various Countries in the Middle East*. New York: UN, 1967.

United Nations Report. "Changing Socio-economic Patterns in the Middle East." Pages 299-314 in Benjamin Rivlin and Joseph S. Szyliowicz (eds.), *The Contemporary Middle East: Tradition and Innovation*. New York: Random House, 1965.

United Nations. General Assembly. *Report of the Commissioner General of the United Nations Relief and Works Agency for Palestine Refugees in the Near East: Official Records, Twenty-seventh Session.* (Supplement No. 13, A/8713.) New York: UN, 1972.

U.S. Agency for International Development. Bureau of Program and Management Services. *Selected Economic Data for the Less Developed Countries.* Washington: AID, 1973.

U.S. Agency for International Development. Bureau for Program and Policy Coordination. Office of Statistics and Reports. *Near East and South Asia: Economic Growth Trends.* Washington: AID, May 1972.

U.S. Agency for International Development. Bureau for Technical Assistance. Office of Population. *Population Program Assistance.* Washington: AID, December 1971.

U.S. Army. Office of the Surgeon General. Medical Information and Intelligence Agency. *Medical and Sanitary Survey on the Hashemite Kingdom of Jordan.* Washington: July 21, 1958 (mimeo.).

U.S. Department of Labor. Bureau of Labor Statistics. *Labor Law and Practice in the Hashimite Kingdom of Jordan.* (BLS Report, No. 322.) Washington: GPO, 1967.

U.S. Department of State. *Jordan: Post Report, July 1972.* Washington: 1972.

U.S. Department of State. Bureau of Intelligence and Research. Office of the Geographer. *Iraq-Jordan Boundary.* (International Boundary Study, No. 98.) Washington. Department of State, April 15, 1970.

———. *Jordan-Saudi Arabia Boundary.* (International Boundary Study, No. 60.) Washington: Department of State, December 30, 1965.

———. *Jordan-Syria Boundary.* (International Boundary Study, No. 94.) Washington: Department of State, December 30, 1969.

U.S. United States Information Agency. *Jordan: A Communications Factbook.* Washington: USIA, 1964.

Uzayzi, R. Z., and Chelhod, J. "L'amour et le mariage dans le désert," *Objets et Mondes* [Paris], IX, No. 3, 1969, 269–278.

Vance, Vick, and Lauer, Pierre. *Hussein of Jordan: My "War" with Israel* (Trans., June P. Wilson and Walter B. Michaels.) New York: William Morrow, 1969.

Van Nieuwenhuijze, C. A. O. "The Near Eastern Village: A Profile." Pages 314–324 in Benjamin Rivlin and Joseph S. Szyliowicz (eds.), *The Contemporary Middle East: Tradition and Innovation.* New York: Random House, 1965.

———. *Social Stratification and the Middle East.* Leyden: E. J. Brill, 1965.

———. *Sociology of the Middle East. A Stocktaking and Interpretation.* (Social, Economic, and Political Studies of the Middle East,

I.) Leiden: E. J. Brill, 1971.

Vatikiotis, P. J. *Politics and the Military in Jordan: A Study of the Arab Legion, 1921-1957.* New York: Praeger, 1967.

Vereté, Mayir. "The Balfour Declaration and Its Makers," *Middle Eastern Studies* [London], VI, No. 1, January 1970, 48-76.

Vester, Bertha Spafford. "Jerusalem, My Home," *National Geographic*, CXXVI, No. 6, December 1964, 831.

————. *Our Jerusalem.* Garden City: Doubleday, 1950.

————. *Supplement to 'Our Jerusalem.'* Jerusalem: Commercial Press, 1954.

von Grunebaum, C. E. "Ramadan." Pages 224-234 in Abdulla M. Lutfiyya and Charles W. Churchill (eds.), *Readings in Arab Middle Eastern Societies and Cultures.* The Hague: Mouton, 1970.

Vouras, Paul P. "Jordan," *Focus*, XVII, No. 6, February 1967, 6.

Wagner, Bernard. *Housing in Jordan.* Amman: n.pub., 1965.

Walter Reed Army Institute of Research. Division of Preventive Medicine. *Jordan (The Hashemite Kingdom of Jordan).* (Health Data Publication, No. 39.) Washington: 1967 (mimeo.).

Wander, H. *Bevölkerungsprobleme in Wirtschaftsaufbau kleiner Lander: das Beispiel Jordanien.* Tübingen, West Germany: J. C. B. Mohr, 1969.

Watt, W. Montgomery. *Muhammed: Prophet and Statesman.* London: Oxford University Press, 1961.

Weightman, George H. "The Circassians," *Middle East Forum* [Beirut], XXXVII, No. 10, December 1961, 26-30.

Wilson, Evan M. "Role of Jerusalem in a Possible Arab Entity." Pages 58-77 in *A Palestine Entity.* (Special Study No. 1.) Washington: Middle East Institute, 1970.

Wolf, Eric. *Peasants.* New York: Holt, Rinehart and Winston, 1966.

Wolf, John B. "Black September: Militant Palestinianism," *Current History*, LXIV, No. 377, January 1973, 5-8, 37.

————. "The Palestinian Resistance Movement," *Current History*, LX, No. 353, January 1971, 26-31, 49-50.

World Christian Handbook, 1968. (Eds., H. Wakelin Coxill, Kenneth Grubb, and Kathleen A. Knapp.) Nashville: Abingdon, 1967.

World Health Organization. *Second Quarterly Report for 1967.* Geneva: WHO, 1967.

————. *Supplement to the Third Report on the World Health Situation, 1965-1966: Part I.* Geneva: WHO, 1968.

World Health Organization. Regional Office for the Eastern Mediterranean. *Annual Report of the Director, 1969-70.* Alexandria, UAR: WHO, 1971.

————. *Annual Report of the Director, 1971-72.* Alexandria, UAR: WHO, 1972.

————. *Annual Report of the Director to the Sixteenth Session of the Regional Committee, 1965-1966.* Geneva: WHO, 1967.

World of Learning, 1971–72. (22d ed.) London: Europa Publications, 1972.

World of Learning, 1972–73, II. (23d ed.) London: Europa Publications, 1972.

The World Survey of Education, V. Paris: United Nations Educational, Scientific and Cultural Organization, 1971.

Wright, Edwin M. "Philosophies of Education in the Middle East," *Viewpoints,* LV, No. 6, July 1966, 8–10.

Wright, G. Ernest (ed.). *The Bible and the Ancient Near East.* Garden City: Doubleday, 1965.

Yacoub, Salah M. "'Bodros'—A Jordanian Front-Line Village Community: A Case in Social Change," *Cornell Journal of Social Relations,* II, No. 1, Spring 1967, 19–36.

Yost, Charles W. "How It Began," *Foreign Affairs,* XLVI, No. 2, January 1968, 304–320.

Zeine, Zeine. *Arab-Turkish Relations and the Emergence of Arab Nationalism.* Beirut: Khayyats, 1966.

(Various issues of the following periodicals were also used in the preparation of this section: *Arab Report and Record* [London], 1969–1973; *Middle East Economic Digest* [London], 1973; *New York Times,* 1973; *Quarterly Economic Review* [London], 1970–1973; and *Washington Post,* 1973.)

Section II. Political

Abboushi, W. F. *Political Systems of the Middle East in the Twentieth Century.* New York: Dodd, Mead, 1970.

Abdullah, King of Jordan. *My Memoirs Completed.* (Translated from the Arabic by Harold W. Glidden.) Washington: American Council of Learned Societies, 1954.

Abidi, Aqil Hyder. *Jordan: A Political Study, 1948–1957.* New York: Asia Publishing House, 1965.

"Agreement for the Determination of Boundaries Between the Hashemite Kingdom of Jordan and the Kingdom of Saudi Arabia," *Middle East Journal,* XX, No. 3, Summer 1968, 346–348.

Akhiemer, Yosef. "The Jordanization of Jordan," *Atlas,* XX, No. 6, June 1971, 30–31.

Al-Marayati, Abid A. *Middle Eastern Constitutions and Electoral Laws.* New York: Praeger, 1968.

Al-Marayati, Abid A., et al. *The Middle East: Its Governments and Politics.* Belmont, California. Duxbury, 1972.

Almond, Gabriel A., and Coleman, James. *The Politics of Developing Areas.* Princeton: Princeton University Press, 1964.

Antonius, George. *The Arab Awakening: The Story of the Arab National Movement.* New York: Capricorn Books, 1965.

Antoun, Richard T. "Conservatism and Change in the Village Community: A Jordanian Case Study," *Human Organization,* XXIV, No. 4, 1965, 4–10.

Aruri, Naseer H. *Jordan: A Study in Political Development (1921–1965).* The Hague: Martinus Nijhoff, 1972.

Badeau, John S. *The American Approach to the Arab World.* New York: Harper and Row, 1968.

Bailey, Clinton. "Cabinet Formation in Jordan," *New Outlook* [Tel Aviv], XIII, No. 8, November 1970, 11–23.

Bayne, E. A. *The Arab-Israeli War of 1967.* (American University Field Staff Report Service, Southwest Asia Series, XVI, No. 4, July 1967.) New York: AUFS, 1967.

Becker, A. S., and Horelick, A. L. *Soviet Policy in the Middle East.* (Report R–504–FF.) Santa Monica: Rand Corporation, 1970.

Berger, Morroe. *The Middle Class in the Arab World.* Princeton: Princeton University Press, 1957.

Berque, Jacques. *The Arabs: Their History and Future.* New York: Praeger, 1964.

Binder, Leonard. *The Ideological Revolution in the Middle East.*

New York: John Wiley, 1964.

Brown, Neville. "After the Showdown: Jordan Is on the Move," *New Middle East* [London], No. 48, September 1972, 20-24.

———. "Jordanian Civil War," *Military Review,* LI, No. 9, September 1971, 38-48.

———. "Jordan's Precarious Truce—How Long Can It Last?," *New Middle East* [London], No. 21, June 1970, 9-13.

———. "Palestinian Nationalism and the Jordanian State," *World Today* [London], XXVI, No. 9, September 1970, 370-378.

Campbell, John C. *Defense of the Middle East.* (Rev. ed.) New York: Praeger, 1960.

Cremeans, Charles D. *The Arabs and the World.* New York: Praeger, 1964.

Davison, W. Phillips. *International Political Communication.* New York: Praeger, 1965.

Dearden, Ann. *Jordan.* London: Robert Hale, 1958.

Evron, Yair. *The Middle East: Nations, Superpowers, and Wars.* New York: Praeger, 1973.

Gibb, H. A. R., and Bowen, Harold. *Islamic Society and the West,* I. London: Oxford University Press, 1951.

Glubb, Sir John Bagot. *Britain and the Arabs.* London: Hodder and Stoughton, 1958.

———. *Syria, Lebanon, Jordan.* New York: Walker, 1967.

Halpern, Manfred. *The Politics of Social Change in the Middle East and North Africa.* Princeton: Princeton University Press, 1965.

———. "Middle Eastern Armies and the New Middle Class." Chapter 7 in John J. Johnson (ed.), *The Role of the Military in Underdeveloped Countries.* Princeton: Princeton University Press, 1962.

Hammond, Paul Y., and Alexander, Sidney S. (eds.) *Political Dynamics in the Middle East.* New York: American Elsevier, 1972.

Harkaby, Yehoshafat. *Arab Attitudes to Israel.* Jerusalem: Israel Universities Press, 1972.

Harris, George L., et al. *Jordan: Its People, Its Society, Its Culture.* New Haven: Human Relations Area Files, 1958.

Howard, Harry N. "Jordan in Turmoil," *Current History,* LXII, No. 365, January 1972, 14-19, 49.

———. "Nationalism in the Middle East," *Orbis,* X, No. 4, 1967, 1200-1213.

Howard, Norman F. "Jordan: The Commando State," *Current History,* LVIII, No. 31, January 1970, 16-20, 49.

Huizinga, J. H. "Can Hussein Survive," *Reporter,* XXXVII, No. 3, September 7, 1967, 34-38.

Hurewitz, J. C. *Diplomacy in the Near and Middle East.* 2 vols. Princeton: Van Nostrand, 1956.

———. *Middle East Politics: The Military Dimension.* New York: Praeger, 1969.

Hurewitz, J. C. (ed.) *Soviet-American Rivalry in the Middle East.* New York: Praeger, 1969.

Hussein, King of Jordan. *Uneasy Lies the Head.* New York: Bernard Geis Associates, 1962.

Ismael, Tareq Y. *Governments and Politics of the Contemporary Middle East.* Homewood, Illinois: Dorsey Press, 1970.

Johnston, Charles. *The Brink of Jordan.* London: Hamish Hamilton, 1972.

Jordan. Ministry of Culture and Information. *The Hashemite Kingdom of Jordan.* Amman: Jordanian Press Foundation, 1973.

Joshua, Wynfred. *Soviet Penetration Into the Middle East.* (Rev ed.) New York: National Strategy Information Center, 1971.

Kerr, Malcolm. *The Arab Cold War, 1958-1967: A Study of Ideology in Politics.* (2d ed.) London: Oxford University Press, 1967.

Khadduri, Majid, and Liebesney, Herbert J. *Law in the Middle East.* Washington: Middle East Institute, 1955.

Khalil, Muhammad. *The Arab States and the Arab League,* I. Beirut: Khayats, 1962.

Khouri, Fred J. *The Arab-Israeli Dilemma.* Syracuse: Syracuse University Press, 1968.

"King Husain on Search for Peace," *Arab Report and Record* [London], No. 3, February 1-14, 1973, 74-76.

"King Husain's 'Secret Circular,'" *Arab Report and Record* [London], No. 10, May 16-31, 1973, 228.

Kirk, George E. *Contemporary Arab Politics.* New York: Praeger, 1961.

Laqueur, Walter Z. *The Middle East in Transition.* New York: Praeger, 1958.

———. *The Struggle for the Middle East.* New York: Macmillan, 1969.

Laqueur, Walter Z. (ed.) *The Israel-Arab Reader: A Documentary History of the Middle East Conflict.* New York: Bantam Books, 1971.

Law, John. "Jordan: A Nation Cracking Apart," *U.S. News & World Report,* LXIX, September 1970, 20-21.

———. "Report from the Scene," *U.S. News & World Report,* LXXIII, August 14, 1972, 47-49.

Lenczowski, George. *The Middle East in World Affairs.* (3d ed.) Ithaca: Cornell University Press, 1962.

———. *Soviet Advances in the Middle East.* Washington: American Enterprise Institute for Public Policy Research, 1972.

Lenczowski, George (ed.). *The Political Awakening in the Middle East.* Englewood Cliffs: Prentice-Hall, 1970.

Longrigg, Stephen H. *The Middle East: A Social Geography.* Chicago: Aldine, 1963.

Lutfiyya, Abdulla M. *Baytin, a Jordanian Village: A Study of Social Institutions and Social Change in a Folk Community.* The Hague: Mouton, 1966.

MacDonald, Robert W. *The League of Arab States.* Princeton:

Princeton University Press, 1965.

Mansfield, Peter. *Nasser's Egypt.* Baltimore: Penguin Books, 1969.

Mansfield, Peter (ed.). *The Middle East: A Political and Economic Survey.* (4th ed.) New York: Oxford University Press, 1973.

Marlowe, John. *Arab Nationalism and British Imperialism: A Study in Power Politics.* New York: Praeger, 1961.

Middle East and North Africa, 1972-73. (19th ed.) London: Europa Publications, 1972.

Mogannam, E. T. "Developments in the Legal System of Jordan," *Middle East Journal,* VI, No. 2, Spring 1952, 194-206.

O'Ballance, Edgar. *The Third Arab-Israeli War.* Hamden: Archon Books, 1972.

Patai, Raphael. *The Kingdom of Jordan.* Princeton: Princeton University Press, 1958.

Patai, Raphael, et al. *Jordan.* New Haven: Human Relations Area Files, 1957.

Pryce-Jones, David. *The Face of Defeat: Palestinian Refugees and Guerrillas.* New York: Holt, Rinehart and Winston, 1972.

Quandt, William B. *Palestinian Nationalism: Its Political and Military Dimensions.* (Report R-782-ISA.) Santa Monica: Rand Corporation, November 1971.

Rafael, Gideon. "UN Resolution 242: A Common Denominator," *New Middle East* [London], No. 57, June 1973, 26-32.

"Reflections on the Quarter, the Middle East: Tense and Volatile," *Orbis,* X, No. 4, 1967, 997-1002.

Rejwan, Nissim. "Jordan: The Accidental Country," *Midstream,* XVI, No. 10, December 1970, 12-22.

Richmond, Sir John. "After the Husain Plan," *New Middle East* [London], LVIII, No. 4, July 1972, 34-37.

Seligman, Lester G. "Elite Recruitment and Political Development." Chapter 4 in J. L. Finkle and R. W. Gable (eds.), *Political Development and Social Change.* New York: John Wiley, 1966.

Sharabi, H. B. *Government and Politics of the Middle East in the Twentieth Century.* Princeton: Van Nostrand, 1962.

———. *Nationalism and Revolution in the Arab World.* Princeton: Van Nostrand, 1966.

Shwadran, Benjamin. *Jordan: A State of Tension.* New York: Council for Middle Eastern Affairs, 1959.

Snow, Peter. *Hussein: A Biography.* Washington: Robert B. Luce, 1972.

Sparrow, Gerald. *Modern Jordan.* London: Allen and Unwin, 1961.

Stravrianos, Leften S. *Middle East: A Culture Area in Perspective.* Boston: Allyn and Bacon, 1966.

Thornburg, Max W. *People and Policy in the Middle East.* New York: W. W. Norton, 1964.

U.S. Department of State. *Background Notes—Jordan.* Washington: GPO, 1972.

———. *The Washington Summit: General Secretary Brezhnev's Visit to the United States, June 18–25, 1973.* Washington: 1973.

"US Vetoes Security Council Resolution," *Arab Report and Record* [London], No. 14, July 16–31, 1973, 332.

Vatikiotis, P. J. *Politics and the Military in Jordan: A Study of the Arab Legion, 1921–1957.* New York: Praeger, 1967.

Wolf, John B. "Black September: Militant Palestinianism," *Current History*, LXIV, No. 377, January 1973, 5–8, 37.

———. "The Palestinian Resistance Movement," *Current History*, LX, No. 353, January 1971, 26–31, 49–50.

Yaari, Ehud. "Fedayeen at the Crossroads: Moment of Truth for Arafat," *New Middle East* [London], No. 57, June 1973, 4–6.

(Various issues of the following periodicals were also used in the preparation of this section: *Arab Report and Record* [London], 1970–1973; *Foreign Broadcast Information Service* [Washington], 1971–1973; *Keesing's Contemporary Archives* [London], Vol. XVI, 1969–Vol. XX, 1973; *Middle East Economic Digest* [London], 1973; *New York Times*, 1973; *Quarterly Economic Review* [London], 1973; and *Washington Post*, 1973.)

Section III. Economic

Abidi, Aqil Hyder. *Jordan: A Political Study, 1948–1957.* New York: Asia Publishing House, 1965.

Agricultural Statistical Yearbook and Agricultural Sample Survey, 1971. Amman: Jordan, Department of Statistics Press, 1972.

American Friends of the Middle East. *The Jordan Water Problem.* Washington: 1964.

Arab Bank Limited. *Annual Report of the Board of Directors, 1971.* Amman: 1972.

Asfour, Edmond. "Problems of Development Planning in Jordan," *Middle East Economic Papers, 1963.* Beirut: Economic Research Institute, American University of Beirut, 1963.

Baer, Gabriel. "Land Tenure in the Hashemite Kingdom of Jordan," *Land Economics,* XXXIII, No. 3, August 1957, 187–197.

——. *Population and Society in the Arab East.* New York: Praeger, 1964.

Balance of Payments Yearbook, XXIV, Washington: International Monetary Fund, 1973.

Burns, Norman. *Point Four in Jordan.* Washington: U.S. Department of State, 1960.

Caponera, Dante A. *Water Laws in Moslem Countries.* Rome: United Nations, Food and Agriculture Organization, 1954.

Carr, Winifred. *Hussein's Kingdom.* London: Leslie Frewin, 1966.

Centre d'Etudes et de Documentation Economiques, Financières et Sociales. *L'Economie des Pays Arabes* [Beirut], February 1972, 20–23.

Dajani, Ali T. *The Industry of Jordan 1967—A Directory of Jordan Industrial Firms.* Jerusalem: Greek Convent, 1967.

El-Ghonemy, Mohamad Riad. "The Role of Land Policy in Agricultural Production and Income Distribution in the Near East." Pages 87–105 in Mohamad Riad El-Ghonemy (ed.), *Land Policy in the Near East.* Rome: United Nations, Food and Agriculture Organization, 1967.

Fisher, Sidney; Kirk, George; and Praner, Robert. "Jordan." Pages 630–636 in *Colliers Encyclopedia,* XIII. New York: Collier, 1968.

Furlonge, Geoffrey "Jordan Today," *Royal Central Asian Society Journal,* LIII, No. 3, October 1966, 277–285.

Gellhorn, Eleanor. *McKay's Guide to the Middle East.* New York: David McKay, 1965.

Glubb, Sir John Bagot. *Syria, Lebanon, Jordan.* New York: Walker, 1967.

Guillaume, Alfred. *Islam*. Baltimore: Penguin Books, 1968.

Hanna, Paul. "Jordan." Pages 209-212 in *Encyclopedia Americana*, XVI. New York: Americana Corporation, 1968.

Harris, George, L., et al. *Jordan: Its People, Its Society, Its Culture*. New Haven: Human Relations Area Files, 1958.

Higgins, Benjamin. *Economic Development*. (Rev. ed.) New York: W. W. Norton, 1968.

Hussein, King of Jordan. *Uneasy Lies the Head*. New York: Bernard Geis Associates, 1962.

International Bank for Reconstruction and Development. *The Economic Development of Jordan*. Baltimore: Johns Hopkins University Press, 1957.

International Monetary Fund. *International Financial Statistics*, XXVI, No. 7, July 1973, 216-219.

———. "Jordan." Pages 212-215 in *International Financial Statistics*, XXVI, No. 8, August 1973.

———. *Nineteenth Annual Report on Exchange Restrictions*. Washington: IMF, 1968.

———. *Twenty-third Annual Report on Exchange Restrictions*. Washington: IMF, 1972.

Israel. Bank of Israel. *The Economy of the Administered Areas, 1969*. Jerusalem: January 1971.

———. *The Economy of the Administered Areas, 1971*. Jerusalem: December 1972.

"The Israeli Administration in Judaea and Samaria," *The Israeli Economist* [Tel Aviv]. XXIV, No. 8, August 1968.

Johns, Richard, and Bonar, John. "Jordan," *Financial Times* [London], March 28, 1973, 16-19.

Jordan. Central Bank of Jordan. *Monthly Statistical Bulletin* [Amman], VIII, No. 12, December 1972, Tables 1-36.

———. *Monthly Statistical Bulletin* [Amman], VIII, No. 2, February 1972, Tables 1-36.

———. *Monthly Statistical Bulletin* [Amman], IX, No. 2, February 1973, Tables 1-36.

———. *Monthly Statistical Bulletin* [Amman], VII, No. 12, December 1971, Tables 1-36.

———. *Monthly Statistical Bulletin* [Amman], VI, No. 12, December 1970, Tables 1-34.

———. *Quarterly Bulletin* [Amman], IX, No. 2, 1968, 5-63.

———. *Annual Report*. Amman: 1967.

———. *Annual Report*. Amman: 1968.

———. *Annual Report*. Amman: 1969.

———. *Annual Report*. Amman: 1970.

———. *Annual Report*. Amman: 1971.

———. *Eighth Annual Report, 1971*. Amman: 1972.

Jordan. Department of Statistics. *Manufacturing Industrial Census*,

1967. Amman: Department of Statistics Press, 1968.

Jordan. Ministry of Culture and Information. *Economic Development of Jordan, 1954–1971*. Amman: Jordanian Press Foundation, 1972.

Jordan. Ministry of National Economy. *Investment Conditions and Opportunities in Jordan*. Amman: Government Printing Office, 1972.

Kanovsky, Eliyahu. "The Economic Aftermath of the Six Day War," *Middle East Journal*, XXII, No. 3, Summer 1968, 278–296.

————. *The Economic Impact of the Six Day War—Israel, the Occupied Territories, Egypt, Jordan*. New York: Praeger, 1970.

Khalil, Muhammad. *The Arab States and the Arab League*. I. Beirut: Khayats, 1962.

Kindleberger, Charles P. *Economic Development*. (2d ed.) New York: McGraw-Hill, 1965.

Kurtzig, Michael E. *Jordan's Agricultural Economy in Brief*. (U.S. Department of Agriculture, Economic Research Service, No. 326.) Washington: GPO, January 1972.

Lerner, Daniel. *The Passing of Traditional Society: Modernizing the Middle East*. Glencoe: Free Press, 1958.

Middle East and North Africa, 1972–73. (19th ed.) London: Europa Publications, 1972.

Narain, R. D., et al. "Population and Food Supply in Asia," *Monthly Bulletin of Agricultural Economics and Statistics* [Rome], XXII, No. 1, January 1973, 1–9.

Nelson, Nina. *Your Guide to Jordan*. London: Alvin Redman, 1966.

Odeh, Hanna S. *The Jordan Valley*. Amman: Government Printing Office, 1968.

Organization for Economic Cooperation and Development. *Development Co-operation, 1972*. Paris: OECD, 1972.

Patai, Raphael. *Jordan*. New Haven. Human Relations Area Files, 1957.

Peretz, Don. "River Schemes and Their Effect on Economic Development in Jordan, Syria, and Lebanon," *Middle East Journal*, XVIII, No. 3, Summer 1964, 293–305.

Pick, Franz. *Pick's Currency Yearbook, 1972*. New York: 1972.

Production Yearbook, 1971. Rome: United Nations, Food and Agriculture Organization, 1972.

Quarterly Economic Review. *Saudi Arabia, Jordan, Annual Supplement, 1972*. London: Economist Intelligence Unit, 1972.

Rizk, E. *The River Jordan*. New York: Arab Information Center, 1964.

Royal Institute of International Affairs. *The Middle East: A Political and Economic Survey*. (2d ed.) London: 1954.

Sfeir, George N. "The Central Bank and the Banking Law of Jordan," *Middle East Journal*, XX, No. 3, Summer 1966, 352–360.

Sparrow, Gerald. *Modern Jordan*. London: Allen and Unwin, 1961.

Stamp, L. Dudley (ed.). *A History of Land Use in Arid Regions*. Paris: United Nations Educational, Scientific and Cultural Organization,

1961.

Statistical Yearbook, 1971. New York: United Nations, Statistical Office, 1972.

Statistical Yearbook, 1972. New York: United Nations, Department of Economic and Social Affairs, 1973.

Statistical Yearbook, 1971, XXII. Amman: Jordan, Department of Statistics Press, 1972.

Tegeler, Henrietta Holm. *The Agriculture of West Asia.* Washington: GPO, 1966.

United Nations Relief and Works Agency. *Bulletin of Economic Development.* (Special Reports on Jordan, No. 14.) Beirut: UNRWA, 1956.

United Nations. Department of Economic and Social Affairs. Statistical Office. *Monthly Bulletin of Statistics,* XXVII, No. 6, June 1973, 1-243.

U.S. Agency for International Development. *A.I.D. Economic Data Book: Near East and South East Asia.* Washington, AID, 1970.

————. *Economic Growth Trends: Near East and South Asia.* Washington: GPO, 1971.

————. *Selected Economic Data for the Less Developed Countries.* Washington: GPO, June 1973.

U.S. Department of Agriculture. *The Agriculture Situation in Africa and West Asia.* (ERS Foreign 354.) Washington: GPO, 1973.

————. *Indices of Agricultural Production in Africa and the Near East, 1962-71.* (ERS Foreign 265.) Washington: GPO, 1972.

U.S. Department of Labor. Bureau of Labor Statistics. *Labor Law and Practice in the Hashemite Kingdom of Jordan.* (BLS Report, No. 322.) Washington: GPO, 1967.

Vouras, Paul P. "Jordan," *Focus,* XVII, No. 6, February 1967, 6.

Ward, Richard J. "Developing the Jordan Economy," *Indian Journal of Economics* [New Delhi], XLVI, October 1965, 147-176.

(Various issues of the following periodicals were also used in the preparation of this section: *Arab Report and Record* [London], 1969-1973; *Middle East Economic Digest* [London], 1973; *New York Times,* 1973; *Quarterly Economic Review* [London], 1970-1973; and *Washington Post,* 1973.)

Section IV. National Defense

Abboushi, W. F. *Political Systems of the Middle East in the Twentieth Century.* New York: Dodd, Mead, 1970.

Abidi, Aqil Hyder. *Jordan: A Political Study, 1948–1957.* New York: Asia Publishing House, 1965.

Abu-Lughod, Ibrahim (ed.). *The Transformation of Palestine.* Evanston: Northwestern University Press, 1971.

Al-Marayati, Abid A. *Middle Eastern Constitutions and Electoral Laws.* New York: Praeger, 1968.

Anderson, James N. D. *Islamic Law in the Modern World.* New York: New York University Press, 1959.

Aruri, Naseer H. *Jordan: A Study in Political Development (1921–1965).* The Hague: Martinus Nijhoff, 1972.

Brown, Neville. "Palestinian Nationalism and the Jordanian State," *World Today* [London], XXVI, No. 9, September 1970, 370-378.

Cooley, John K. "Israelis Put Down Roots in Arab Soil," *Christian Science Monitor,* May 30, 1973, Section 2, 7.

Cramer, James. *The World's Police.* London: Cassell, 1964.

Dearden, Ann. *Jordan.* London: Robert Hale, 1958.

Dupuy, T. N., et al. *The Almanac of World Military Power.* Harrisburg: Stackpole Books, 1970.

Europa Year Book—1972, I: International Organizations. London: Europa Publications, 1972.

Glubb Pasha. *The Middle East Crisis: A Personal Interpretation.* London: Hodder and Stoughton, 1957.

Glubb, Sir John Bagot. *Britain and the Arabs.* London: Hodder and Stoughton, 1958.

———. *A Soldier with the Arabs.* New York: Harper, 1957.

———. *The Story of the Arab Legion.* London: Hodder and Stoughton, 1948.

Harris, George L., et al. *Jordan: Its People, Its Society, Its Culture.* New Haven: Human Relations Area Files, 1958.

Hoagland, Jim. "Israeli Attitude Toward Arab Land Return Hardens," *Washington Post,* June 5, 1973, A14.

Hollman, Dieter. "Profile of Yasir Arafat Drawn," *Horizont* [East Berlin], April 1973, 14-15. [Translated by U.S. Department of Commerce, Office of Technical Services, Joint Publications Research Service (Washington). JPRS: 58,860, *Translations on Near East,*

No. 944, April 26, 1973, 1–6.]

Hovey, Harold A. *U.S. Military Assistance: A Study of Policies and Practices.* New York: Praeger, 1965.

Howard, Harry N. "Jordan in Turmoil," *Current History,* LXII, No. 365, January 1972, 14–19, 49.

Howard, Michael, and Hunter, Robert. *Israel and the Arab World: The Crisis of 1967.* (Adelphi Papers.) London: Institute of Strategic Studies, 1967.

Hurewitz, J. C. *Middle East Politics: The Military Dimension.* New York: Praeger, 1969.

Jarvis, Claude Scudamore. *Arab Command: The Biography of Lieutenant Colonel F. G. Peake Pasha.* London: Hutchinson, 1943.

Johnson, John J. (ed.) *The Role of the Military in Underdeveloped Countries.* Princeton: Princeton University Press, 1962.

Johns, Richard. "The Creeping Settlement," *Financial Times* [London], May 16, 1973, 8.

Jordan. Laws, Statutes, etc.
A Collection of Laws and Regulations. Amman: Government Printers, 1960.
Constitution. Amman: Government Printing Office, 1965.

Jordan. *Monthly Statistical Bulletin* [Amman], IX, No. 2, February 1973, tables 29 and 31.

Khouri, Fred J. *The Arab-Israeli Dilemma.* Syracuse: Syracuse University Press, 1968.

Kimche, David, and Bawly, Dan. *The Sandstorm.* New York: Stein and Day, 1968.

Lerner, Daniel. *The Passing of Traditional Society: Modernizing the Middle East.* Glencoe: Free Press, 1958.

Lias, Godfrey. *Glubb's Legion.* London: Evans Brothers, 1956.

Liesbesney, Herbert J. "Stability and Change in Islamic Law," *Middle East Journal,* XXI, No. 1, Winter 1967, 16–34.

Little, Tom. "The Nature of the Palestinian Resistance Movement," *Asian Affairs* [London], LVII (New Series I), Pt. I, June 1970, 157–169.

Mansfield, Peter. "Jordan." Page 449 in *Britannica Book of the Year: 1970.* Chicago: William Benton, 1970.

———. "Jordan." Pages 429–431 in *Britannica Book of the Year: 1971.* Chicago: William Benton, 1971.

———. "Jordan." Page 399 in *Britannica Book of the Year: 1972.* Chicago: William Benton, 1972.

———. "Jordan." Pages 393–394 in *Britannica Book of the Year: 1973.* Chicago: William Benton, 1973.

Mansfield, Peter (ed.). *The Middle East: A Political and Economic Survey.* (4th ed.) New York: Oxford University Press, 1973.

Middle East and North Africa, 1972–73. (19th ed.) London: Europa Publications, 1972.

The Military Balance: 1972–1973. London: International Institute for Strategic Studies, 1972.

Military Dictionary: English-Arabic. Amman: General Headquarters, The Arab Legion, 1952.

Mogannam, E. T. "Developments in the Legal System of Jordan," *Middle East Journal,* VI, No. 2, Spring 1952, 194–206.

Nakleh, Emile A. "The Anatomy of Violence: Theoretical Reflections on Palestinian Resistance," *Middle East Journal,* XXV, No. 2, Spring 1971, 180–200.

O'Ballance, Edgar. *The Third Arab-Israeli War.* Hamden: Archon Books, 1972.

Patai, Raphael. *The Kingdom of Jordan.* Princeton: Princeton University Press, 1958.

Peake, Frederick G. (Peake Pasha). *A History of Jordan and Its Tribes.* Coral Gables: University of Miami Press, 1958.

Pryce-Jones, David. *The Face of Defeat: Palestinian Refugees and Guerrillas.* New York: Holt, Rinehart and Winston, 1972.

Quandt, William B. *Palestinian Nationalism: Its Political and Military Dimensions.* (Report R–782–ISA.) Santa Monica: Rand Corporation, November 1971.

Reich, Bernard. *Crisis in the Middle East, 1967: Implications for U.S. Policy.* (Report RAC–R–39.) Washington: Research Analysis Corporation, February 1968.

Seton-Williams, M. V., and Hitchins, Verity Elizabeth. "Jordan." Pages 81–84 in *Encyclopaedia Britannica,* XIII. Chicago: William Benton, 1969.

Sharabi, Hisham. *Palestine Guerrillas: Their Credibility and Effectiveness.* (U.S. Department of State, Office of External Research, Foreign Affairs Research Paper No. 11049.) Washington: FAR, 1970.

Shwadran, Benjamin. *Jordan: A State of Tension.* New York: Council for Middle Eastern Affairs, 1959.

Snow, Peter. *Hussein: A Biography.* Washington: Robert B. Luce, 1972.

Sparrow, Gerald. *Hussein of Jordan.* London: George G. Harrop, 1940.

———. *Modern Jordan.* London: Allen and Unwin, 1961.

Statistical Yearbook, 1971, XXII. Amman: Jordan, Department of Statistics Press, 1973, p. 185.

United Nations. *International Review of Criminal Policy, No. 21.* (ST/SOA/Ser. M/21.) New York: UN, 1963.

———. *Study of the Right of Everyone to Be Free from Arbitrary Arrest, Detention, and Exile.* (E/CN. 4/826/Rev. 1.) New York: UN, 1964.

———. *Third United Nations Seminar on the Prevention of Crime and Treatment of Offenders.* (ST/TAO/Ser. C/81.) New York: United Nations Educational, Scientific and Cultural Organization, 1966.

United Nations. Bureau of Social Affairs. *Comparative Survey of Juvenile Delinquency, Part Five: Middle East.* (ST/SOA/SD/1/

Add.4/Rev.1.) New York: UN, 1965.

United Nations. Department of Economic and Social Affairs. *International Review of Criminal Policy*, No. 19. (ST/SOA/Ser. M/19.) New York: UN, 1962.

United Nations. Economic and Social Council. *Second United Nations Seminar for the Arab States on the Prevention of Crime and The Treatment of Offenders*. (ST/TAO/Ser. C/42.) New York: United Nations Educational, Scientific and Cultural Organization, 1959.

U.S. Arms Control and Disarmament Agency. *World Military Expenditures: 1971*. (Publication No. 65.) Washington: July 1972.

U.S. Department of Defense. *Military Assistance Facts*. Washington: GPO, 1968.

——. *Military Uniforms*. Washington: GPO, n.d.

U.S. Department of State. Bureau of Intelligence and Research. *World Strength of the Communist Party Organizations: Twenty-fourth Annual Report*. (Department of State Publication No. 8658.) Washington: June 1972.

Vance, Vick, and Lauer, Pierre. *Hussein of Jordan: My "War" with Israel*. (Trans., June P. Wilson and Walter B. Michaels.) New York: William Morrow, 1969.

Vatikiotis, P. J. *Politics and the Military in Jordan: A Study of the Arab Legion, 1921-1957*. New York: Praeger, 1967.

Wolf, John B. "Black September: Militant Palestinianism," *Current History*, LXIV, No. 377, January 1973, 5-8, 37.

——. "The Palestinian Resistance Movement," *Current History*, LX, No. 353, January 1971, 26-31, 49-50.

Yaari, Ehud. "Arafat's Moment of Decision," *New Middle East* [London], No. 57, June 1973, 4-6.

(Various issues of the following periodicals were also used in the preparation of this section: *Arab Report and Record* [London], 1969-1973; *Middle East Economic Digest* [London], 1973; *New York Times*, 1973; *Quarterly Economic Review* [London], 1970-1973; and *Washington Post*, 1973.)

GLOSSARY

dinar—Monetary unit of Jordan, abbreviated JD and divided into 1,000 fils. In 1950 par value was established with the IMF (*q.v.*) at US$2.80 equal JD1; as a result of the February 1973 devaluation of the United States dollar, the value in mid-1973 was US$3.11 equal JD1.

fedayeen (sing., fedayee)—Arab commandos or guerrillas.

fellahin (sing., fellah)—Peasant or agricultural worker.

IBRD—International Bank for Reconstruction and Development; also known as the World Bank.

IDA—International Development Association. An affiliate of IBRD and a part of the World Bank Group. Became operational in 1960.

imam—Prayer leader of an Islamic congregation.

IMF—International Monetary Fund.

Israeli-occupied Territory—West Bank (*q.v.*).

JD—Jordanian dinar (*q.v.*).

East Bank—That portion of Jordan east of the Jordan River, the Dead Sea, and the series of wadis from the Dead Sea to the Gulf of Aqaba. Roughly the former Amirate of Transjordan (see fig. 1).

Palestinian—Narrowly, a citizen of the British mandated territory of Palestine (1922–48). Generally, a Muslim or Christian native or descendant of a native of the region between the Egyptian Sinai and Lebanon and west of the Jordan River-Dead Sea-Al Aqaba line who identifies himself primarily as other than an Israeli.

sharia—Body of Islamic law. Courts applying this law known as sharia courts.

sharif (Arabic pl., *ashraf*)—An individual who claims to be and is accepted as a descendant of the Prophet Muhammad through his daughter Fatima.

shaykh—Tribal chief. Frequently seen in English as sheikh or sheik.

Sunna—The "example" provided by the Prophet Muhammad's acts and sayings as recalled and recorded by his closest followers, who were known as the Companions. The Sunna is accepted by Sunni Muslims as the model of correct behavior.

Sunni—The larger branch of Islam known for its adherence to the Sunna (*q.v.*). Almost all Muslims in Jordan are Sunni.

Tapline (Trans-Arabian Pipeline)—A 1,068-mile, thirty-inch diameter pipeline completed in 1950 to transport petroleum from the Aramco (Arabian American Oil Company) oil fields in Saudi Arabia to the shipping facilities of the Mediterranean port of Sidon, Lebanon, crossing Jordan and Syria on the way. An eight-inch diameter pipe-line connects Tapline with the Jordanian refinery at Az Zarqa and supplies Jordan's requirements of crude petroleum.

Transjordanian—Narrowly, a citizen of the Amirate (Princedom) of Transjordan (1922–46). Generally, a Muslim or Christian native of the region east of the Jordan River-Dead Sea-Al Aqaba line and within the approximate boundaries of the contemporary state of Jordan, that is, of the East Bank (*q.v.*).

ulama (Arabic sing., *alim*)—Collective term for recognized Islamic scholars.

UNRWA—United Nations Relief and Works Agency for Palestine Refugees in the Near East.

West Bank—That portion of Jordan west of the Jordan River and the Dead Sea. Area was seized by Israel in the 1967 war and in late 1973 remained Israeli-occupied Territory (see fig. 1).

INDEX

artisan enterprises. *See* handicrafts
arts: 122–130
Aruri, Naseer: 73, 86
As Safi: 51, 53
As Salt: xiv, 38, 47, 51, 55
Asad, President Hafiz al: 166
Aun, Sharifa Dina Abdul Hamid al: 33
awqaf (*see also* Ministry of Awqaf, Islamic Affairs, and Holy Places): 63, 184
Ayubi, Haytam: 150
Az Zarqa: 4, 29, 51, 53; cost of living, 191, 192; dam, 208, 219; population, 55, 85; refinery, 54, 215, 220; River, 45
Azazimat tribe: 78
Azraq ash Shishan oasis: 55
Azzam, Samira: 124

Baath Party: 28, 40, 156, 158, 159
Baghdad Pact: 27, 29, 31, 158, 159, 160
Bahai sect: 72
Bahri, Jamil: 126
balance of payments: 196, 200
Balfour Declaration: 17, 18
Bani Atiya tribe: 79
Bani Khalid tribe: 79
Bani Sakhr tribe: 78, 79
banking system: 189–190
beduins: 2, 4, 14, 66, 80–81, 87; nomadic life, 45, 54, 55, 78, 79, 105, 109; representation in government, 136, 139; tribal law, 138
Ben-Moshe, Eliezer: 74
Berji, Yusuf al: 151
Bernadotte, Folke: 23
birth control: 57
birth rate: 58
bismallah: 66
Black September group: 151, 154, 155, 169
book publishing: 121
border problems: 31, 34, 53
Boullata, Issa: 125
Boullata, Kamal: 127
boundaries: xiv, 41, 42–44, 51, 79
Bourguiba, Habib: 165
Brezhnev, Leonid: 164
budget, government: x, 5, 184, 185, 186, 187, 188; military, 228–229, 231; teachers, 99, 100
Bunche, Ralph: 23

cabinet: 134, 146
Cairo Conference of 1964: 34, 163
calendar, Muslim: 61
camels: 78, 109, 211, 237
Canaan: 8, 9
Canada: 215
cement: 194, 196, 218, 220

censorship. *See* civil rights
census: 42, 54, 56; agriculture, 207
Central Bank of Jordan: 180, 189
Central Treaty Organization (CENTO). *See* Baghdad Pact
chambers of commerce: 194
Chechen people: 75
Chelhod, Joseph: 78, 89
children: 88
China: Nationalist, 172; People's Republic of, 120, 172, 198, 199
Christianity: ix, 10–11, 65, 75, 84, 108, 109; churches, 70; government and, 68, 136, 139, 147; holy places, 69, 70, 71
Chrorou, Fadil: 151
Churchill, Winston: 19
Circassians: 75, 84, 136, 139, 147
citrus crops: 203, 210
civil rights: 133, 137; freedom of religion, 65, 68; freedom of speech, 5, 68, 114, 115, 137
civil service. *See* government: labor force
civil war of 1970: 6, 152, 223
climate: ix, 47–49
commandos. *See* Palestinian guerrillas
communications: 113–122
communist countries (*see also* Soviet Union): 120, 148
Communist Party of Jordan: (*see also* National Front party): 222, 240
conscription: 227
constitutions: ix, 20, 22, 131, 132–134, 222
construction: 60, 217
cooperatives, agricultural: 194, 205
copper: 49, 51, 215
cost of living: 105, 106, 109, 191; Amman, 106, 179, 192; per capita income, 181
Council of Ministries: 135–136
court systems (*see also* religious courts): x, 132, 138, 239
credit: 189–190, 194; agriculture, 203, 204, 209
crime: 238
crops (*see also* marketing of crops): 45, 202, 209, 210
Crusades: 12
Cuba: 120
currency: 190
customs duties: 188
Cyprus: 120
Czechoslovakia: 171

Damascus Protocol: 16
Daoud, Mohammad: 152
Dar al Islam: 11
Dayan, Moshe: v, 36

5, 24, 37, 169–171, 186; military aid, 30, 31 32, 225, 228, 229, 230–231, 233, 234, 235: trade, 198, 199

United States Agency for International Development (AID): 189, 231

United States Information Service (USIS): 120

United States Military Assistance Program (MAP): 229, 230

University of Jordan: 99, 101, 104, 110; library, 121

urban areas: 4, 54, 55, 83–85, 91, 109; housing, 105, 106; sanitation, 107

Uzayzi, R. Z.: 89

villages and rural areas: 55, 107, 109; administration, 81–83, 140, 141; agriculture, 202; development, 219; police, 237; radio, 118–119

vocational and technical education: 60, 93, 97, 103, 105, 226

Wadi al Arabah: 46
Wadi al Hasa: 47, 49, 209
Wadi al Mawjib: 209
Waldheim, Kurt: 165
Waqf land: 206
water supply (*see also* irrigation; Jordan River; rainfall): ix, 4, 107, 108, 182, 206
weapons: 233
West Bank (*see also* Israeli-occupied Territory): 8, 23, 24, 36, 50, 51; administrative

divisions, 44; education in, 94, 99, 105; holy places, 68, 177; population, 41, 55, 57, 58

West Germany: 34, 120, 171; aid, 37, 189, 231

wheat: 203, 209, 210

windstorms: 48–49, 107–108

women: education, 91, 100, 103, 104, 105; employment, 59, 90–91; religion and, 62, 67; status, 86, 88–89, 90, 91, 121; suffrage, 136; writers, 123–124

Women's Federation of Jordan: 57

Woodhead Commission: 21

World Bank (IBRD): 172, 181, 208

World Council of Churches: 111

World Health Organization: 108, 172

World War I: 7, 16, 17

World Zionist Organization: 15, 18, 19, 21

Yahya, Razzaq: 150

Yamani, Ahmad al: 150

Yamani people: 76

Yarmuk River: 45, 47, 54; dam, 208, 219

Yemen: 22, 23

Yom Kippur War. *See* Arab-Israeli War of October 1973

Yugoslavia: 171, 198, 199

Zarqa affair: 29

Zeeyza airport: 54

Zein, Princess: 33

Zionism: 7, 8, 14, 15, 17, 18, 21, 22

PUBLISHED AREA HANDBOOKS

550–65	Afghanistan	550–30	Japan
550–98	Albania	550–34	Jordan
550–44	Algeria	550–56	Kenya
550–59	Angola	550–50	Khmer Republic (Cambodia)
550–73	Argentina	550–81	Korea, North
550–66	Bolivia	550–41	Korea, Republic of
550–20	Brazil	550–58	Laos
550–168	Bulgaria	550–24	Lebanon
550–61	Burma	550–38	Liberia
550–83	Burundi	550–85	Libya
550–166	Cameroon	550–163	Malagasy Republic
550–96	Ceylon	550–45	Malaysia
550–159	Chad	550–161	Mauritania
550–77	Chile	550–79	Mexico
550–60	China, People's Rep. of	550–76	Mongolia
550–63	China, Rep. of	550–49	Morocco
550–26	Colombia	550–64	Mozambique
550–67	Congo, Democratic Rep. of (Zaire)	550–35	Nepal, Bhutan and Sikkim
550–91	Congo, People's Rep. of	550–88	Nicaragua
550–90	Costa Rica	550–157	Nigeria
550–152	Cuba	550–94	Oceania
550–22	Cyprus	550–48	Pakistan
550–158	Czechoslovakia	550–46	Panama
550–54	Dominican Republic	550–156	Paraguay
550–155	East Germany	550–92	Peripheral States of the Arabian Peninsula
550–52	Ecuador	550–42	Peru
550–150	El Salvador	550–72	Philippines
550–28	Ethiopia	550–162	Poland
550–167	Finland	550–160	Romania
550–29	Germany	550–84	Rwanda
550–153	Ghana	550–51	Saudi Arabia
550–87	Greece	550–70	Senegal
550–78	Guatemala	550–86	Somalia
550–82	Guyana	550–93	South Africa, Republic of
550–164	Haiti	550–95	Soviet Union
550–151	Honduras	550–27	Sudan, Democratic Republic of
550–165	Hungary	550–47	Syria
550–21	India	550–62	Tanzania
550–154	Indian Ocean Territories	550–53	Thailand
550–39	Indonesia	550–89	Tunisia
550–68	Iran	550–80	Turkey
550–31	Iraq	550–74	Uganda
550–25	Israel	550–43	United Arab Republic (Egypt)
550–69	Ivory Coast		

550-97	Uruguay	550-55	Vietnam, South
550-71	Venezuela	550-99	Yugoslavia
550-57	Vietnam, North	550-75	Zambia

* U.S. GOVERNMENT PRINTING OFFICE: 1974—585-917 (PO3)